THE ORIGINS OF THE KEYNESIAN
REVOLUTION

To my parents

The Origins of the Keynesian Revolution

The Development of Keynes' Theory of Employment and Output

Robert W. Dimand

Stanford University Press
Stanford, California
1988

Stanford University Press
Stanford, California
© 1988 Robert W. Dimand
Originating publisher: Edward Elgar Publishing
  Aldershot
First published in the U.S.A. by
  Stanford University Press, 1988
Printed in Great Britain
ISBN 0–8047–1525–4
LC

Contents

Acknowledgements

Chapters 2, 3 and 4 of this study are based on my doctoral dissertation at Yale University. I am grateful to the members of my dissertation committee, James Tobin, Katsuhito Iwai and Lorie Tarshis, for their advice and encouragement. I have learned much of what I know about macroeconomics and about Keynes from them, but I must absolve them of any responsibility for the result. Robert B. Bryce and Lorie Tarshis have kindly permitted me to make use of notes that they took while attending Keynes' lectures. I am indebted to Lorie Tarshis and William Scott for discussions of economics at Cambridge, where they were students in the 1930s.

William N. Parker has been for me, as for other Yale economics students, the ideal that all directors of graduate studies should strive to become. While teaching at Carleton University I was fortunate to have among my colleagues Eric G. Davis, who drew my attention to the crucial role of Hawtrey, T. K. Rymes, who is editing the students' notes on Keynes' lectures, and P. Nicholas Rowe.

I am grateful to the Eastern Economic Association for permission to incorporate in chapter 2 of this book material previously published as a paper in the *Eastern Economic Journal*, and to the Royal Economic Society which awarded that paper a prize in an essay competition for members of the society under the age of thirty, on the occasion of the centenary of Keynes' birth.

While a graduate student I received fellowships from Yale University, the Social Sciences and Humanities Research Council of Canada and the Government of Quebec (Fonds FCAC). It was a great stroke of luck that my Yale teaching fellowship enabled me to be a teaching assistant to James Tobin in his course on 'The Keynesian Revolution and the Counter-Revolutions', and to William Parker and Richard Levin in their course on the history of economic thought, while I was writing my dissertation – no other teaching assistant can ever have been as fortunate in his course assignments.

Most of all, I am deeply grateful for the support, help and encouragement that I have received from my parents.

Introduction

Although there have been many works written about Keynes, there is room for another to re-examine the development of Keynes' thought from orthodox Cambridge monetary theory to the *General Theory* in light of new controversies about what the *General Theory* is and in light of extremely important new evidence. *The General Theory of Employment, Interest and Money*, John Maynard Keynes' great book, was regarded by economists for many years as simply a special case of classical theory, where the money wage rate happened to be rigid for arbitrary reasons, or where workers suffered money illusion, caring irrationally about nominal wages instead of real wages. Keynes' theory was held to be traditional classical theory with new labels, the familiar neoclassical marginal product of capital, for example, being disguised as the marginal efficiency of capital. Once the myth was abandoned that Keynes alone among leading economists had advocated public works in the Depression, a vast array of academic supporters of demand stimulus were acclaimed as predecessors of Keynes. Robert Clower and Axel Leijonhufvud forced economists to take a new look at the *General Theory* by showing that the book was not about arbitrary wage rigidity or money illusion, but about the possibility of co-ordination failure in a monetary economy.[1]

The reappraisals of the economics of Keynes, distinguished by Leijonhufvud from later Keynesian economics, tended to examine the *General Theory* in isolation, but this could be misleading. When Keynes wrote the *General Theory*, he assumed that his readers would be familiar with the portfolio approach to money demand and the pricing of capital assets in his *Treatise on Money*. To understand Keynes' achievement in the *General Theory*, it is necessary to examine how it builds upon and extends his earlier work, and how it differs from the work of his contemporaries. His earlier writings in

1

monetary theory were eclipsed by the success of the *General Theory*. It is now forgotten that the *Treatise* was received by the economics profession as an innovative, revolutionary work. The four-volume set of *Critical Assessments* of Keynes, edited by J. Cunningham Wood, reprints the reviews of the *General Theory* and later articles on Keynes, but no reviews of the *Treatise*; indeed, nothing written before 1936.[2] Although the reappraisal of the economics of Keynes has shown the need to take another look at the *General Theory* in the context of the evolution of Keynes' thought, this need was not filled by such work as that of Axel Leijonhufvud, who wrote in the introduction to his book: 'I would emphasize strongly from the outset that this doctrine-historical objective is strictly secondary ... to put [Keynes'] analytical achievements in proper historical perspective is not a major concern of this study.'[3]

The availability of previously unexploited evidence presents a great chance for historical study of the development of Keynes' theory of a monetary economy. The Royal Economic Society's edition of Keynes' *Collected Writings* provided much new material. Until Hawtrey's comments on the *Treatise* and Keynes' reply were published in 1973 in Volume XIII of Keynes' writings, it was not possible to appreciate Hawtrey's role in the development of the multiplier. Before Volume XXIX came out in 1979 with newly discovered papers, historians of economics knew that members of the 'Cambridge Circus' had written Keynes a manifesto about his spring 1932 lectures but did not yet have the manifesto itself or Keynes' notes for his lectures. Above all, students' notes on Keynes' lectures, taken by Robert Bryce from 1932 to 1934, by Lorie Tarshis from 1932 to 1935 and by several other students, have been recovered and are being edited for publication by Thomas K. Rymes of Carleton University. Don Patinkin has cited passages from these lecture notes showing the presence of the multiplier theory of effective demand in the 1933 lectures, and its absence from those of 1932,[4] but there is more to be learned from this source, such as Keynes' 1934 account of the difference between his marginal efficiency of capital and Fisher's internal rate of return. Patinkin has made important use of the newly published material on Keynes, notably in his 1976 and 1980 reviews of several volumes of the *Collected Writings*. While Patinkin concentrated on the appearance in Keynes' thought of the theory of effective demand, the recognition of changes in the level of output as a force equilibrating investment and saving, the present study examines the development and synthesis of four elements of Keynes' theory of the level of employment and output in a monetary economy: the multiplier theory of effective demand, the liquidity preference theory of the interest rate, the marginal efficiency of capital theory of investment, and the analysis of the failure of the labour market to clear.

Because of this focus, the present study traces the roots of these building blocks of Keynes' *General Theory* in his earlier works on monetary theory and his popular writings on unemployment. I also examine the role of other economists in the development of Keynes' theory; for example, the role of Hawtrey, Giblin, Kahn and Warming in the development of the multiplier from the crude version used by Keynes and Henderson in 1929 to the version employed in the *General Theory*. I also compare Keynes' analysis of how unemployment can arise, and what policies could diminish it, with discussion of the topic by some of his contemporaries, to find out the extent to which Keynes' analysis was distinctive, rather than simply a reflection of the conventional wisdom of his time.

Any book on the development of Keynes' thought will necessarily be controversial. I have no illusions that I have said the last word on the subject. Like Keynes, 'I do not hope to be right. I hope to make progress.'[5]

NOTES

1. Clower (1965); Leijonhufvud (1968). See also Hines (1971); Bliss (1975a).
2. Wood (1983).
3. Leijonhufvud (1968), 9, 12.
4. Patinkin (1976), 79; (1982), 21–3.
5. Quoted by E. Johnson, in E. Johnson and H. Johnson (1978), 16.

1   The open-economy macroeconomics of Keynes' *Tract on Monetary Reform*

Keynesian macroeconomics grew out of an earlier tradition of Cambridge monetary theory, which Keynes had not only mastered and taught but to which he had made major contributions. The habit of reading Keynes' *General Theory* without reference to his earlier writings has led to the prevalence of several myths about Keynes. Because the *General Theory* was the only one of his books to restrict its formal analysis to a closed economy, Keynes has come to be regarded as an economist who ignored the effect of international trade and capital flows on macroeconomic stabilization. Most students of international finance would be surprised to read Arthur Bloomfield's claims, written in 1947, that 'Keynes was the first to develop a systematic theory of the forward exchanges' and that 'Keynes (with the possible exception of Fisher) was the first modern writer to emphasize the internal-vs.-external stability conflict, and to recommend a flexible exchange rate policy'.[1] Similarly, although Keynes has sometimes been dismissed as an economist for whom 'money does not matter' or as the inflationist depicted by Buchanan and Wagner,[2] he had a strong theoretical understanding of the causes, effects and costs of inflation, and was concerned to insulate the British economy from imported inflation or deflation.

Keynes' writings on international finance, from his first book on *Indian Currency and Finance* (1913) to his final article on 'The Balance of Payments of the United States', published posthumously in 1946, are united by his continuing concern with the balance of payments constraint imposed on domestic monetary policy by the gold standard. He judged exchange rate regimes by their conse-

4

quences for domestic stabilization, and regarded stabilization of the price level and of output as more important than stabilization of the exchange rate. This concern was behind his opposition to Britain's return to the gold standard in 1925, his proposal for a tariff to offset the overvaluation of the pound in March 1931, and his prompt abandonment of the tariff proposal when Britain left the gold standard in September of that year. In *Indian Currency and Finance*, Keynes drew on his experience at the India Office from 1906 to 1908 to analyse the scope for monetary management in the Indian gold exchange standard, which differed from the gold standard by not allowing the public to present banknotes for redemption in bullion. The fluctuating exchange rates and sharply differing national inflation rates after the First World War offered Keynes further material for monetary theory.

In 1922 Keynes wrote thirteen articles on aspects of international finance for a series of supplements on *Reconstruction in Europe*, which he edited for the *Manchester Guardian Commercial*. The 20 April 1922 supplement included three articles by Keynes on 'The Stabilisation of the European Exchanges – a Plan for Genoa', 'The Theory of the Exchanges and "Purchasing Power Parity"', and 'The Forward Market in Foreign Exchanges', the last two of which were revised and combined as the third chapter of his *Tract on Monetary Reform* in the next year. These articles were followed on 27 July by 'The Consequences to Society of Changes in the Value of Money' and 'Inflation as a Method of Taxation', papers which Keynes revised as the first two chapters of the *Tract*. Although Keynes was the editor of the *Economic Journal*, he preferred to expound the theory of inflation and of exchange stabilization to a wider, non-academic audience which could affect public policy, and then reprint four of the articles, along with two additional chapters, in a 'tract for the times', which also came out in an American edition, and was quickly translated into German, into French and, by Piero Sraffa, into Italian. Despite the timeliness of the *Tract*'s composition, and although Keynes was an orthodox classical economist on the theory of output when he wrote it, he continued to regard it as being of interest. When Keynes compiled his *Essays in Persuasion* in 1931, he included three of the five chapters of the *Tract*, indicating that the *Tract* is relevant to the understanding of his later views.

THE THEORY OF MONEY AND INFLATION

Cambridge monetary theory was presented to a wider audience with the publication of A. C. Pigou's 'The Value of Money' in the *Quarterly Journal of Economics* in 1917 and Alfred Marshall's *Money, Credit and Commerce* in 1923, compiled when Marshall was in his eighties but written in part more than fifty years before. Keynes regarded *Money, Credit and Commerce* as a mere shadow of the book Marshall could have written earlier, judging by Marshall's lectures on money which Keynes attended in 1906. Keynes had, however, a great admiration, repeatedly expressed in his prewar lectures on the theory of money[3] and later in his edition of Marshall's *Official Papers*, for Marshall's extensive evidence before the Gold and Silver Commission (1887–8) and the Indian Currency Commission (1899). Keynes' exposition of the quantity theory of money in the *Tract* follows Marshall and Pigou in starting from the public's desired holdings of cash and demand deposits. He noted that Irving Fisher's *Purchasing Power of Money* (1911), which Keynes had reviewed in the *Economic Journal*, differed from the Cambridge cash-balance approach by starting from the volume of transactions, but held this to be a difference in exposition rather than substance.[4]

While the earlier Cambridge tradition had dealt with the fixed exchange rate world of the gold standard, Keynes wrote in a context of inconvertible paper currency. He took the supply of money to be exogenously controlled by the central bank, and wrote the money market clearing condition

$$n = p(k + rk')$$

where n is the number of currency notes in circulation, p an index number of the cost of living, k the number of consumption-units of purchasing power the public wishes to hold as cash, k' the number of units of purchasing power the public wishes to hold as demand deposits against cheques, and r the proportion of deposit liabilities that the banks choose to hold as cash reserves.

In the *Tract*, as in his prewar lectures, Keynes referred ironically to Goschen's remark that 'there are many persons who cannot hear the relation of the level of prices to the quantity of currency affirmed without a feeling akin to irritation'.[5] Such persons would have been further irritated by the *Tract* which held that the money supply was fully under the control of the central bank under an inconvertible paper standard, and that the demand for money was a stable function of a few variables. While Pigou had linked the demand for cash balances only to the volume of transactions, and hence to income, explicitly assuming a constant ratio of total transactions to the total resources of the economy (without considering whether wealth might be more appropriate than income for the 'total resources'), Keynes related k and k' to both real income and the cost of holding money. When examining the demand for money in periods of hyperinflation, Keynes related money demand to the inflation rate rather than to the nominal interest rate, since in such cases the inflation rate accounted for almost the entire opportunity cost of holding money instead of bonds. He noted that in Germany the note issue increased 200-fold from December 1920 to June 1923, while the price level rose 2500-fold, a dramatic 92 per cent decrease in demand for real money balances.[6] Keynes was emphatic that the high rate of monetary growth, by raising the cost of holding money, was responsible for the rising velocity of circulation and the reduced real quantity of money, so that the fact that prices rose faster than the money supply was consistent with the price inflation being caused by the monetary growth.

The value of money collapsed in several European countries after the First World War. Austrian prices reached 14,000 times their prewar level, notwithstanding the best efforts of the distinguished economist Joseph Schumpeter as the first Finance Minister of the Austrian Republic. Prices rose to 23,000 times their prewar level in Hungary, to 2,500,000 times in Poland, and even more in Russia. When the German hyperinflation was finally halted, one trillion paper marks (that is, one million million paper marks) had the same value as one gold mark.[7] These countries experienced a flight from money and a collapse of demand for real money balances.

In 'Inflation as a Method of Taxation', which was incorporated in the *Tract*'s chapter on 'Public Finance and the Value of Money', Keynes examined the way in which a government could acquire command over real resources from holders of money and, to the extent that the inflation was not anticipated when the bonds were issued, of public debt by means of currency creation and inflation. The inflation tax, which Keynes first discussed in a Treasury memorandum in 1915,[8] provided a positive explanation of why governments overwhelmed by wartime increases in their public debt far exceeding their postwar capacity for taxation would resort to hyperinflation, despite its social costs. 'A government can live for a long time, even the German government or the Russian government, by printing paper money. That is to say, it can by this means secure the command over real resources, resources just as real as those obtained by taxation. . . . It is the form of taxation which the public find hardest to evade and even the weakest government can enforce, when it can enforce nothing else.'[9]

> The active and working elements in no community, ancient or modern, will consent to hand over to the rentier or bond-holding class more than a certain proportion of the fruits of their work. When the piled-up debt demands more than a tolerable proportion, relief has usually been sought in one or other of two out of the three possible methods. The first is repudiation. But, except as the accompaniment of revolution, this method is too crude, too deliberate, and too obvious in its incidence. The victims are immediately aware and cry out too loud; so that, in the absence of revolution, this solution may be ruled out at present, as regards *internal* debt, in Western Europe.
>
> The second method is currency depreciation, which becomes devaluation when it is fixed and confirmed by law. In the countries of Europe lately belligerent, this expedient has been adopted already on a scale which reduces the real burden of the debt by from 50 to 100 per cent. In Germany the National Debt has been by these means practically obliterated, and the bond-holders have lost everything. In France the real burden of the debt is less than a third of what it would be if the franc stood at par; and in Italy only a quarter. The owners of small savings suffer quietly, as experience shows, these enormous depredations, when they would have thrown down a government which had taken from them a fraction of the amount by more deliberate but juster instruments.[10]

Drawing on his discussions with Soviet financial experts at the Genoa Conference of 1922, Keynes presented the Soviet government's estimates of its revenues from the inflation tax.[11] Noting that the tax base for the inflation tax would be eroded as inflation reduced demand for real money balances, Keynes showed that there would be a revenue-maximizing rate of inflation.[12] Keynes observed that the special cost of inflationary finance was not the transfer of purchasing power from holders of cash and bonds to the government, but was rather the reduction in the real quantity of money because of the effect of higher opportunity costs on demand. The abandonment of money as a medium of exchange, and the consequent search and transactions costs of barter loomed large for Keynes among the social costs of hyperinflation.[13] It is unfortunate that the economics profession did not pay proper attention to this chapter of the *Tract*, as can be seen from Harry Johnson's account of the concept of 'forced saving':

> This is a concept, which after 40 years of monetary theorizing, we can understand pretty well. All it amounts to is that, if you inflate the money supply of an economy, this will drive up prices; and the rise in prices will cause people to try to restore their real balances; and, to do that, they have to spend less on goods and services. So, you are extracting goods and services from them through the inflationary process. This is known in the modern literature as 'the inflation tax.'[14]

All of this was in Keynes' *Tract*, but not in the writings of Marshall and Pigou. Thomas Paine, considering the consequences of financing the American War of Independence by the issue of Continental bills ('not worth a Continental'), had identified currency depreciation as a form of taxation: 'As while they pay the former they do not suffer the latter, and as when they suffer the latter they did not pay the former the thing will be nearly equal.'[15] Keynes was the first, however, to point to the effect of the inflation rate of the demand for real money balances as the source both of the revenue-maximizing inflation rate and of the social cost of anticipated inflation.

Keynes also trenchantly analysed the effects of unanticipated inflation in a world of nominal contracts. Testifying before the Colwyn Committee on National Debt and Taxation in 1924, Keynes urged that the Treasury issue 'bonds of which the capital and interest would be paid not in a fixed amount of sterling but in such amount of sterling as has a fixed commodity value as indicated by an index number'.[16] In the absence of such indexation, higher than expected inflation would transfer command over purchasing power from lenders to borrowers and, until contracts expired, reduce the real value of nominal wages, salaries and rents. The chance of such unexpected redistribution would result in risk premiums in nominal contracts.[17]

Even though 'money is simply that which the State declares from time to time to be a good legal discharge of money contracts',[18] prolonged price stability had conditioned the public to treat money values as real values. The gold parity of the pound sterling, for example, had prevailed from its establishment by Sir Isaac Newton as Master of the Royal Mint in 1717 until the outbreak of the First World War, excepting only the Napoleonic Wars and their aftermath from 1797 to 1821. Keynes noted that the British price level was the same in 1844 as in 1881 and in 1914. From 1826 to 1914, British prices never rose more than 30 per cent above the level of 1844, 1881 and 1914, and never fell more than 30 per cent below that level.[19] As a result, drastic changes in the price level were not expected.

> So rooted in our day has been the conventional belief in the stability and safety of a money contract that, according to English law, trustees have been encouraged to embark their trust funds exclusively in such transactions, and are indeed forbidden, except in the case of real estate (an exception which is itself a survival of the conditions of an earlier age), to employ them otherwise.
>
> German trustees were not released from a similar obligation until 1923, by which date the value of trust funds invested in titles to money had entirely disappeared.[20]

Partly because of this conventional faith in price stability, Keynes felt that the nominal rate of interest would adjust sluggishly to high rates of inflation, and noted that in Germany, even though the money rate of interest was 100 per cent per month, this rate lagged behind the rates of inflation and of exchange rate depreciation, so that the real rate was negative.[21] Irving Fisher was also concerned,[21] in his Geneva lectures on *The Money Illusion* (1928), that expectations of inflation had appeared to adjust only adaptively in the German and other hyperinflations, so that the real interest rate and real wages could be affected by changes in inflation in the short run. Fisher's analysis of inflation, which resembled that of Keynes' *Tract*, led him to pioneering estimation of distributed lags, as a way to investigate the adaptive expectations hypothesis, and to calculation of the correlation between unemployment and changes in the price level.[22]

Keynes made careful use of the distinction between real and nominal interest rates in the *Tract*. Although this distinction is usually traced to Irving Fisher's *Appreciation and Interest* (1896), Keynes identified the first clear exposition as having been given in the concluding note to Book VI, chapter vi, of Marshall's *Principles of Economics* (1890), restated in Marshall's Note to the Indian Currency Committee (1899), where Marshall also cited Fisher.[23] Keynes' command of this point, to which he returned in the *Treatise on Money* (1930), is interesting in the light of Harry Johnson's observation that:

> The restatement of the quantity theory of money did include one important and genuinely novel element, drawn not from Keynes but from his

predecessors in monetary theory; this consisted in its emphasis on the Fisherian distinction between the real and the money rate of interest and on the expected rate of price inflation or deflation as determining the difference between the two.[24]

THE THEORY OF THE FOREIGN EXCHANGES

Having explained the incentive for governments to inflate the money supply and the prices level, and the social costs of doing so, Keynes turned, in his chapter on 'The Theory of Money and the Foreign Exchanges', to the effects of inflation on the exchange rate. Keynes determined the price level in the *Tract* from the ratio of an exogenous money supply (given floating exchange rates) to a stable demand for real money balances that depended on real income and the rate of inflation. No theory of the level of real income was offered, although Keynes accepted that inflation and deflation could have real effects, at least in the short run, because of gradually adapting expectations and because the nominal interest rate could not fall below zero. Given national price levels, if there are 'a number of independent systems of inconvertible paper, what basic fact determines the rates at which units of the different currencies exchange for one another? The explanation is to be found in the doctrine, as old in itself as Ricardo, with which Professor Cassel has latterly familiarised the public under the name of "purchasing power parity"'.[25] In his memorial article on Marshall in 1924, Keynes paid tribute to the presentation of the purchasing power parity theory of exchange rates in a memorandum appended by Marshall to his evidence before the Gold and Silver Commission in 1888, part of the memorandum reappearing in Appendix C of *Money, Credit and Commerce*. Keynes quoted a synopsis of the theory from Marshall's memorandum:

> Let B have an inconvertible paper-currency (say roubles). In each country prices will be governed by the relation between the volume of currency and the work it has to do. The gold price of the rouble will be fixed by the course of trade just at the ratio which gold prices in A bear to rouble prices in B (allowing for cost of carriage).[26]

Because of arbitrage, the prices of tradable goods could not differ across countries, when calculated in the same currency, by more than the costs of transport and tariffs. Pigou, writing on 'Some Problems of Foreign Exchange' in the *Economic Journal* (1920) and on 'The Foreign Exchanges' in the *Quarterly Journal of Economics* (1922), discussed possible deviations from purchasing power parity due to the existence of non-traded goods, since it would be only the prices of traded goods which would be equalized directly, not the purchasing power of money.[27] Following Pigou, Keynes argued that 'if capital and labour can freely move between home and export industries without loss of relative efficiency, ... and if the fluctuations in price are solely due to monetary influences', there would still be a tendency towards equalizing the purchasing power of money. Unfortunately, Keynes weakened the force of this analysis by adding another assumption, that 'there is no movement in the "equation of exchange"', that is, in the terms of trade, which amounts to assuming his conclusion that PPP holds. Keynes went beyond Pigou to observe that even if all goods were traded, if the different national price indices were constructed with different weights, then changes in relative prices of goods, due to technical progress, changes in factor prices or demand shifts, would cause deviations from measured PPP.[28] Keynes went on to present monthly data from August 1919 to June 1923 on the dollar value of sterling, francs and lire, and to conclude that 'The figures show that quantitatively speaking, the influences which detract from the precision of the purchasing power parity theory have been in these cases small, on the whole, as compared with those which function in accord with it'.[29] Keynes thus accepted PPP as an empirical matter, not on grounds of theory except under special assumptions, so that he felt free to write in 1935 that 'No one now puts faith in the famous "purchasing-power-parity" theory of the foreign exchanges, based on index numbers'.[30] His acceptance of the theory in 1922 and 1923 reflected his belief that the monetary fluctuations of the time were so great as to swamp other influences, and his assumption in his earlier writings that balance of payments equilibrium would be preserved by price and exchange rate changes, rather than by income changes.

Having established the rate of exchange depreciation as the difference between national rates of inflation, as a corollary of PPP, Keynes went on to be, in Bloomfield's words, 'the first to develop a systematic theory of the forward exchanges, with the central proposition that the forward discount or premium on the exchange rate between two currencies tends to equal the difference between short-term interest rates in the two centers'.[31]

Forward quotations for the purchase of the currency of the dearer money market tend to be cheaper than spot quotations by a percentage per month equal to the excess of the interest which can be earned in a month in the dearer market over what can be earned in the cheaper. It must be noted that the governing factor is the rate of interest obtainable for short periods, so that a country where, owing to the absence or ill-development of an organised money market, it is difficult to lend money satisfactorily at call or for very short periods, may, for the purposes of this calculation, reckon as a low interest-earning market, even though the prevailing rate of interest for longer periods is not low at all. This consideration generally tends to make London and New York more attractive markets for short money than any Continental centres.[32]

Keynes discussed other possible reasons for divergence of the forward premium or discount from the short-term interest rate differential, apart from limited opportunities for short-term lending in some countries. Even when risk from exchange rate variation was covered by forward transactions, there was still default risk: 'The possibility of financial trouble or political disturbance, and the quite appreciable probability of a moratorium in the event of any difficulties arising, or of the sudden introduction of exchange regulations which would interfere with the movement of balances out of the country.... In the case of Roumania or Poland, for example, this factor is, at times, the dominating one.'[33]

> But there is a further contingency of considerable importance which occurs when speculation is exceptionally active and is all one way. It must be remembered that the floating capital normally available, and ready to move from centre to centre for the purpose of taking advantage of moderate arbitrage profits between spot and forward exchange, is by no means unlimited in amount, and is not always adequate to the market's requirements.... [An] abnormal discount can only disappear when the high profit of arbitrage between spot and forward has drawn fresh capital into the arbitrage business.

Keynes criticized attempts to distinguish speculative dealings in foreign exchange from dealings to hedge commercial transactions, and opposed official exchange regulations intended to discourage speculation, explaining that speculators and arbitrageurs perform a vital service.[34]

While noting the causes of possible deviations from purchasing power and interest rate parity, Keynes equated the rate of exchange rate appreciation or depreciation to differences between inflation rates, the spread between spot and forward exchange rates to the nominal interest differential, and the difference between real and nominal interest rates to the expected rate of inflation. Because he held, as did Irving Fisher, that expectations adjusted to actual inflation only sluggishly, Keynes' analysis allowed real interest rates, calculated *ex post*, to differ systematically across countries. 'So few persons understand even the elements of the theory of the forward exchanges that there was an occasion in 1920, even between London and New York, when a seller of spot dollars could earn at the rate of 6 per cent per annum above the London rate for short money by converting his dollars into sterling and providing at the same time by a forward sale of the sterling for reconversion into dollars in a month's time.'[35] Before accepting this evidence of an unexploited profit opportunity and of the possibility of systematically beating the market, however, one should recall that 1920 was the year when currency speculation reduced Keynes' net assets from £16,000 to a negative figure of almost £2,000.[36]

THE CONFLICT OF INTERNAL AND EXTERNAL STABILITY

Keynes held that while dearer money in one financial centre under the gold standard would cause a gold inflow and money supply increase to restore interest rate and purchasing power parity with a fixed exchange rate, only the spread between spot and forward rates would have to adjust under an inconvertible paper standard.[37] Flexible exchange rates would allow the money supply to be set at a level appropriate for domestic stabilization. From the *Tract* to Bretton Woods, Keynes believed that short-term stability of the exchange rate, to reduce the risks of international transactions, should be accompanied by long-term flexibility, which would leave monetary and fiscal policy free to achieve domestic stabilization goals. In the *Tract*, as in *The Economic Consequences of Mr Churchill*, his attack on the return to the prewar gold parity in 1925, Keynes urged that a fixed exchange rate be sacrificed for the sake of price level stability. Both imported inflation and deflation were to be avoided.

Keynes opposed importing inflation through fixed exchange rates when other countries inflated their currencies because inflation would reduce the real quantity of money and make nominal contracts riskier. He had an equally lively sense of the costs of deflation, which he strongly rejected as a means of preserving a pegged exchange rate. Because nominal interest rates cannot be negative when money carries an own-rate of interest of zero and has a negligible storage cost, even correctly anticipated deflation can affect the real rate of interest. In the *Tract*, Keynes recognized the existence of what he later came to term a liquidity trap at a nominal interest rate of zero. 'When prices are falling 30 to 40 per cent between the average of one year and that of the next, as they were in Great Britain and in the United States during 1921, even a bank rate of 1 per cent would have been oppressive to business, since it would have corresponded to a very high rate of real interest. Anyone who could have foreseen the movement even partially would have done well for himself by selling out his assets and staying out of business.'[38] The British deflation of 1921, which was accompanied by a sharp increase in unemployment, resulted from a British attempt to move closer to the prewar dollar/sterling parity at a time when United States prices were falling. When Britain completed the restoration of the prewar parity in 1925 Keynes warned, in *The Economic Consequences of Mr Churchill*, that the competitive position of British goods in the world market could be restored only by a decline in British prices and money wages, and that considerable unemployment would be needed to drive down money wage rates.

In the *Tract*, Keynes rejected the claim that the deflation required to restore the exchange rate of $4.86 to the pound sterling was a necessary act of justice to prewar bondholders. The great wartime increase in public debt had occurred after Britain suspended convertibility into gold, so that the deflation would be a transfer of real wealth from borrowers and from taxpayers as a whole to creditors whose loans had largely been made in inflated, inconvertible paper currency. Keynes cited an article on 'Devaluation versus Deflation' by Irving Fisher in the eleventh of the *Manchester Guardian* Commercial Reconstruction supplements (7 December, 1922), in which Fisher estimated that money contracts in the prewar United States had been an average of one year old.[39] Keynes' protest against the redistribution of wealth to bondholders and the increased burden on the taxpayers of a return to the gold standard echoed the protest of William Cobbett in his *Paper Against Gold* (1817) a century earlier. The Napoleonic Wars had been financed by expanding the National Debt in the period of floating exchange rates and currency inflation after the Bank of England stopped paying out gold in 1797.

Restoration of the prewar gold parity in 1821 benefited fundholders, who had bought government stock with depreciated paper, at the expense of all taxpayers.[40] Keynes wrote in the comfort of King's College, Cambridge, Cobbett in Newgate Prison because of an article on military discipline, but their indignation was the same.

Keynes warned in the *Tract* that deflation would reduce real output and increase unemployment:

> Comparatively free from the burden of internal debt, and free also from serious budgetary deficits, Czechoslovakia was able in the course of 1922, in pursuance of the policy of her finance minister, Dr Alois Rasin, to employ the proceeds of certain foreign loans to improve the exchange value of the Czech crown to nearly three times the rate which had been touched in the previous year. The policy has cost her an industrial crisis and serious unemployment. To what purpose? I do not know.... Pursuing a misguided policy in a spirit of stern virtue, she preferred the stagnation of her industries and a still fluctuating standard.[41]

Keynes' opposition to the deflation required to restore the prewar gold and dollar parity of sterling was persistently misunderstood and misrepresented by the City Editors (that is, the financial editors) of the London newspapers, who felt that they had refuted Keynes by showing that in the past prices had been less stable under inconvertible paper currency than under the gold standard. Keynes was moved to write to the City Editor of the *Morning Post* on 1 August, 1925:

> I must also state what your City Editor must surely know well, that to assert that the management of the currency in the country prior to the readoption of gold had my approval, is a gross travesty of my opinions. I criticicised it repeatedly and vehemently.
> It is typical of the silliness and utter lack of intellectual standards by which this controversy is carried on by City Editors that because I am in favour of managing the currency *with a view to stability of prices*, I am therefore supposed to be in favour of managing it *with a view to instability of prices*. Sometimes I am said to have favoured deflation, as in your columns, and sometimes inflation, as in the columns of your contemporaries.[42]

Keynes proposed to reconcile internal and external balance by stabilizing the purchasing power of money at its current level, pegging the exchange rate at the level which would satisfy purchasing power parity at that price level. This would not be the same as simply pegging the exchange rate at its current level, because by 1925 the exchange rate of the pound sterling had already appreciated above that level on speculation about the return to gold. Keynes' desire to free monetary policy from the need to achieve the prewar parity and then to maintain a fixed exchange rate was not shared in the Bank of England, the Treasury, the City of London or the London School of Economics, but he was not alone. Four other Cambridge economists, John Clapham, Claude Guillebaud, Frederick Lavington and Dennis Robertson, presented a report on *Monetary Policy* to the British Association, advocating return to gold at a lower parity.[43] In the United States, Irving Fisher of Yale urged monetary management to stabilize the price level, not the exchange rate. By 1930 and 1931, when Keynes was supporting an import tariff and export bounty to offset the overvaluation of the pound, Ralph Hawtrey, the only economist in the Treasury, favoured devaluation.

In his *Treatise on Money* in 1930, Keynes again discussed exchange rate flexibility as a means of allowing monetary policy to be used for the pursuit of internal balance:

> With a local standard the dilemma, which sometimes faces a Central Bank, that it may be impossible to preserve both internal equilibrium and external equilibrium at the same time, presents itself much less acutely. If the Central Bank is free to vary both the rate of foreign exchange and its market-rate of interest, applying appropriate doses of each at the right moment, there is much less risk of the loss of wealth and output due to the prevalence of general unemployment. For direct changes in the price of foreign-trade goods can be largely substituted for unemployment as the first link in the causal chain whereby external equilibrium is preserved and restored. Its disadvantage is to be found in the diminished mobility that it means (if that is a disadvantage) for foreign lending.[44]

In the *Treatise*, where the capital account of the balance of payments ('foreign lending') was a function of the covered interest-rate differential, Keynes proposed an interest-equalization tax on British residents' income from overseas securities, to allow the real interest rate on British securities to differ from that in the rest of the world by the amount of the tax.[45]

CONCLUSION

In the *General Theory*, Keynes labelled the Cambridge tradition of monetary theory, represented by Pigou, as classical, for lacking a theory of the level of output in a monetary economy. Keynes was not only thoroughly familiar with Cambridge monetary theory, but in the *Tract* had made major contributions to it: inflation as a tax on money balances and government bonds, the reduction in the real quantity of money as a social cost of inflation, the revenue-maximizing rate of inflation, and the nominal interest rate differential as the forward premium or discount in the foreign exchange market. None of these can be found, for example, in Pigou's articles on the value of money and on the foreign exchanges. Keynes' analysis of the index number problem with purchasing power parity, when relative prices change and goods have different weights in different national indices, was also original. He continued to regard the *Tract* as sufficiently valuable to reprint three of its five chapters in his *Essays in Persuasion*. His lasting concern with the costs of inflation can be seen in his four articles in *The Times* in 1937, discussing whether government borrowing for increased defence spending would be inflationary even though there was still substantial unemployment,[46] and in the analysis of how to close the inflationary gap by means of taxation and deferred pay in *How to Pay for the War* (1940).[47] Keynes' grasp of the classical mechanism of automatic balance of payments adjustment, displayed in the *Tract*, can also be seen in his final paper, 'The Balance of Payments of the United States' (1946), which argued that there would be no lasting dollar scarcity because balance of payments surpluses would raise United States prices and income, and lower the US interest rate, sufficiently to restore equilibrium.[48]

Keynes was a classical economist when he wrote the *Tract*, in the sense of lacking a theory of the determination of the level of output in a monetary economy or of the equilibrating effect of changes in the level of output (as opposed to prices), but discussion of the consequences of deflation, given that the nominal interest rate cannot fall below zero and that nominal wages may be sticky, is suggestive of his later work. To understand the development of Keynes' thought, one must understand his starting point. Keynes started from the Marshallian foundations of Cambridge monetary theory, but he was an important contributor to this theory, not just an expositor of accepted doctrine.

NOTES

1. Bloomfield (1947), 298.
2. Buchanan and Wagner (1977). Contrast Humphrey (1981).

3. Keynes (1983), xII, 689–783.
4. Keynes (1923), 62n. The review of Fisher is in Keynes (1983), xI.
5. *Ibid.*, 61.
6. *Ibid.*, 46. Rudolf Havenstein, president of the Reichsbank, felt that since monetary growth was slower than price inflation, money creation was not keeping up with the needs of trade, but hoped that thirty-eight new, high-speed printing presses, supplied by thirty paper mills working overtime, would enable the Reichsbank to catch up.
7. Garraty (1978), 154.
8. Keynes (1972), xvi; H. Johnson, in E. Johnson and H. Johnson (1978), 118.
9. Keynes (1923), 37.
10. *Ibid.*, 54. The third, unused method was a capital levy. Reparations and inter-Allied war debts were, in effect, repudiated after 1931.
11. *Ibid.*, 49.
12. *Ibid.*, 40.
13. *Ibid.*, 45–6 gives time series on the real quantity of money in Germany, Austria and Russia during their inflations.
14. H. Johnson, in E. Johnson and H. Johnson (1978), 142.
15. Paine, quoted by Mathias (1979), 290.
16. Keynes, quoted by Humphrey (1974), 241.
17. Keynes (1923), 1.
18. *Ibid.*, 8.
19. *Ibid.*, 10.
20. *Ibid.*, 7 and 7n.
21. *Ibid.*, 19–23, on the distinction between real and nominal interest rates.
22. Fisher (1926).
23. Keynes (1951), 165.
24. H. Johnson, in E. Johnson and H. Johnson (1978), 195, 245.
25. Keynes (1923), 71.
26. Keynes (1951), 166–7.
27. Pigou (1920), 467; Pigou (1922), 64–5.
28. Keynes (1923), 73–6.
29. *Ibid.*, 81, 83–7.
30. Keynes (1935), 361.
31. Bloomfield went on to say that 'Keynes' contributions in this field and their great influence of interwar thinking and policy cannot be analyzed here'. Bloomfield (1947), 298.
32. Keynes (1923), 103–4.
33. *Ibid.*, 105.
34. *Ibid.*, 109, 112–13.
35. *Ibid.*, 109.
36. Moggridge, in Keynes (1983), xII.
37. Keynes (1923), 114.
38. *Ibid.*, 23.
39. *Ibid.*, 121–2.
40. Cobbett (1817).

41. Keynes (1923), 120.
42. Pollard (1970), 49.
43. *Ibid.*, 7.
44. Keynes (1930), ı, 362. The discussion of flexible exchange rates in pp. 356–63. Foreign lending, as a function of the covered interest differential, is discussed on ı, 131–2, 161–6, 213–16, 326–42.
45. *Ibid.*, ıı, 315.
46. Hutchison (1977).
47. Keynes (1940), Trevithick (1975).
48. Keynes (1946).

2 Equilibrium and disequilibrium in Keynes' *Treatise on Money*

In the preface to his *Treatise on Money*, Keynes announced that:

> My object has been to find a method which is useful in describing not merely the characteristics of a static equilibrium, but also those of disequilibrium, and to discover the dynamic laws governing the passage of a monetary system from one position of equilibrium to another.[1]

Although the format of the work is that of a full-blown, comprehensive treatise on monetary theory and institutions, the theoretical heart of the *Treatise* is Keynes' application of new, incompletely worked out analytical tools to the economic problems of Britain in the 1920s. The work is worth re-examination because the *General Theory*, which has shaped the thinking of even such a well-known critic of Keynesian macroeconomics as Milton Friedman,[2] would have been a different book had Keynes not written the *Treatise* first. Since his concern in writing the *General Theory* was to make good the *Treatise*'s lack of a theory of output, Keynes felt no need to restate aspects of monetary theory on which his views were well known and basically unchanged. For example, the liquidity preference theory of the interest rate expounded in the *General Theory* takes as given the much lengthier discussion of asset markets and portfolio choice in the *Treatise*. Nowadays, however, the *General Theory* is no longer read by a public acquainted with the *Treatise*, so that Keynes' failure to restate material from his earlier book has led increasingly to misunderstanding of the later Keynes as an economist for whom 'money doesn't matter'.

The *Treatise* illuminates the work of Clower, Leijonhufvud, Benassy, Iwai and others[3] who interpret Keynesian macroeconomics not as a long-run competitive equilibrium with sticky wages, but rather as a protracted disequilibrium or as a shifting short-period equilibrium subject to volatile expectations, quantity constraints on transactions and uninsurable uncertainty. As the definitive statement of his central message, these economists propose Keynes' 1937 article in the *Quarterly Journal of Economics*,[4] which emphasizes uncertainty, imperfect information, changes in expectations, and costs and time lags in adjusting expectations and behaviour. In fact, such concerns recall the dependence of investment in the *Treatise* on windfall profits or losses that surprise entrepreneurs and cause them to revise their expectations of the potential profitability of investment projects. Similarly, recent treatment of the multiplier as a process through time, rather than as a tool for comparative static analysis, shows its links to the period analysis of the *Treatise* and of D. H. Robertson's studies of economic fluctuations. Keynes' reliance on disequilibrium analysis in the *Treatise* and his insistence on the continuous evolution of his thought indicate that these disequilibrium interpretations of the *General Theory* are not simply pulled out of thin air. A close reading of the *Treatise*, in fact, shows that they were part and parcel of Keynes' thought for at least a decade.

New classical economists and other critics of Keynes reject his claim to have derived an unemployment equilibrium, arguing that the existence of involuntary unemployment indicates 'the non-execution of some perceived mutually advantageous trades'.[5] The growing consensus that the *General Theory* does not provide a theory of long-run unemployment equilibrium should not reduce interest in the work, however, since economists are concerned with the phenomenon of involuntary unemployment even when it occurs in situations not normally classified as equilibria. The disequilibrium interpretation of the *General Theory* suggests that the methodological break between that book and the *Treatise* was not as sharp as has usually been supposed. As Keynes warned in the preface to the *General Theory*:

> The relation between this book and my *Treatise on Money*, which I published five years ago, is probably clearer to myself than it will be to others; and what in my own mind is a natural evolution in a line of thought which I have been pursuing for several years, may sometimes strike the reader as a confusing change of view. This difficulty is not made less by certain changes in terminology which I have felt compelled to make.[6]

THE FUNDAMENTAL EQUATIONS

Keynes intended the *Treatise* as a definitive treatment of money, which would confirm his stature as a serious academic scholar, rather than just the author of stinging polemics on the Versailles Peace Treaty, the return to the gold standard, and the Treasury's opposition to Lloyd George's public works proposals. Consequently, its two volumes contain material ranging from Book II on index numbers, drawing on the essay on index numbers with which Keynes won the Adam Smith Prize in 1908, to speculations on whether the profit inflation engendered by the influx of Spanish treasure from Mexico and Peru into Europe made the achievements of Shakespeare and his contemporaries possible. The theoretical heart of the *Treatise*, however, consists of Books III and IV, in which Keynes presents his Fundamental Equations for the value of money and discusses the dynamics of the price level. Since the terminology of the *Treatise* is not the familiar one of post-*General Theory* macroeconomics, it is necessary to describe the Fundamental Equations before proceeding to consider the concepts of equilibrium and disequilibrium used by Keynes in the *Treatise*.

Keynes' Fundamental Equations are variations of the Equation of Exchange first presented in *The Purchasing Power of Money*, the classic 1911 exposition of the quantity theory of money by the Yale economist Irving Fisher. The version popularized by Fisher is $MV = PT$, where M is the quantity of money, V its velocity of circulation, P the price level and T the volume of transactions. Keynes' formulation in the *Treatise* differs from Fisher's version by emphasizing the distinction between the purchasing power of money and the average price level of transactions. This emerged from Keynes' view that a significant part of the money supply served to finance asset transfers rather than the sale of output. The Cambridge cash balance version of the quantity theory, the $M = kPT$ presented by Marshall and Pigou, and by Keynes in *A Tract on Monetary Reform*,[7] closely resembled Fisher's theory since it was primarily concerned with transactions demand for cash balances and with determination of a price level P that was not the reciprocal of the purchasing power of money.[8]

Keynes' two Fundamental Equations for the price level of consumption goods and for the price level of output as a whole are tautologies, but are converted into equilibrium conditions by the imposition of behavioural constraints on the variables in the equations. Keynes himself noted, after deriving his Fundamental Equations, that:

> These conclusions are, of course, obvious and may serve to remind us that all these equations are purely formal; they are mere identities; truisms which tell us nothing in themselves. In this respect they resemble all other versions of the Quantity Theory of Money. Their only point is to analyse and arrange our material in what will turn out to be a useful way for tracing cause and effect, when we have vitalised them by the introduction of extraneous facts from the actual world.[9]

The equations for the price level of consumption goods and services is derived from the definition of saving as the difference between the normal (expected) earnings of factors of production and consumption expenditure. (See Table 2.1 for definition of symbols.)

$$P \cdot R \equiv E - S$$

$$\equiv \frac{E(R+C)}{O} - S \qquad \text{from the identity } O \equiv R + C$$

$$\equiv \frac{E}{O} \cdot R + I' - S \qquad \text{from the definition } I' \equiv (C/O)E$$

$$P \equiv \frac{E}{O} + \frac{I'-S}{R} \qquad \text{First Fundamental Equation}$$

$$P \equiv \sum_{i=1}^{2} \frac{M_i V_i}{O} + \frac{Q_1}{R} \equiv W_1 + \frac{Q_1}{R}$$

This expression says that the price of consumption goods equals earnings per unit of output plus windfall profits in the consumption goods sector per unit of that sector's output. Earnings are equal to the quantity of money times its velocity of circulation.[10] Profits, Q, constitute a windfall to entrepreneurs, the excess of the value of current output over the earnings of the factors of production (including the return on capital). Since profits are $(PR + I) - E$, then $Q \equiv I - S$ by the definition of saving as the difference between earnings and consumption expenditure. Q_2, profits in the investment goods sector, will be $I - I'$, the excess of the market value of the current output of capital goods over their cost of production. Q is the sum of Q_1 and

Table 2.1   Symbols used in A Treatise on Money

O	total output of goods in physical units, $O \equiv R + C$
R	volume of consumption goods and services flowing on market in a given time period
C	net increase in stock of investment goods in physical units
E	earnings of factors of production: cost of production
S	saving: difference between money–income and money–expenditure on current consumption, $S \equiv E - PR$
P	price level of consumption goods and services, reciprocal of the purchasing power of money
P'	price level of investment goods
π	price level of output as a whole
I	value of current output of investment goods
I'	cost of production of current output of investment goods
Q	windfall profits (or losses) in the economy as a whole; not included in E or S
Q_1	windfall profits in the consumption goods sector
Q_2	windfall profits in the investment goods sector, $Q \equiv Q_1 + Q_2$
W	rate of earnings (not just wages) per unit of human effort
W_1	rate of earnings per unit of output, E/O
e	coefficient of efficiency, defined by $W \equiv eW_1$, so that e measures units of output per unit of human effort
M_1	Income deposits: cash deposits held by individuals
M_2	Business deposits: cash deposits held by entrepreneurs
M_3	Savings deposits: held as investments, not to finance expenditures
V_i	velocity of circulation of M_i, $i = 1, 2, 3$
L	foreign lending (private capital account)
B	foreign balance (current account)
G	gold outflow or other balancing transactions, $G \equiv L - B$

Q_2, so that profits in the production of consumer goods, Q_1 equals $I' - S$. This can be derived by noting that Q_1 is the excess of the market value of the output of consumer goods over the earnings of the factors of production employed in that sector, $PR - (E - I')$, and substituting in the definition of saving used in the *Treatise*.

Keynes' Fundamental Equation for the price level of output as a whole is derived in a manner analogous to his first equation:

$$\pi O \equiv PR + P'C$$

$$\pi \equiv \frac{PR + P'C}{O}$$

$$\pi \equiv \frac{(E - S) + I}{O}$$

$$\pi \equiv \frac{E}{O} + \frac{I - S}{O} \qquad \text{Second Fundamental Equation}$$

$$\pi \equiv W_1 + \frac{Q}{O} \quad \equiv \sum_{i=1}^{2} \frac{M_i V_i}{O} + \frac{Q}{O} \quad [11]$$

These 'equations' are, of course, identities which as yet have no economic content. Keynes provided such content by incorporating the functional dependence of investment, saving and velocity on the rate of interest, and of investment on windfall profits in the previous period. He explained the determination of the interest rate in terms of portfolio balance, emphasizing demand for money as an asset. The level of output was fixed in the short run by full employment of available resources. Each period's investment decisions affect the full employment level of output in the next period by changing the capital stock. Windfall profits (or losses) are the difference between investment and saving in the current period, and, together with the interest rate, determine what investment will be in the next period. The Fundamental Equations thus provide the framework for a dynamic model of a capitalist economy.

CONCEPTS OF EQUILIBRIUM IN THE TREATISE

Equilibrium may be defined in three different ways in economics: in terms of satisfaction and mutual consistency of agents' expectations, as a position of rest (or steady-state growth path) or as a situation where markets clear. The *Treatise* links the first two senses of equilibrium. When entrepreneurs' expectations are satisfied, windfall profits will be zero and the entrepreneurs will have no incentive to revise their investment decisions. If expectations turn out to be mistaken and windfall profits or losses occur, the resulting changes in investment will cause the economy to deviate from steady-state growth. Failure of markets to clear, although discussed in connection with credit rationing and two isolated passages on sticky wages, is not analysed systematically or made a focus of attention in the *Treatise*.

This is a serious deficiency in a work which was motivated by concern with the persistence of high rates of unemployment in Britain in the 1920s, which Keynes interpreted as the protracted failure of a market to clear.

The driving force in the economic system of the *Treatise* is 'profits', Q. Keynes restricts Q to unanticipated profits or losses of entrepreneurs, and excludes such windfalls from income or saving. Windfalls are treated, in effect, as entering directly into the capital accounts of entrepreneurs without appearing on their income accounts. The equation $Q = I - S$, intended by Keynes as a definitional identity, contains the behavioural implication that windfall profits or losses go entirely into changes in entrepreneurs' asset holdings, not into capitalists' consumption. Interest on capital, normal remuneration of entrepreneurs and anticipated monopoly gains are all considered part of the earnings of factors of production rather than part of profits.

When Q is positive, entrepreneurs increase their planned production for the next period, and, conversely, they cut back on production plans when Q is negative. Since investment decisions depend directly on the anticipated stream of earnings from a proposed investment and inversely on the interest rate (cost of capital), two interpretations of the role of Q are possible, though both are offered in the *Treatise* as though they were identical. Through most of the *Treatise*, Q is an *ex post* realization, a measure of surprise that serves entrepreneurs as an additional piece of information in forming expectations of profitability. If they regard their environment as stochastic, repeatedly mistaken expectations may be necessary before expectations are revised. Otherwise the windfall profit or loss might be interpreted as simply a random shock without any implications for future profitability.

In one passage, however, Keynes observed that

> We have spoken so far as if entrepreneurs were influenced in their prospective arrangements entirely by reference to whether they are making a profit or loss on their current output as they market it. In so far, however, as production takes time ... and in so far as entrepreneurs are able at the beginning of a production-period to forecast the relationship between saving and investment at the end of this production-period, it is obviously the anticipated profit or loss on new business just concluded, which influences them in deciding the scale on which to produce and the offers which it is worthwhile to make to the factors of production. Strictly speaking, we should say that it is the *anticipated* profit or loss which is the

mainspring of change, and that it is by causing anticipations of the appropriate kind that the banking system is able to influence the price-level.[12]

Windfall profit or loss, Q as a measure of surprise cannot have an anticipated value other than zero. One cannot expect an unexpected gain. Clearly, this passage treats Q as an *ex ante* measure of above normal profitability or of quasi-rents to be obtained from an investment project because of the difficulty competitors have in swiftly increasing the stock of investment goods to a desired level. This version of Q resembles the q theory of investment: Keynes' Q_2 ($Q_2 = I - I'$) is greater than, equal to, or less than zero, as Tobin's q, which is I/I', the ratio of the market value of new investment goods to their cost of production, is greater than, equal to, or less than one.

According to Keynes:

> The essential characteristic of the entity which we call *Profits* is that its having a zero value is the usual condition in the actual economic world of to-day for the equilibrium of the purchasing power of money. It is the introduction of this *fact* from the real world which gives significance to the particular Fundamental Equations which we have selected and saves them from the character of being mere identities.[13]

In this passage, the key equilibrium condition of the economic system of the *Treatise on Money* appears in the incongruous guise of an empirical fact. In equilibrium, Q, its components Q_1 and Q_2, and, in an open economy, the balance of payments G are all equal to zero.[14] No unanticipated profits or losses are then experienced in either the capital goods or consumer goods sector, so expectations are satisfied. Furthermore, entrepreneurs have no reason to alter their offers to hire factors of production, so production in the next period will be the same as production in the current period (or will continue to grow at the same steady rate). Expectational equilibrium coincides with equilibrium as a position of rest. Since investment is not constrained to equal depreciation, this equilibrium should be interpreted as a steady state growth path, with the stock of investment goods and the level of production growing at rates set by the exogenous growth of population and technical knowledge. Keynes mentioned three per cent per annum as an example of a plausible steady rate of growth of output in a progressive community, and pointed out that for price stability the quantity of money would have to grow at the same rate as output, so that the first term of each Fundamental Equation would remain constant.[15] With a constant money supply, the price level would decline steadily and the nominal rate of interest lie below the real rate.

In the *Treatise*, Keynes was concerned with stabilization of the purchasing power of money and of the price level of output as a whole as a means to stabilize production and employment. The relevant equilibrium for Keynes' purposes in the *Treatise* is not a constant price level (if the exogenous supply of money is constant), but the $I=S$, $Q_1=Q_2=O$ expectational equilibrium which keeps production on its steady state growth path, barring such exogenous shocks as wars, demand shifts or innovations in technology or organization.

Although aggregate profits in each sector are zero in equilibrium, Keynes follows the Marshallian rather than the Walrasian tradition by allowing individual entrepreneurs to experience windfall profits or losses, provided that these cancel out in aggregate. Keynes implicitly assumes that one entrepreneur with an unanticipated profit of $10X$ will increase his offers to factors of production by exactly as much as ten entrepreneurs with losses of X apiece reduce their offers.

Keynes refers to:

equilibrium – i.e. when the factors of production are fully employed, when the public is neither bullish nor bearish of securities and is maintaining in the form of savings-deposits neither more nor less than the 'normal' proportion of its total wealth, and when the volume of savings is equal both to the cost and to the value of the new investments.[16]

The last clause is simply the zero windfall profits condition, $I=I'=S$, and the second means that securities prices, and hence interest rates, are not expected to change. Equilibrium is seen as a situation in which entrepreneurs have no incentive to change their behaviour. The issue of equilibrium as the clearing of markets for factors of production is less clear but more important. The *Treatise* presents no theory of output other than determination of the level of production by full employment of stocks of resources which are given by past investment decisions and exogenous factors such as population growth and natural resource endowment.

In *The Economic Consequences of Mr Churchill* and later criticism of Britain's return to the gold standard, Keynes blamed a mistaken monetary policy for the persistence of widespread involuntary unemployment. This belief informed his composition of a treatise on the pure and applied theory of money. The rate of unemployment remained above 10 per cent in Britain in every year except one between 1921 and the outbreak of the Second World War. The Clyde shipyards, Lancashire cotton textile mills, and Midlands and Welsh coal mines were export industries, made especially vulnerable to overvaluation of sterling by specific sectoral weaknesses. Millions of tons of merchant shipping had been launched around the world to meet transport needs during the First World War, creating a stock of cargo vessels in excess of peacetime needs. The decision taken by Winston Churchill and Admiral Sir John Fisher to switch the Royal Navy from coal to oil power and to buy a controlling interest for the Admiralty in the Anglo-Persian Oil Company was merely the most striking instance of a trend away from the use of coal as a fuel for ships. The war disrupted textile exports, so, since the technology was relatively simple and Asian labour costs low, Indian, Chinese and Japanese textile producers expanded their capacity and output to capture former British markets in Asia. India, which absorbed one-third of the cotton textile production of Lancashire on the eve of the First World War, imported almost no British textiles twenty years later, and went on to become a net exporter of cotton textiles to Britain.[17]

Keynes argued that both the absorption of displaced workers into new jobs in other industries and regions and the recovery from the recession of 1920–1 were choked off by Britain's return to the gold standard in 1925, when the pound sterling was pegged at $4.86 even though its free market value was then $4.40.[18] Since no alteration was made in the nominal value of debts and other contracts when the prewar parity was restored, creditors received a transfer of real wealth from the rest of the community. Deflation of wages and prices was necessary for adjustment to foreign competitive pressures under the new exchange rate, but resistance to wage cuts resulted in both continued unemployment and industrial unrest culminating in the General Strike of 1926, which grew out of a coal strike following an attempt to cut coal miners' wages. Keynes' work in the following years was divided between popular essays and speeches advocating remedies for unemployment, and the elaboration of a formal body of monetary theory which would support his views on monetary policy.

Keynes' concern that the labour market might fail to clear without government intervention goes as far back as a letter he wrote to his mother on 10 August 1914, in his first few days at the Treasury at the beginning of the First World War. In that letter he wrote: 'Where money can be spent on capital improvement, a large part of it going in payment of labour which might otherwise be unemployed, the argument for spending it is very strong.'[19] The labour market is not analysed explicitly in the *Treatise* because Keynes felt that the topic fell outside the confines of a work on monetary theory, and so he restricted his direct comments on employment to *obiter dicta*. Concern with unemployment and market clearing remained at the back of his mind none the less, and reappeared in the *General Theory*.

FAILURE OF MARKETS TO CLEAR

Keynes attributes unemployment, whether of labour or of other resources, to downward rigidity of the earnings of the factors of production. In so far as workers and the owners of other factors of production are able to reduce their earnings to the equilibrium level but stubbornly refuse to do so, their unemployment is voluntary. Keynes discusses the emergence of unemployment due to such rigidities in the course of examining the consequences of a decline in investment caused by an increase in the bank rate. The 'natural rate' in the following quotation is the equilibrium rate of interest, r, which equates $I(r)$ to $S(r)$.

> At this stage, therefore, we have a fall both in P and in P', consequent losses to *all* classes of entrepreneurs, and a resulting diminution of the volume of employment which they offer to the factors of production at the existing rate of earnings. Thus a state of unemployment may be expected to ensue, and to continue, until the rise in the bank-rate is reversed or, by chance, something happens to alter the natural-rate of interest so as to bring it back to equality with the new market rate.
>
> Moreover, the longer this state of affairs continues, the greater is the volume of unemployment likely to be. For, at first, entrepreneurs may continue to offer employment on the old terms, even though it involves them in losses, partly because they are tied up with long-period contracts with the factors of production which they cannot quickly get out of, and partly because it will be worthwhile, so long as they hope and believe that the period of loss will be fairly short, to avoid the expenses of closing down and starting up again. But as time goes on, these motives will gradually lose their effect and cease to operate.
>
> Finally, under the pressure of growing unemployment, the rate of earnings – though, perhaps, only at long last – will fall.[20]

In this passage of the *Treatise*, Keynes treats unemployment as the result of nominal factor price rigidity in the face of shocks to the demand for factors of production. He mentions contracts and doubt, in a stochastic world, about the permanence of demand shocks as barriers to speedy adjustment, but does not discuss the causes of wage rigidity at that point in his book. A possible explanation is offered sixty-four pages later: 'If the money-rates of remuneration of the *different* factors of production could be reduced simultaneously and in an equal proportion, no one need suffer.... But there is generally no means of securing this.'[21] Keynes refers to differences in bargaining power and length of contracts (including debts) as reasons why all nominal incomes cannot be reduced to their new equilibrium levels in step with each other. Resistance to wage cuts thus represents the refusal of one group to bear a disproportionate share of the burden of adjustment while bondholders and workers with unexpired contracts gain from the increased purchasing power of money. In the absence of across-the-board wage bargaining between a single federation representing employers and a single trade union group unencumbered by a carry-over of intertemporal contracts fixed in nominal terms, no trade union would wish to be the first to accept wage cuts, in case the cuts did not become general or affect money incomes other than wages.

It is important to remember that this theory has been pieced together from two widely separated passages in a book which provides no formal analysis of the labour market and does explain the determination of the level or duration of unemployment. The Fundamental Equations are formulae for the determination of the price level, not output or employment, and the only dynamic processes discussed at length in the *Treatise* are price fluctuations. The core of the economic theory of the *Treatise* assumes that adjustments occur in prices rather than quantities. Not until the second chapter of the *General Theory* does Keynes give appropriate emphasis in his published work to the explanation of the cause of consequences of downward rigidity of nominal wages presented in the two passages quoted from the *Treatise* above. As he puts the matter there,

> the struggle about money-wages primarily affects the *distribution* of the aggregate real wage between different labour-groups, and not its average amount per unit of employment, which depends, as we shall see, on a different set of forces. The effect of combination on the part of a group of workers is to protect their *relative* real wage. The *general* level of real wages depends on the other forces of the economic system.... Every trade union will put up some resistance to a cut in money-wages, however

small. But since no trade union would dream of striking on every occasion of a rise in the cost of living, they do not raise the obstacle to any increase in aggregate employment which is attributed to them by the classical school.[22]

Despite subsequent commentary, this relative wage explanation of downward rigidity of nominal wages does not depend in any way on the concept of 'money illusion', as developed by Irving Fisher in a series of lectures published under that title two years before the completion of the *Treatise*.[23] Fisher pointed to widespread confusion between real and nominal changes during the German hyperinflation of 1922 and 1923, due to attitudes ingrained during the prolonged price stability of the preceding century, and called for education of the public about the difference between real and nominal interest rates and between real and money wages. In Keynes' theory, workers do not mistake a reduction in money wages for a reduction in real wages. Rather, they correctly perceive the distributional problems associated with adjusting real wages under decentralized bargaining and staggered, multiperiod contracts. 'There may exist no expedient by which labour as a whole can reduce its *real* wage to a given figure by making revised *money* bargains with the entrepreneurs.'[24]

But while labour and product markets are assumed to clear through most of the *Treatise*, financial markets generally are not. While Keynes regarded the US money market as a close approximation to a pure auction market in which all buyers and sellers are satisfied, the British market typically had a fringe of unsatisfied borrowers willing to pay prevailing rates of interest but kept out of the market by credit rationing. The Bank fixed both the bank rate (the rate at which it would discount notes presented to it by deposit banks) and the quantity of bank money without having to keep them in a market-clearing relationship. The Bank kept control over the terms at which credit was offered and the abundance of credit through the use of 'terror, agreement and convention' to induce the co-operation of the banking system in rationing loans. The 'terror' referred to is the fear that the Bank would use its power to alter the stock of bank money to make its official bank rate effective. In addition, the Bank of England had a formal agreement with the London clearing banks under which they paid an interest rate on their savings deposits two points below the official bank rate. A significant body of custom and tradition linked interest rates on loans to the bank rate.[25]

In so far as there exists both an unsatisfied fringe of would-be entrepreneur-borrowers and a fringe of unemployed factors of production, an injection of additional money into the economy can increase employment at existing rates of remuneration.[26] Thus, if downward wage rigidity leads to unemployment, the existence of credit constraint makes expansionary monetary policy effective as a means of eliminating involuntary unemployment. This provides a rationale for Keynes' advocacy in the *Treatise* of expansionary open-market operations and bank rate reductions undertaken jointly by the Bank of England and the Federal Reserve Board to remedy 'the slump of 1930'.[27] However, the failure of the money market to clear is simply taken as an institutional datum, and no explanation is offered in the *Treatise*, other than an appeal to convention for the otherwise irrational behaviour of presumably profit-seeking bankers. This irrationality is especially difficult to explain in view of the fact that the Bank of England remained privately owned until 1945, and that in the interwar period its directors were keenly interested in the Bank's ability to pay dividends to its shareholders, a concern which could conflict with use of the Bank's powers for economic management. Despite this weakness, Keynes' linkage of credit rationing and unemployment is suggestive for current theories of disequilibrium in systems of interrelated markets in which obstacles to market clearing in one market (such as a liquidity trap) cause disequilibrium elsewhere in the model.

Keynes notes in the *Treatise* one other instance of quantity adjustment rather than price adjustment: Ralph Hawtrey's theory that liquid capital (inventories of finished goods) acts as a buffer for short-period changes in investment in fixed and working capital or in demand, thus obviating the need for any fluctuation in prices. Keynes objects that carrying charges on liquid stocks (which include warehouse and insurance costs as well as interest and the depreciation of perishable and fashion-sensitive goods) are sufficiently high to preclude the holding of inventories large enough to play a significant role as a buffer. He also attempts to show that interest accounts for only a small part of carrying costs, so that liquid stocks are not interest-sensitive. This is part of a running controversy he had with Hawtrey over the relevant interest rate for policy purposes. Hawtrey emphasized the short-term rate, which enters into inventory-holding decisions, while Keynes stressed the long-term rate, which affects investment in fixed capital.[28] In the derivation of his Fundamental

Equations, Keynes assumes that the flow of goods and services available for consumption consists entirely of perishable products which have to be sold immediately in auction markets for whatever they will bring.[29] In his comments on Hawtrey, Keynes overlooks the key general implication that adjustments can occur in quantities rather than prices. This point was brought home to him after the completion of his book when Hawtrey, commenting on page proofs circulated by Keynes, criticized the *Treatise*'s implicit assumption of constant output.[30]

INVESTMENT, SAVING AND THE RATE OF INTEREST

In *A Treatise on Money*, investment decisions depend on anticipated streams of earnings and on the rate of interest (cost of capital). Expectations of profitability depend on past values of Q_1, windfall profits in the production of consumer goods and services, and Q_2, windfall profits in the production of investment goods, with different weights in the investment function reflecting the differing capital intensities of the sectors. 'Surprises', represented by non-zero profits, are the channel through which entrepreneurs absorb information about market conditions. An unexpected profit makes an entrepreneur more optimistic, and induces him to invest in expanding productive capacity. Changes in the level of investment can thus be written as a function of windfall profits and of the change in the rate of interest:

$$\Delta I = I_t - I_{t-1} = f(r_t - r_{t-1}, Q_{1t-1}, Q_{2t-1}) \tag{1}$$

with $f_1 < 0, f_2 > 0, f_3 > 0$, where f_i is the partial derivative of function f with respect to its ith argument. That is, an increase in the long-term interest rate reduces investment, while windfall profits increase investment by leading entrepreneurs to purchase investment goods to enable them to increase their output. The level of investment in any period, as the sum of the past changes in the level of investment, depends on the current interest rate and on all the past windfall profits and losses.

Keynes accepts Schumpeter's theory of entrepreneurial innovation in organization and technology as the explanation of major movements in investment in fixed capital, and hence as the principal exogenous shocks setting off cyclical fluctuations in economic activity: 'Apart from the many minor reasons why these should fluctuate, Professor Schumpeter's explanation of the major movements may be unreservedly accepted.' However, there is no indication that Keynes had read Schumpeter's *Theory of Economic Development* (which did not appear in English translation until 1934), since he goes on to note: 'This convenient summary of Professor Schumpeter's views is taken from Wesley Mitchell, *Business Cycles*', which was Keynes' main source for Continental theories of the trade cycle.[31] Keynes wished elsewhere in the *Treatise* that 'my knowledge of the German language was not so poor (in German I can only clearly understand what I know already! so that *new* ideas are apt to be veiled from me by the difficulties of the language)'.[32]

In the *Treatise*, saving depends positively on the rate of interest. Decisions on how much to save are not made by the same people who decide on the proportion of investment goods to consumption goods and services; and entrepreneurs, lacking perfect foresight, must make production decisions before knowing the results of the saving decisions.[33] This allows investment to differ from saving, and corresponds to divergence between *ex ante* or planned investment and saving in the *General Theory*. Such a divergence appears in the *General Theory* as an unintended change in inventories, but in the *Treatise*, where output is assumed perishable, it is a windfall gain or loss on the sale of current output. (In the *Treatise*, S is not necessarily identical with planned or desired saving but may include some forced saving due to the 'inflation tax' on money balances.)

Richard Lipsey has pointed out that the identity of I with $Q+S$ in the *Treatise* and of *ex post* I with *ex post* S in the *General Theory* is purely a question of choice of definitions, and that the discussion in many macroeconomic textbooks of dynamic forces which ensure that this identity holds are misguided.[34] What matters is whether I and S are equal *ex ante* under their *Treatise* definitions and, if they are not, whether the economy possesses equilibrating forces that move them toward equality. Because of a failure to recognize the functional dependence of saving on the level of income, such forces are absent from the *Treatise*. Thus there is only an unstable 'knife-edge' equilibrium (as in the Harrod-Domar growth model).

The *Treatise*'s treatment of saving suffers from the lack of a concept such as the consumption function, which plays such an important role both in Kahn's articles on the multiplier and in the *General Theory*. This is seen most clearly in Keynes' parable of the effects of the introduction of a 'Thrift Campaign' (increase in saving) in a community devoted entirely to the production and consumption of bananas. Such a campaign reduces the selling price of bananas and causes unexpected losses for entrepreneurs. Since attempts by entrepreneurs to reduce their losses by cutting wages or laying off workers will reduce spending on bananas by exactly as much as costs of production are reduced, losses will be unchanged. Savings still exceed investment. Curtailment of investment, which occurs as losses make entrepreneurs pessimistic about future profitability, will increase losses by making $I-S$ even more negative.

> Thus there will be no position of equilibrium until either (a) all pro-
> duction ceases and the entire population starves to death; or (b) the thrift
> campaign is called off or peters out as a result of the growing poverty; or
> (c) investment is stimulated by some means or other so that its cost no
> longer lags behind the rate of saving.[35]

Keynes' consideration of what Patinkin termed a 'coroner solution'[36] shows that he failed to grasp the implications of saying that the thrift campaign could peter out because of growing poverty: saving falls as income falls. Instead, in the parable Keynes implicitly assumes that the marginal propensity to consume was unity, and that the quantity of planned saving is independent of the level of income.

This problem may explain why the *Treatise* does not repeat the case for public works projects to reduce unemployment put forward by Keynes and Hubert Henderson in their 1929 pamphlet *Can Lloyd George Do It?* and in articles in *The Nation and Athenaeum*.[37] Their argument rested on the rounds of secondary employment generated when the workers on the public works projects spent their wages, but without a theory of leakages of spending into saving and imports, it appeared that government expenditure of one farthing might suffice to employ all of Britain's one million unemployed, were it not for time lags in the successive rounds of spending. The *Treatise*'s assumption that Q, the unanticipated change in the value of entrepreneurs' assets, does not affect their consumption indicates that investment can generate the saving to finance itself. (Saving, in the last sentence, means that part of income, whether anticipated or unanticipated, which is used to acquire assets instead of being spent in consumption.) It was not until Kahn's article that the other half of the problem was solved. His analysis showed that after successive rounds of spending the multiplier converged to a finite value.[38]

The market rate of interest at which $I(r)$ equals $S(r)$ is called the natural rate of interest, a term Keynes borrowed from the Swedish economist Knut Wicksell.[39] At the natural rate, the second term of each of the Fundamental Equations would be zero. Unlike Wicksell, Keynes did not identify the natural rate with the marginal productivity of capital, mainly because he held that to be a part of value theory rather than monetary theory. Keynes went so far as to apologize that his chapters on fluctuations in the rate of investment 'are of the nature of a digression, which is doubtfully in place in a Treatise on Money but has to be included because the fluctuations in the rate of investment have not been treated, sufficiently for my purpose, elsewhere'.[40] In the *General Theory*, with its analysis of the labour market and of the marginal efficiency of investment, he abandoned this severe compartmentalization.

Investment, saving and the velocities of circulation are all functions of the rate of interest.[41] The price level of investment goods (P'), an inverse function of the rate of interest, clears asset markets by inducing wealth-owners to hold the exogenously given volume of savings deposits (M_3) and the stock of investment goods, including the flow of newly-produced ones coming on the market for the first time in the current period. P' is thus determined by the disposition of the public to 'hoard' money, an early version of liquidity preference. Given the rate of new investment and its cost of production, the price level of consumption goods is determined by the public's disposition to save, since investment decisions determine what resources remain available to produce consumption goods, while saving decisions determine how much of income is spent on them. Keynes presented these equilibrium conditions as though they were definitions: 'The price-level of investments as a whole, and hence of new investments, is that price-level at which the desire of the public to hold savings-deposits is equal to the amount of savings-deposits which the banking system is willing and able to create.'[42]

At this point, it is possible to write down the short period equilibrium for the model implicit in Books III and IV of the *Treatise*:[13]

Exogenous variables: Reserves and r set by the central bank, foreign interest rate and price level (r_F, π_F) exogenous, O (Output) set by full employment of inherited factors of production.

$$I \equiv S + Q \tag{2}$$
$$I(r, Q_{-1}) = S(r) \tag{3}$$
$$\pi O \equiv E + Q \tag{4}$$
$$PR \equiv E - S \tag{5}$$
$$O \equiv C - R \tag{6}$$
$$P'C \equiv I \tag{7}$$
$$V_i = V_i(r) \qquad i = 1, 2 \tag{8}$$
$$E \equiv M_1 V_1 + M_2 V_2 \tag{9}$$
$$M_3 = m(P') \tag{10}$$
$$\text{Reserves} = f(M_1, M_2, M_3) \tag{11}$$
$$L \equiv B + G \tag{12}$$
$$L(r/r_F) = B(\pi / x\pi_F) \tag{13}$$

Equation (3) is the internal equilibrium condition that there be no windfall profits or losses (zero Q). Equation (13) is the external equilibrium condition that overseas lending, determined by foreign and domestic rates of return, equals the trade balance, dependent on the terms of trade, so that there are no balancing international gold flows (changes in the net foreign assets of the monetary authority). Foreign variables are exogenous to a small open economy, and, in keeping with Keynes' contributions to his 1929 *Economic Journal* debate with Ohlin about German reparations and the transfer problem, income effects on the trade balance are neglected. The variable x in equation (13) is the exchange rate (stated as the price of foreign exchange, domestic currency per unit of foreign currency). The interest rate has a negative effect on investment and foreign lending, and a positive effect on saving and the velocities of circulation.

The public's 'bearishness', or propensity to hoard in equation (10), combined with a given stock of savings deposits, gives P', the price level of investment goods. Equation (10) is the equilibrium condition that wealth-owners achieve the desired composition of their portfolios, given asset prices. Together with the rate of interest and last period's Q, which determine how much entrepreneurs will spend on investment goods, P', the price of investment goods which induces wealth-owners to hold the existing stocks of assets, yields a value for C, the volume of real investment, from equation (7). The identity that C and R must add up to O, the full employment level of output, then determines the volume of consumption goods and services. (Keynes' selection of an abbreviation for Output which so closely resembles zero is not one of his happier choices of symbols.)

The rate of interest determines the velocities of circulation, so the volume of income-deposits created by the banking system determines the level of money income, E. From equations (2) and (3), Q is zero in equilibrium, so with saving, $S(r)$, determined by the interest rate, the volume of income-deposits and the interest rate, acting through E, set values for the price levels P and π.

When the interest rate happens to be the natural rate which equates I and S in equation (3), this is a simple, standard quantity theory of money model of equilibrium. However, it is an unstable system that will be in equilibrium only if the banking system – meaning primarily the central bank – sets the market rate of interest equal to the natural rate. If the banking system fails to do this, windfall profits or losses will emerge and, through the investment function, will generate cumulative divergence from equilibrium. While the central bank may not know the natural rate of interest, which changes as technology changes, Keynes assumes that it can tell whether the market rate is above or below the natural rate by observing profit inflation or deflation. If the banking system does not set the appropriate interest rate, there is no force in this model which would restore equilibrium.

Under a floating exchange rate system, the exchange rate sets the terms of trade so that the trade balance offsets foreign lending. Under this system, the r_F term in equation (12) would be expanded to account for anticipated changes in exchange rates. With the exchange rate pegged under the gold standard, the burden of adjustment falls on the domestic price level and interest rate as gold flows alter the level of reserves in the banking system. Alternatively, the monetary authority pursues monetary policy intended to prevent gold outflows. Keynes urged that in the event of inconsistency between conditions for internal and external equilibrium, the exchange rate be allowed to change so that monetary policy can pursue the goal of domestic price stabilization, which will in turn stabilize output. In the model of the *Treatise*, cumulative inflation or deflation can be avoided only by the central bank setting the appropriate interest rate. Keynes firmly rejected a policy of defending the gold value of the pound sterling by pegging the domestic market rate of interest to the foreign interest rate, because this would surrender the opportunity to use *r* as an instrument for domestic stabilization.

Given that Britain was tied to the gold standard, the *Treatise's* proposed remedy for 'the slump of 1930' was concerted international action by central banks, perhaps orchestrated by the Bank for International Settlements, to lower interest rates. During the financial crisis of summer 1931, when it was clear that co-ordinated action by central banks was lacking or inadequate, Keynes advocated a protective tariff to ease the foreign balance constraint on British domestic monetary policy. It is significant that he dropped this proposal immediately when the pound was floated in September 1931.

CUMULATIVE PROCESSES

Keynes considered it possible that a divergence between the market and natural rates of interest could generate either cumulative inflation, as in Germany, Austria, Hungary and Russia in the years after the First World War, or cumulative deflation, as in the wake of the Wall Street panic of October 1929 or the Kreditanstalt crash of 1931. He argued that in a closed economy (such as the world as a whole), with cheques as the only means of payment and no cash reserves held by the banks or public, 'it is evident that there is no limit to the amount of bank-money which the banks can safely create *provided that they move forward in step'*.[44] This is a restatement of Wicksell's case of a pure credit economy, in which the banking system, unconstrained by any need for cash reserves or any cost of production of money, can lend as much as they choose and count on these loans generating an equal quantity of bank deposits. On the other hand, no single bank can expand on its own, because many of the deposits created by its loans would be at other banks.

The market rate and the natural rate of interest are both real rates, adjusted for anticipated changes in the purchasing power of money.[45] As long as the market rate is below the natural rate, *I* is greater than *S*, windfall profits are being received, and entrepreneurs have an incentive to increase investment still further, thus perpetuating the disequilibrium. Of course, since resources are assumed to be fully employed, entrepreneurs as a group cannot expand their total output, although they bid against each other for factors of production in an attempt to do so. This implicit assumption has a surprising consequence:

> If entrepreneurs choose to spend a portion of their profits on consumption (and there is, of course, nothing to prevent them from doing this), the effect is to *increase* the profit on the sale of liquid consumption-goods by an amount exactly equal to the amount of profits which have been thus expended. This follows from our definitions, because such expenditure constitutes a diminution of saving, and therefore an increase in the difference between I' and S.... Thus profits, as a source of capital increment for entrepreneurs, are a widow's cruse which remains undepleted, however much of them may be devoted to riotous living.[46]

This precursor of Kalecki's 'capitalists get what they spend' alters Keynes' usual assumption in the *Treatise* that entrepreneurs do not consume out of windfall profits. However, this does not invalidate the identity $I = S + Q$, since the entrepreneurs' consumption decisions are taken as affecting the disposition of their normal remuneration and as diminishing S. By reducing their saving and shifting the $S(r)$ function in toward the origin, the entrepreneurs raise the natural rate of interest. Since, as we have seen, the market rate of interest is tied by 'terror, agreement and convention' to the bank rate set by the central bank, the natural rate rises above the market rate, setting off cumulative inflation. Strictly speaking, Keynes' Fundamental Equations show that prices are above their equilibrium levels when I is greater than S and windfall profits are being received, but not that prices are rising. What drives the cumulative process is the investment function, equation (1) above, which causes the gap between I and S to keep growing once it has come into existence.

Keynes classifies changes in W_1, the earnings of factors of production per unit of output, as income inflation or deflation, and changes in Q as profit inflation or deflation, dividing the latter into commodity or capital inflation (or deflation) according to whether it acts through Q_1 or Q_2.[47] He suggests that a profit inflation, but not an income inflation, may be needed to redistribute consumption from unproductive to productive use (consumption of working capital by workers rather than consumption by rentiers) as a means of expanding employment and, with a lag, output.

> The evil of not creating wealth would be greater than the evil that the wealth, when created, should not accrue to those who have made the sacrifice, namely, to the consumers whose consumption has been curtailed by the higher prices consequent on the Profit Inflation.[48]

If downward rigidity of factor earnings creates unemployment, monetary policy can be used to eliminate the unemployment through a cumulative profit inflation generated by a reduced market rate of interest. Keynes fails, however, to advise the central bank on how to ensure that its actions generate only a profit inflation rather than an income inflation. If one insists on retaining Keynes' definition of Q as unanticipated gains or losses rather than his sometime usage of it as a measure of above-normal profit opportunities, it is not clear that a cumulative process, which would become expected as it went along, could continue to generate surprises. The existence of an excess supply of labour means that W_1 is stuck above its equilibrium value due to market structure, so that income inflation will not occur until full employment is achieved. Under full employment, it would no longer be possible for the central bank to reallocate resources from consumption to investment through expansionary monetary policy, since income inflation would result as soon as the public understood the policy.

The cumulative process continues until the market rate and the natural rate are equated, either through the banking system deciding to change the market rate of interest, or through changes in the natural rate.[49] The two major means of altering the natural rate to establish equilibrium, a falling schedule of the marginal efficiency of investment and the consumption function linking the level of saving to income, appear in the *General Theory* but not in the *Treatise*.

CONCLUSION

The economic theory of the *Treatise*, as outlined above, embodies an approach that is not alien to that of the *General Theory*, but is rather an incomplete version of it, one that requires further elaboration of the investment and saving functions and of the emergence of involuntary unemployment in the labour market. Keynes' detailed discussion of monetary institutions and of the balance between 'bear' and 'bull' opinion in securities markets provides the setting for the liquidity preference theory of the rate of interest, while his stress on the importance of reducing interest rates to expand production debunks the legend that money is unimportant in Keynesian economics. Keynes' remarks on unemployment and the inability of workers to simultaneously adjust their money incomes so as to equilibrate real wages are clear anticipations of the *General Theory*'s treatment of the labour market. The emphasis in the *Treatise* on uncertainty, imperfect foresight of entrepreneurs and windfall profits or losses as surprises causing alteration of expectations is in line with interpretations of the *General Theory* put forward by Keynes himself in his article in the *Quarterly Journal of Economics* in 1937 and revived by several recent commentators, notably Clower, Leijonhufvud and Davidson. The incorrect treatment of technical progress in the first Fundamental Equation, pointed out by Hansen, and the careless handling of identities and equations are comparatively minor faults, and were easily repaired.

The principal failing of the *Treatise* was that it neither incorporated the passages on unemployment into a theory of the level of output, nor turned from price dynamics to fluctuations in output and employment. Keynes' final verdict on the *Treatise* was:

> When I finished it, I had made some progress towards pushing monetary theory back to becoming a theory of output as a whole. But my lack of emancipation from preconceived ideas showed itself in what now seems to be the outstanding fault of the theoretical parts of that work (namely, Books III and IV), that I failed to deal thoroughly with the effects of *changes* in the level of output. My so-called 'fundamental equations' were an instantaneous picture taken on the assumption of a given output. They attempted to show how, assuming the given output, forces could develop which involved a profit-disequilibrium, and thus required a change in the level of output. But the dynamic development, as distinct from the instantaneous picture, was left incomplete and extremely confused.[50]

Keynes' development from the *Treatise* to the *General Theory* can thus be seen as a continuing struggle to remedy deficiencies in the earlier work and to round out its analysis. This suggests that in fact Keynes did not abandon a concern with expectational disequilibrium and its links with market failure, rigidities and instability of the economic system, and replace it with efforts to derive a long-run competitive equilibrium with involuntary unemployment, as some have argued. Instead of a sharp, total break, there was a considerable degree of continuity in his thought, though this was partially masked by his subsequent changes in terminology and forms of exposition.

NOTES

1. Keynes (1930), I, v.
2. Patinkin (1969), and exchange between Patinkin and Friedman in Gordon (1973).

3. Clower (1965); Leijonhufvud (1968); Benassy (1975); Iwai (1981).
4. Keynes (1937).
5. Barro (1977), quoted in Gordon (1981), 494.
6. Keynes (1936), xxi–xxii.
7. Marshall (1923); Pigou (1917); Keynes (1911, 1923).
8. Field (1981), 13.
9. Keynes (1930), I, 138.
10. Alvin Hansen (1932) pointed out that Keynes had implicitly assumed the same rate of technical progress in the two sectors, a criticism which Keynes accepted in an exchange of notes in the *American Economic Review* – see Keynes (1932). Hansen and Herbert Tout (1933) presented a suggestion by Erik Lundberg for eliminating this problem, using definitions proposed by Ragnar Frisch. W_1 in Keynes' First Fundamental Equation was replaced by W_r, the rate of earnings per unit of consumers' goods, calculated as $(E-I')/R$. While Keynes' slip concerning index numbers was unfortunate in a work that devoted so many pages to exposition of the theory of index numbers, Hansen went much too far in claiming to have caught 'A Fundamental Error in Mr. Keynes' *Treatise on Money*'. See Adarkar (1933); Rübner-Petersen (1934); Hart (1933).
11. The sum of $M_1 V_1$ and $M_2 V_2$ appears here where Keynes wrote $M_1 V_1$, to make his notation consistent with his discussion.
12. Keynes (1930), I, 159.
13. *Ibid.*, I, 156–7.
14. *Ibid.*, I, 151.
15. *Ibid.*, I, 258.
16. *Ibid.*, I, 146–7.
17. Harnetty (1972).
18. Keynes (1925); Moggridge (1969).
19. Quoted by Edel (1979), 222–3.
20. Keynes (1930), I, 206–7.
21. *Ibid.*, I, 271.
22. Keynes (1936), 14–15.
23. Fisher (1928) focused attention on money illusion, a concept recognized in his own and others' earlier work. Fisher's pioneering articles on adaptive expectations, distributed lag estimation and a statistical relationship between inflation and unemployment, which attracted little notice when first published in the 1920s, developed out of his studies of money illusion.
24. Keynes (1936),13.
25. Keynes (1930), II, 364–7.
26. *Ibid.*, I, 263.
27. *Ibid.*, II, 386–7.
28. *Ibid.*, II, 130–7.
29. *Ibid.*, I, 176–8.
30. E. G. Davis (1980); Calabre (1980). Cf. E. G. Davis (1981); Spreng (1976); Deutscher (1984).
31. Keynes (1930), II, 95–6.
32. *Ibid.*, I, 199n.

33. *Ibid.*, I, 174.
34. Lipsey (1972).
35. Keynes (1930), I, 178. Cf. Keynes (1981), xx, 78, 80.
36. Patinkin (1976). Cf. Patinkin (1982), 15.
37. Keynes and Henderson (1929).
38. Kahn (1931). Hawtrey provided a similar analysis at about the same time in correspondence with Keynes. See E. G. Davis (1980) and Chapter 4 below.
39. Keynes (1930), I, 155, 186.
40. *Ibid.*, II, 95.
41. *Ibid.*, I, 218: 'A change in bank-rate may in itself modify the velocities of circulation by changing the amount of sacrifice involved in holding balances.'
42. *Ibid.*, I, 26.
43. Klein (1947), 189–92, differs from this model by omitting the dependence of I on Q (my equation (1)), and by taking M_1, M_3 and V_1 as each being exogenous, resulting in an overdetermined model.
44. Keynes (1930), I, 26.
45. *Ibid.*, I, 197. V_1 and V_2 depend, however, on the nominal market rate of interest rather than on the real rate.
46. *Ibid.*, I. 139.
47. *Ibid.*, I, 155.
48. *Ibid.*, II, 126.
49. Wicksell (1907).
50. Keynes (1936), xxii.

3 The reception of the *Treatise on Money* and its relation to the economics of the time

Was there ever a Keynesian revolution? That there was a significant difference between John Maynard Keynes' approach to macroeconomics and the contemporary conventional wisdom of the economics profession has been challenged in recent years. Until the 1970s, the accepted view was that Keynes' ideas were different. Books by Robert Lekachman and Michael Stewart, written during the golden days of the 'New Economics' in the 1960s, reflected the belief that Keynes pioneered public works and deficit spending to remedy unemployment in contrast to a consensus among economists and policymakers that wage cuts would put people back to work as long as confidence was maintained by sound policies of balancing the budget and adhering to the gold standard.[1] Perhaps the first modern doubts were posed by Herbert Stein, who argued that if the Keynesian revolution was about public works instead of wage cuts, it was no revolution: Herbert Hoover pressured businessmen to desist from wage cuts and advocated contracyclical timing of public works projects, while J. Ronnie Davis has documented similar views among Jacob Viner and his colleagues at the University of Chicago.[2] Even Arthur Pigou, singled out by Keynes in the *General Theory* as the archclassical theorist, largely agreed with Keynes on policy, as is shown below. On the side of theory, several distinguished Swedish economists, notably the Nobel laureates Gunnar Myrdal and Bertil Ohlin, were convinced that before the publication of the *General Theory* they had already developed all the essentials of Keynesian macroeconomics out of the tradition of Wicksellian monetary theory.

The reception accorded by economists to Keynes' *Treatise on Money* and to his lectures and pamphlets on remedies for unemployment can tell us a great deal about the state of macroeconomic theory, especially in the English-speaking world, on the eve of the *General Theory*. Contemporary discussion can illuminate such questions as the extent of professional consensus on stabilization policy, the theoretical foundations used to support various policy proposals, and how Keynes' work was perceived in relation to that of his contemporaries. The issue of the perceived continuity of Keynes' work is particularly interesting because of the importance of the *Treatise* for the claim that modern use of disequilibrium dynamics to provide microeconomic foundations of analyses of involuntary unemployment and the effectiveness of active monetary and fiscal policy has a legitimate Keynesian pedigree, and is not simply an *ad hoc* rationalization of a failed theory.

A REVIEW OF THE REVIEWS

The *Treatise* has been so eclipsed by the *General Theory* in the consciousness of the economics profession that it is startling to note that Sir Josiah Stamp was referring to the *Treatise* when he proclaimed: 'In many respects I regard Mr. Keynes' work as the most penetrating and epoch-making since Ricardo.'[3] Charles Hardy was also writing about the *Treatise* when he predicted that 'the serious work of the next generation on business cycles, central banking, and international finance will be more profoundly modified as the result of this than of any other book which has been published since the war'.[4] This reaction was not limited to the English-speaking countries: Achille Loria, in a review which appeared as the lead article in *La Riforma Sociale*, pronounced the *Treatise* 'a masterly intellectual obelisk, sculpted, it is true, with hieroglyphs and arabesques, of which some are bizarre and others hard to decipher, but adorned in every part with august and magnificent characters and rearing its dazzling summit into the hyper-space of creative thought'.[5] The *Treatise* was assured attention because of the identity of its author, who had achieved international celebrity in debates over the Versailles Peace Treaty, the economic burden of reparations and Britain's return to the gold standard. It is striking that the lead article in the issue of *La Riforma Sociale* following Loria's review of the

Treatise was again devoted to Keynes: a critique of his proposal for a revenue tariff.[6] If Peter Drucker's memory is to be trusted, Karl Polanyi attempted to persuade his fellow editors at *Die Oester-reichische Volkswirt* (The Austrian Economist) that their year-end review for 1927 should include 'a piece about an English economist, Keynes is his name; the man, you know, who wrote about the *Economic Consequences of the Peace* in 1919–20. He's coming out with new and exciting theories that stand traditional economics on its head.' It must be noted, however, that the other editors rejected this suggestion as firmly as they rejected Polanyi's proposals for an article discussing Stalinism as a new form of Oriental despotism and for 'a piece on the fall of agricultural prices on the world markets – it foreshadows a serious economic depression in a few years' time'.[7] Joseph Schumpeter wrote to Keynes: 'I do not think that any scientific book has been looked for with so universal an impatience – in our time at least – as yours is',[8] adding a month later that it was 'truly a Ricardian *tour de force*' and predicting over-optimistically that 'it will ever stand out as a landmark in its field'.[9]

Keynes and Macgregor, the editors of the *Economic Journal*, entrusted reviewing the *Treatise* to Sir Josiah Stamp. Although he was an applied economist specializing in taxation and national income accounting rather than a theorist, Stamp had a status in the economics profession closely parallel to that of Keynes. Stamp's long service as secretary of the Royal Statistical Society, editor of its journal, chairman of the largest railway company in the British Isles and chairman of the governing body of the London School of Economics resembled Keynes' career as secretary of the Royal Economic Society, editor of its journal, chairman of the National Mutual Life Assurance Society and Bursar of King's College, Cambridge. Their many non-academic commitments kept either from holding a formal university appointment as professor or lecturer. They served together on such Whitehall bodies as the Economic Advisory Council (1930–9) and the Chancellor's Consultative Council in the wartime Treasury, and each was raised to the peerage for his public service. Stamp was a director of the Bank of England, his seat on the Court of Directors going to Keynes upon Stamp's death.[10] Stamp was uniquely placed to speak for the intersection of the economics profession and the policy establishment: when John Gunther suggested ten names for an inner circle of the English ruling classes, he named 'the great economist Sir Josiah Stamp' in company with such figures as Baldwin, Chamberlain, Montague Norman and Lord Salisbury.[11]

Stamp's enthusiastic review emphasized the separation of investment and saving decisions in the *Treatise* and the book's acceptance, following from this separation, of 'temporary disequilibrium, adjustable by a changed rate of interest, as a chronic state of affairs in society'.[12] This view of an unstable economy in which monetary policy is effective contrasts sharply with new classical macroeconomics' vision of an inherently stable private sector disrupted by unanticipated actions of the monetary authority. Stamp pointed out the affinity between the deflationary effect of saving in the *Treatise* and the underconsumption doctrines of John Hobson, who was later hailed as a precursor in the *General Theory*, and Foster and Catchings, American heretics outside the mainstream of economics. Stamp noted the important distinction that the cause of deflation in the *Treatise* was saving that was not matched by a decision to invest, while for the underconsumptionists, oversaving was synonymous with overinvestment. Both shared a concern with investment and saving as crucial influences on the price level and the credit cycle, however. Stamp provided a concise summary of Keynes' trade cycle theory, noting its implications for government investment (public works) as well as for interest rate policy:

> [I]n Mr. Keynes' analysis, the purchasing power withheld from consumption-goods lowers the demand and the price, and produces business losses which, put crudely here, are 'financed' by that very excess of purchasing power transferred to saving. At some subsequent date it may be possible to create an excess of *investment* over savings, and reverse the process, but this is a mere equivalence and not an absorption of the original error. Dynamically, *at the moment* when private investment is less than savings, the surplus of the latter might be prevented from financing losses by being absorbed in public investment which creates a demand for the right commodities and prevents a deflation of their price on the supply existing.[13]

Keynes' innovation was in theory, not primarily in policy proposals:

> In the realm of pure theory and analysis, I am convinced that our sense of indebtedness to him will continually grow. It was not only stout Cortez upon a peak in Darien who had a Pacific to stare at! And the days of pathbreakers are clearly not yet ended.[14]

Keats' exaltation upon first looking into Chapman's Homer, which came to Stamp's mind in reviewing the *Treatise*, was also recalled by Kenneth Boulding:

> I shall never forget the excitement, as an undergraduate of reading Keynes' *Treatise on Money* in 1931. It is a clumsy, hastily written book and much of its theoretical apparatus has now been discarded. But to its youthful readers it was a peak in Darien, opening up vistas of uncharted seas – 'Great was it that dawn to be alive, and to be young was very heaven!'[15]

The longest journal review of the *Treatise* was a forty-one page review by John H. Williams of Harvard which appeared as a lead article in the *Quarterly Journal of Economics*. Like Stamp, Williams was a scholar whose opinions had weight both in academic circles and among policy-makers, for he combined for many years the positions of Dean of the Graduate School of Public Administration at Harvard and economic adviser to the Ferderal Reserve Bank of New York, including service from 1936 to 1947 as the Bank's vice-president for research. His review was generally favourable: 'As one who has rather a prejudice against big books I can merely say that I have seldom read two large volumes with as much pleasure.'[16] Like Stamp, Williams noted that Keynes differed from the Foster and Catchings 'oversaving' theory by distinguishing the acts of saving and investment,[17] and he praised Keynes for seeing the special significance of savings deposits for portfolio choice and the determination of interest rates: 'So far as I know all theories previous to Keynes' have failed to make use of the statistical division of deposits into demand and time.'[18] Much of the review was an appraisal of the statistical sections of the *Treatise*: there were at the time, for example, no official statistics on the money supply so Keynes had to construct his own estimates. Williams caught one crucial theoretical point missed by other reviewers, Keynes' vacillation between profits as realized windfalls and profits as perceived opportunities to earn more than the normal competitive rate of return on new investments.[19] Williams stressed that expectations form the basis of investment and production decisions, and that windfall profits as surprises matter only as one source of new information for entrepreneurs to use in forming expectations about future profitability. Realized profits are important not in their own right but because of the absence or incompleteness of other sources of information on future market conditions.

Williams' over-all opinion of the *Treatise* was warm enough for Keynes' publishers to quote it on the jacket of reprints of the book: 'It exhibits a rare combination of penetration in theoretical analysis, grasp of mathematical statistical analysis, and felicity of expression. I cannot hope to give a just impression of its scope and richness.'[20] However, he expressed scepticism about the effectiveness of the monetary policy advocated in the *Treatise*, on the grounds that expansionary open-market operations might bid up factor earnings instead of reducing the real rate of interest, and he felt that the 'fundamental equations' were unimportant compared to such major contributions of the *Treatise* as its analysis of the effect of the interest rate on investment and the price level.

The most incisive appraisal of the *Treatise* was by Charles Hardy of the Brookings Institution, who reviewed the first volume, on the pure theory of money, in the *American Economic Review*, and the second volume, on the applied theory of money, in a review article in the *Journal of Political Economy*. After terming the book 'a masterly analysis, comprehensive, penetrating', Hardy explained the intellectual lineage of the *Treatise*:

> In a field which has been perhaps more intensively cultivated during recent years than any other branch of economics, Keynes says much that is new, much more that is new to those who do not read German, still more to those who do not read either German or D. H. Robertson.... In analyzing the causes of discrepancies between the rate of saving and the rate of formation of capital, Keynes follows closely in the footsteps of Wicksell, whose work he brings almost for the first time to the attention of readers of English.[21]

This last comment is particularly interesting in light of Keynes' subsequent reputation for taking scant notice of his Swedish predecessors. Hardy's opinion was shared by Lionel Robbins, who, in his introduction to the English translation of Wicksell's *Lectures*, wrote in 1934 that 'largely as a result of the writings of Professor Hayek and Mr. J. M. Keynes, his [Wicksell's] theories concerning the rate of interest and the price level have become more widely known and his reputation is on the increase'.[22]

Hardy corrected a slip in Keynes' handling of Irving Fisher's distinction between real and nominal interest rates, reminding Keynes that it is anticipated price changes which matter, not past ones, except in so far as experience forms the basis for expectations, as with adaptive or extrapolative expectations.[23] Keynes was aware of Fisher's distinction and, apart from the one passage noted by Hardy, used it correctly in the light of Harry Johnson's claim that

> The restatement of the quantity theory of money did include one important and genuinely novel element, drawn not from Keynes but from his predecessors in monetary theory; this consisted in its emphasis on the Fisherian distinction between the real and money rate of interest and on the expected rate of price inflation or deflation as determining the difference between the two.[24]

Hardy noted that the 'fundamental equations', being tautologies, are not testable propositions, that the natural rate of interest is not directly observable, and that the empirical parts of the *Treatise* offer historical illustrations but not inductive proofs of Keynes' theories. He failed to note that it is possible to test the specification of the investment and saving functions and estimate their parameters, although the body of techniques for doing so was largely undeveloped when Hardy wrote, and that the natural rate of interest can then be obtained from the intersection of the investment and saving schedules. Despite Hardy's remark that 'the central point in the Wicksell doctrine, and the one on which Mr Keynes relies throughout the book, is impervious to inductive proof or disproof', the functional dependence of investment and saving on the rate of interest rather than on other variables such as the level of current income (through the accelerator and the propensity to save) is refutable, so that the theory of the natural rate is an operationally meaningful theorem in Samuelson's sense.[25]

Hardy felt that 'Professor Keynes' program of monetary reform contains less that is new than does his theoretical analysis'.[26] He pointed out the crucial flaw in the *Treatise*, the unconscious shift 'from the stabilization of business activity to the stabilization of prices' as a goal:

> All this analysis Mr Keynes forgets when he reaches his practical program. The stabilization of the price level emerges either as an end in itself or as a standard so closely tied to the ultimate objective as to be practically identified with it.[27]

This was the main problem Keynes struggled with on the road to the *General Theory*. Indeed, he was already aware of it when the *Treatise* was published. In September 1930 Keynes received both Ralph Hawtrey's criticism of the implicit assumption of constant output, and the first draft of Richard Kahn's article on the multiplier, which pointed the way to a theory of the level of employment and output.[28] Keynes and his circle were already dissatisfied with this aspect of the *Treatise* while the rest of the economics profession was still coming to grips with this book. For example, Lorie Tarshis arrived in Cambridge from the University of Toronto as 'the *Treatise*'s most devout believer', thanks to A. F. Wynne Plumptre, a former student of Keynes who had come to teach in Toronto two years earlier with a hundred copies of the first printing of the *Treatise* in his luggage for his students. Tarshis was disconcerted to discover that Keynes' lectures were no longer an exposition of the *Treatise*, and instead reflected Keynes' groping toward a theory of output, along with such unfamiliar concepts as the liquidity trap.[29]

Alvin Hansen, then a professor at the University of Minnesota, published a three-paragraph note entitled 'A Fundamental Error in Keynes' "Treatise on Money"' in the *American Economic Review* in 1932, pointing out that Keynes' first 'fundamental equation' was valid beyond the base-year only if technical progress proceeded at the same pace in the capital goods and consumption goods sectors. Keynes accepted this criticism in a reply in the same journal, and suggested ways in which the fault could be remedied. Hansen and Herbert Tout made further suggestions on this point the next year, in the inaugural issue of *Econometrica*.[30] The necessary modifications are not extensive – the 'fundamental error' can claim that name only because it is an error in a 'fundamental equation'. A more important point is Hansen and Tout's criticism that divergence between investment and saving cannot cause windfall profits or losses because the divergence *is* the windfall, Keynes having defined 'profits' Q as $I-S$. What matters here, however, is the functional dependence of changes in I between periods on realized values of Q. A divergence between I and S in the current period will generate a larger profit disequilibrium in the next period by changing I. The causal forces at work are reflected not in the tautological 'fundamental equations' but in the functional specification of the variables appearing in the 'equations'.

Hansen and Tout make the odd comment that, if Keynes' definitions of investment and saving are discarded, 'the equations then fall to the ground'. Surely any equation can be made incorrect by redefining the variables. Once they look beyond the 'fundamental equations', though, we often find suggestive and helpful analysis. The position which Keynes' book seems to us to hold may perhaps be made clear if we compare it to another masterly work. Without making any absolute comparisons, we may liken it in some respects to *Das Kapital* of Karl Marx. Here is a work which plowed deeply into ground only lightly dug before, which did so inadequately by developing a fundamentally incorrect theoretical structure, and yet withal a work which contained a multitude of correct ideas, greatly obscured by the unsatisfactory nature of the foundations, yet offering a host of illuminating suggestions. Both the truth and the error have been used by ardent protagonists in the political arena to support practical policies in which they believe. The likeness of the *Treatise on Money* to *Das Kapital* in all these respects is striking.[31]

Dennis Robertson, Reader in Economics at Cambridge University, wrote on the *Treatise* in the *Economic Journal*. Robertson had been Keynes' student before the First World War and later worked very closely with him, so closely that the preface to Robertson's *Banking Policy and the Price Level* (1926) says that in Chapters V and VI 'neither of us now knows how much of the ideas therein contained is his and how much mine'. He was distinctly cool toward the *Treatise*, however, and seized on two passages which revealed serious flaws in the work. One was the parable of the banana plantation, in which an autonomous decision by savers to save more causes a cumulative deflation that would continue until either investment is exogenously stimulated (by public works or lower interest rates), the population starves to death, or 'the thrift campaign peters out because of growing poverty'. Robertson failed to catch the implicit assumption that the falling level of income fails to restore equilibrium by reducing saving, but he did argue that since savers can save only by acquiring some asset, someone must   be making abnormal profits from the bidding up of 'mechanical banana-cutters' which would balance the losses of the banana growers.[32]

Robertson also criticized Keynes' widow's cruse passage, which held that if entrepreneurs decided to consume out of profits, this would increase profits by as much as entrepreneurs' spending increased. He showed that since Keynes had explicitly ruled out any rise in cost (factor earnings) per unit of output and tacitly assumed away 'the possibility that output, and thus *aggregate* costs, can be increased', the widow's cruse followed from the truism that all money must be somewhere: 'the money spent on any day by one entrepreneur must be found at nightfall in the bank balance of another'. Since Robertson thanked James Meade in a footnote 'for putting me on the right track' about constancy of output,[33] this insight into the widow's cruse fallacy seems to be due to Keynes' 'Circus', of which Meade was a member while spending the 1930–1 academic year at Cambridge. This ranks with the saving function as one of the crucial first steps beyond the *Treatise*, but it should be noted that Robertson used the possibility of changes in the level of output only to expose the widow's cruse fallacy, and did not yet recognize its wider implications. Moreover, the implicit constancy of output in the *Treatise* was pointed out to Robertson by one of the members of the celebrated Cambridge Circus that worked through and criticized the *Treatise*, rather than being independently noted by Robertson. It is undeniable, however, that Robertson singled out the passages which most clearly display important flaws in the framework of the *Treatise*, flaws of far greater significance than the index number problem described by Hansen as 'a fundamental error'.

A. C. Pigou, Professor of Economics at Cambridge, wrote a brief, unsympathetic review for *The Nation and Athenaeum*. He viewed Keynes' formulae as mere variants of the Cambridge cash-balance version of the quantity theory of money, which was true of the first terms of the fundamental equations, but neglected the profits terms of Keynes' equations. The most that Pigou would concede was that Keynes' version might be handier to use and would perhaps be even more suggestive of useful lines of thought.[34] Pigou was an extreme outlier among the reviewers, finding little new or worthy of remark in the *Treatise*, and publishing this deflating opinion in a journal of which Keynes was both chairman of the editorial board and the major shareholder.

Friedrich Hayek, the newly-appointed Tooke Professor of Economic Science and Statistics at the London School of Economics, devoted considerably more attention to the *Treatise* than Pigou did. Hayek's 'Reflections on the Pure Theory of Money of Mr Keynes' was a long, two-part review of the first volume of the *Treatise* and appeared in *Economica* in August 1931 and February 1932. While finding much to praise in the *Treatise*, Hayek criticized Keynes for not making use of the Austrian capital theory of Böhm-Bawerk, refined by Wicksell. Hayek argued that deflation was a necessary phase of the business cycle in which inefficient producers were weeded out and excessive prolongation of the time structure of production was corrected. Economic contraction would halt and reverse the lengthening of the period of production during overinvestment, and would itself be brought to an end by a new expansion, without creating any cumulative processes requiring policy intervention. 'Hayek went so far as to speak of an "enormous advance." Nevertheless, Keynes replied not without irritation. As he himself remarked on another occasion, authors are difficult to please.'[35] Keynes had no wish to bring Austrian capital theory into his macroeconomics, a stand which enabled him to keep out of the prolonged and angry debate between Frank Knight of Chicago and Hayek which revealed a number of ambiguities and paradoxes in the Austrian concept of an average period of production.[36]

Keynes' reply to the first half of Hayek's review appeared, together with Hayek's rejoinder, in the November 1931 issue of *Economica*. This exchange led to a heated correspondence between Keynes and Hayek from December 1931 to February 1932, of which eleven letters survive, including a letter from Hayek to Keynes on Christmas Day with a reply the same day. Hostilities reopened in March with a harsh review by Piero Sraffa, one of the Cambridge Circus, in the *Economic Journal* of Hayek's *Prices and Production*, a book which Keynes had criticized in his reply to Hayek's review of the *Treatise*. Sraffa's review was followed in print by a reply from Hayek, a rejoinder by Sraffa and a note by Keynes denying Hayek's claim that Sraffa had misinterpreted the *Treatise* in the course of his review of Hayek's book. There was also further correspondence between Hayek and Keynes on the submission of Hayek's reply to Keynes as editor of the *Economic Journal*.

Considering the extent and complexity of this debate and the remarkable abilities of Hayek, Keynes and Sraffa as economic theorists, it is astonishing how little light is provided by this extended case of people talking past each other. At the end of Hayek's review, the most heavily annotated article in the surviving copies of Keynes' journals, Keynes protested: 'Hayek has not read my book with that measure of "goodwill" which an author is entitled to expect of a reader. Until he does so, he will not know what I mean or whether I am right.'[37] But how much goodwill or understanding is displayed in this comment on Hayek's book in Keynes' reply?

> The book, as it stands, seems to be one of the most frightful muddles that I have ever read, with scarcely a sound proposition in it beginning with page 45, and yet it remains a book of some interest, which is likely to leave its mark on the mind of the reader. It is an extraordinary example

of how, starting with a mistake, a remorseless logician can end up in Bedlam.[38]

The only suitable comment on this sorry episode was made by Keynes in a note to Sraffa and Kahn: 'What is the next move? I feel that the abyss yawns – and so do I. Yet I can't help feeling that there *is* something interesting in it.'[39]

There was general agreement among the professional reviewers, excepting Pigou, that the *Treatise* was startlingly novel, and that the innovation was primarily in theoretical underpinnings (rather than in policy prescriptions) and in the analysis of the effect of interest rates on investment and the price level (rather than the 'fundamental equations'). Reviewers such as Hayek and Robertson, who were strongly critical of some propositions in the *Treatise*, shared this view with more sympathetic commentators like Stamp and Williams. Modern economists should note that the reviews indicate considerable openness to new theories even among established senior scholars, and reflect considerable dissatisfaction with the ability of the existing body of economic theory to explain the trade cycle. Significantly, the reviewers displayed no commitment to the 'Treasury view' that expansionary monetary and fiscal policy would be ineffective in stimulating economic activity. On the contrary, Keynes' policy recommendations in the *Treatise* and in *Essays in Persuasion* were accepted as unremarkable, if not generally acceptable, while his theoretical justification for the effectiveness of interest rate reductions was seized upon as novel and exciting. Interestingly, none of the reviewers commented on Keynes' analysis, totalling less than two pages, of concern with relative wages in an environment of decentralized bargaining and staggered multiperiod contracts as a rational explanation of downward rigidity of money wages and thus a cause of unemployment during deflation.[40]

It is curious that while Boulding and Tarshis, who were greatly taken with the *Treatise* when they read it as students, were convinced Keynesians after the publication of the *General Theory*, more senior economists tended to react differently to the two books. Williams, Schumpeter and Hardy,[41] whose praise of the *Treatise* is quoted above, were much cooler toward the *General Theory*. On the other hand, Hansen, who dismissed the 'fundamental equations' as without practical significance, moved from initial sharp criticism of the *General Theory* to become Keynes' most prominent American disciple.

Among works of economics published in 1930, only Irving Fisher's *Theory of Interest* came close to commanding as much attention as the *Treatise* was accorded, and Keynes' book evoked stronger emotions, whether as extravagant acclaim or sharp criticism. The reception of the *Treatise* suggested widespread agreement with the content (although certainly not the wording) of Michal Kalecki's statement, in a 1932 review for a Polish journal of Keynes' Halley Stewart lecture on 'The World's Economic Crisis and the Way of Escape', that Keynes was 'the most serious contemporary bourgeois economist'.[42]

THE TREASURY VIEW AND ITS ACADEMIC SUPPORTERS

While Keynes was not alone among economists in his view of the appropriate economic policy to reduce unemployment and control fluctuations, he was at odds with the consensus of political opinion, which was supported by a substantial number of leading economists. This consensus was expressed in January 1935 by the Principal Private Secretary to the Chancellor of the Exchequer in his minutes of a Treasury meeting called to consider a response to yet another Lloyd George speech urging expansionary fiscal policy:

> There was of course universal agreement that public works as a remedy for unemployment are quite futile. Any programme that could possibly be financed or got going within a reasonable period would not employ more than 3 per cent of the unemployed for say a year or two. At the end of that time the men go back on the dole.[43]

Opposition in Britain to deficit spending on public works as a remedy for unemployment and, until 1931, to leaving the gold standard was bipartisan. Its best known instance was Winston Churchill's 1929 budget speech, together with the supporting memoranda submitted by the Treasury and other departments in rebuttal of Lloyd George's public works proposals of that year. The same views were held by Prime Minister Ramsay MacDonald and Chancellor of the Exchequer Philip Snowden in the succeeding Labour government. Snowden argued that 'an expenditure which may be easy and tolerable in prosperous times becomes intolerable in a time of grave industrial depression'.[44]

The standard scholarly presentation of the Treasury view, that public spending simply displaced private spending, was made in 1925 by Ralph Hawtrey, the Assistant Secretary in charge of the Financial Enquiries Branch of the Treasury, in an article entitled 'Public Expenditure and the Demand for Labour' in *Economica*, the journal of the London School of Economics.[45] This article relied on what later became known as 'crowding out', the argument that government borrowing and spending would discourage private investment by bidding up the rate of interest. Hawtrey, a self-taught economist who served as visiting professor of economics at Harvard in the autumn of 1928, was greatly respected by Keynes, to whom he was linked through their membership in the Apostles, a society of Cambridge graduates which was at the centre of the Bloomsbury group. Hawtrey's comments on the proofs of the *Treatise*, which Keynes showed him shortly before publication, criticized the implicit assumption of constant output and provided a clear numerical example of the multiplier. Despite his part in the development of the multiplier, Hawtrey, a firm believer in a monetary theory of the trade cycle, restated the Treasury case against the effectiveness of fiscal policy in 'Public Expenditure and Trade Depression' in the *Journal of the Royal Statistical Society* in 1933.[46]

Fiscal policy was prevented from serving as an instrument of economic stabilization not only by arguments about crowding out, but also by a bipartisan consensus that a substantial budget surplus should be realized each year as a contribution to the National Debt Sinking Fund for debt reduction. In the fiscal years 1920–1 to 1928–9, surpluses adding up to £736 million were put into the Sinking Fund. In 1928–9, for example, the British government spent £460 million (excluding interest on the debt) and added £76 million to the Sinking Fund.[47] These surpluses were piled up despite the fact that, from 1921 to the outbreak of the Second World War, British unemployment dipped below 10 per cent in only one year. The leaders of the Labour Party shared Conservative views on debt reduction: in 1923 Ramsay MacDonald condemned suggestions that an unexpected revenue surplus be used for housing, insisting that it should go to the Sinking Fund instead. In 1926, Philip Snowden criticized for not going far enough Churchill's Economy (Miscellaneous Provisions) Act, which reduced Treasury contributions to health insurance and the Unemployment Insurance Fund to allow for increased debt reduction.[48] When Snowden warned of a projected budget deficit of £23 million in his budget speech of April 1931, laying the groundwork for tax increases and spending cuts in the near future, the apparent deficit existed only because £60 million for reduction of the National Debt was counted as an expenditure.[49]

Until the gold outflow of August and September 1931 made defence of the gold parity of sterling impossible, monetary policy to stimulate economic activity was ruled out by the need to maintain the pegged exchange rate. The general acceptance of this constraint is aptly illustrated by the former Labour Party minister who exclaimed, when Britain left the gold standard on 21 September 1931: 'They never told us we could do that.'[50] Keynes' proposal for a 'managed currency', reiterated in the *Treatise*, was rejected by the Chamberlain-Bradbury Committee, whose report guided the return to the gold standard in 1925, on the grounds that the managers would face inevitable political temptation to resort to inflationary policies. Furthermore, there was widespread agreement in the political arena with the opinion expressed by Snowden in *The Observer* in 1926 that a return to the gold standard was a necessity which need not be preceded by a healthy balance of trade because 'a stable currency is one of the essentials of a healthy state of trade'.[51]

During the return to gold in 1925 and in the budget speech in 1929, Winston Churchill, the Conservative Chancellor of the Exchequer (1924–9), presented the orthodox Treasury view of his advisers, Lord Bradbury and Sir Otto Niemeyer, the Treasury representatives on the Chamberlain-Bradbury Committee, and of Montague Norman, the Governor of the Bank of England. Despite this, Churchill was the one leading figure in government with strong private qualms about the wisdom of Treasury advice. When in May 1929, a month after Churchill's budget speech, the government issued a White Paper entitled 'Memoranda on Certain Proposals Relating to Unemployment', in reply to Lloyd George, the only departmental memorandum not signed by the responsible minister was the Treasury memorandum, which was issued on the sole responsibility of the Treasury staff.[52] Particularly striking is a note from Churchill to Niemeyer in February 1925, while the decision to return to gold was being made:

> The Treasury have never, it seems to me, faced the profound significance of what Mr Keynes calls the 'paradox of unemployment amid dearth'. The Governor shows himself perfectly happy in the spectacle of Britain possessing the finest credit in the world simultaneously with a million and

a quarter unemployed.... On the other hand I do not pretend to see even 'through a glass darkly' how the financial and credit policy of the country could be handled so as to bridge the gap between a dearth of goods and a surplus of labour; and well I realise the danger of experiment to that end. The seas of history are full of famous wrecks. Still if I could see a way, I would far rather follow it than any other. I would rather see Finance less proud and Industry more content.

You and the Governor have managed this affair. Taken together I expect you know more about it than anyone else in the world. At any rate alone in the world you have had an opportunity over a definite period of years of seeing your policy carried out. That it is a great policy, greatly pursued, I have no doubt. But the fact that this island with its enormous resources is unable to maintain its population is surely a cause for the deepest heartsearching.[53]

Although he was not happy with the situation, Churchill felt that he had no choice but to follow the views of his advisers and the weight of informed public opinion. His past tenure of the Home, Admiralty, Munitions, War, Air and Colonial portfolios had not provided him with the necessary experience and confidence in matters of finance which he would have needed to challenge the Treasury staff, the Bank of England and such senior colleagues as Austen Chamberlain, the Foreign Secretary. Chamberlain, as a former Conservative Chancellor of the Exchequer, had been chosen by Snowden, the Labour Chancellor, to chair the committee which recommended a return to the gold standard at the prewar parity. After serving as Financial Secretary to the Treasury, Chamberlain had become Chancellor of the Exchequer in 1903 (at the time of his father's resignation from the Cabinet), held the Exchequer again in Lloyd George's postwar coalition, and led the Conservative Party in 1921–2. The only other ex-Chancellor in the Cabinet, apart from Prime Minister Stanley Baldwin, was Chamberlain's younger half-brother, Neville Chamberlain, the Minister of Health. Financial recommendations issued under Austen Chamberlain's name could not lightly be rejected.

Churchill's political position was in stark contrast to that of Chamberlain. He had crossed the floor of the House from Conservatives to Liberals in 1904, after his constituency association repudiated him for criticizing Arthur Balfour's administration, a contretemps apt to be remembered unkindly by such Conservatives as Balfour, who in 1925 was Lord President of the Council in Baldwin's Cabinet. In the November 1922 general election, Churchill, standing as a Coalition Liberal, lost his seat at Dundee,

Scotland, by 10,000 votes to a prohibitionist named Scrymgeour, whom he had defeated by 18,000 votes in 1918 and had defeated at every election since 1908. Standing as a Liberal Free Trader at West Leicester in the December 1923 general election, Churchill lost by 4000 votes, and was shouted down at election meetings by cries of 'What about the Dardanelles?'. When he stood as an Independent and Anti-Socialist candidate at a by-election for the Abbey Division of Westminster in March 1924, the official Conservative candidate put up posters proclaiming 'Dundee didn't. West Leicester laughed. Westminster won't!'. Westminster didn't, by a margin of forty-three votes.[54] Finally, in November 1924, Churchill was returned as a Constitutionalist for Epping, with the support of the local Conservative constituency association. He was surprised and pleased to be offered the Exchequer in Baldwin's Cabinet, the portfolio his father had held in 1886 and for which he had been passed over by Lloyd George in the 1921 Cabinet shuffle. Despite joining the government, Churchill did not rejoin the Conservative Party and its *alter ego*, the Carlton Club, for another year. His lack of a regional electoral base (comparable to the Chamberlain dynasty in Birmingham) and of standing in the Conservative Party (of which he was not even a member when the decision to return to gold was taken) made Churchill's position at the Treasury far too shaky to reject the report of the Chamberlain-Bradbury Committee or the Treasury view in general. His services could too easily be dispensed with, as Baldwin and Neville Chamberlain demonstrated in the National Government from 1931 to 1939.

With Churchill's private doubts about the Treasury view kept firmly private, political opposition to conventional economic wisdom in Britain came, apart from the Liberal platform of 1929, from groups considered on the fringe of respectability: Oswald Mosley's New Party in the 1931 election, Lloyd George's family circle of 'independent Liberals' who had broken with both the official Liberal Party and the National Liberals after the formation of the National Government, and Lord Beaverbrook's Empire Crusade, which was primarily concerned with tariff preference for the Dominions and tariff protection for agriculture.

The political consensus in the United States was also far removed from the 'managed currency' views of the *Treatise on Money* and the countercyclical fiscal policy advocated in *Essays in Persuasion*. Herbert Hoover came to the Presidency with an outspoken record as

Secretary of Commerce of urging that public works projects be carried out in periods of slump rather than of expansion. He also differed from the British Treasury view when he reacted to the stock market crash of 1929 by inviting groups of businessmen to the White House to ask them to refrain from cutting wages. The practical effect of these views was, however, negated by two overriding concerns of Hoover: he was committed to maintaining the fixed value of the dollar in terms of gold, and he would not support public works programmes financed by borrowing rather than by taxes. Faced with a budget deficit when falling national income slashed tax revenues, Hoover called for and signed the Federal Revenue Act of 1932, which raised the top-bracket income tax rate from 24 per cent to 63 per cent, and nearly doubled tax rates on lower incomes. This combination of tax increases with a tight money policy to protect a fixed exchange rate was carried in the face of a United States unemployment rate of 23.6 per cent in 1932.[55] Hoover did, at least, aim merely at a budget in which revenues equalled expenditures, whereas in Britain, Baldwin and Churchill, MacDonald and Snowden strove to achieve large surpluses for debt reduction.

Franklin Roosevelt denounced Hoover's budget deficits in a speech in Pittsburgh during the 1932 election campaign, though at bottom he was a pragmatist without deep commitment to either balanced budgets or the gold standard. Until August 1934, President Roosevelt's Budget Director was Lewis Douglas, who wrote memoranda to the President warning him that not only Roosevelt's place in history but 'conceivably the immediate fate of western civilization' depended on balancing the budget. One of Douglas' first acts in office was to draft an order halting all government construction projects begun under the Hoover Administration, an order which Roosevelt signed, possibly without realizing its implications. According to Marriner Eccles, 'The naked, rusting girders of the Department of Commerce Building in Washington stood for months as a token of Roosevelt's resolve to balance the budget.' The gold standard exacted comparable devotion: when the Supreme Court voted five to four that Congress acted within its power in abrogating the 'gold clause' in contracts, Justice James Clark McReynolds lamented that the Constitution was 'gone'.[56]

Many independent commentators shared these views. Walter Lippmann charged that Hoover's budget message of December 1931 'offers the spectacle of the government of the richest country in the world unwilling to economize enough and unwilling to tax enough to balance its accounts'. The distinguished historian Allan Nevins, in his introduction to a collection of Lippman's columns published in 1932, praised this observation: 'It will be noted that Mr Lippmann was insistently calling for a program of budget-balancing as a first and fundamental step toward recovery before any of our political leaders did so.'[57]

Clearly the bipartisan conventional wisdom guiding public policy in the 1930s provided something for a Keynesian Revolution to overturn. Though research has exploded the myth that the established economists of the day were united in supporting wage cutting as a cure for unemployment and in opposition to deficit-financed government spending and monetary expansion, economists' doubts about the gold standard and annually balanced budgets, unsupported by theoretical arguments, had no impact on mainstream political opinion. Furthermore, an outspoken and articulate body of professional economists backed the Treasury view without reservations. In England the largest group of economists with such views was centred around Professors Edwin Cannan, T. E. Gregory, Friedrich Hayek and Lionel Robbins of the London School of Economics.

Gregory campaigned for a policy of deflation to achieve and preserve the prewar gold parity of sterling in a series of books such as *The First Year of the Gold Standard* (1926) and in essays, collected as *Gold, Unemployment and Capitalism* (1933), in addition to being one of the authors of the orthodox majority report of the Macmillan Committee on Finance and Industry (1929–31). Keynes signed the dissenting minority report. Gregory, writing in 1926, lambasted Keynes for conferring respectability on those who resisted the necessary adjustment to a lower price level: 'whilst it is not desirable to increase unemployment, reduce money wages and offend working class sentiment without good reason, it is useless to allow working class sentiment to govern monetary policy'. Lionel Robbins, in his book *The Great Depression* (1934), and his LSE colleague F. C. Benham, in *British Monetary Policy* (1932), argued that the gold parity of sterling should have been defended in 1931 with a high bank rate and a courageous deflation. They blamed this failure of political will on Keynes and other advocates of a managed currency who, in Robbins' words, 'encouraged the belief that the stable price-level was the be-all and end-all of monetary policy'.[58] Robbins warned in the *Lloyds Bank Monthly Review* in October 1932, at a time when 22 per

cent of the British work force was unemployed: 'If we are to avoid
inflationary disturbances, the authorities in different financial centres
must work the gold standard on lines much more severe than those
which have been the rule in recent years.'[59] As a member of the
Economic Advisory Council, Robbins joined with the business representatives on the Council to oppose the compromises on public
works, a revenue tariff and expansionary monetary policy worked
out among Keynes, Pigou, Stamp and Henderson, the activist economists on the Council. His firm stand earned him Keynes' ironic
praise in the *General Theory* as a classical economist whose policy
recommendations were consistent with his theory.[60]

Keynes offered, briefly in the *Treatise* and at greater length in the
General Theory, two arguments against wage-cutting as a cure for
unemployment. In a world of decentralized collective bargaining and
overlapping contracts, nominal wage bargaining was about relative
wages of different groups of workers, and could not alter the real
wage to clear the labour market. Even if money wages could be
lowered without such calamities as the 1926 General Strike or 1931
Invergordon naval mutiny, this would fail to stimulate economic
activity because of reduced demand by workers and the effect of
lower prices on real wages. Professor Edwin Cannan of the London
School of Economics brushed aside Keynes' arguments on both
issues in the most prominent place available: the first Presidential
Address to the Royal Economic Society's annual meeting after a
lapse of 'a considerable number of years', published in the *Economic
Journal* in September 1932. Cannan had assured the Chamberlain-
Bradbury Committee that 'managed currency' was all very fine in
theory but quite impracticable because a monetary authority unconstrained by the gold standard could not be trusted to resist inflation.
He was equally emphatic in 'The Demand for Labour', declaring that
'general unemployment is in reality to be explained almost in the
same way as particular unemployment.... General unemployment
appears when asking too much is a general phenomenon'. Cannan
decried the reduction of labour mobility by trade unions which
placed restrictions on admission to trades and insisted on the same
wages for experienced and inexperienced workers. On policy, he
endorsed reduction of nominal wages to eliminate mass unemployment:

> So-called 'fixed interest' should be allowed to be eaten away by defaults
> and stoppages without too much attention being given to the injustices

involved. Money-wages and salaries should be allowed to be reduced without resistance to the reductions being backed by the state and public opinion.[61]

In the preface to his collection of articles, *Economic Scares*, in which he reprinted 'The Demand for Labour' in 1933, Cannan observed that 'it seems at the present time to be the urgent duty of every economist to do all he can to allay the fear of insufficiency of work which is giving rise to all sorts of crazy schemes of social reorganization'.[62] An argument, similar to Cannan's, that trade unions contribute to unemployment by pushing up wages and restricting labour mobility, was presented at length in *The Theory of Collective Bargaining* (1930) by W. H. Hutt, a London School of Economics graduate teaching at the University of Cape Town (where he was promoted in 1931 to Professor and Dean of the Faculty of Commerce).

With the gold standard and a balanced budget ruling out expansionary monetary and fiscal policy, only wage-cutting was left as a remedy for unemployment. Blame for impeding the fall of nominal wages fell on unemployment benefits as well as on trade unions. Winston Churchill, in two articles 'On the Abuse of the Dole' in the *Daily Telegraph* in March 1930, denounced 'the folly of all plans of marching off the unemployed in gangs and battalions to artificially fomented public works, and profession thereby to remedy unemployment', and called for firmness against 'the ne'er-do-well, or the confirmed sturdy loafer, or the Bolshevik misfit, or other members of the tribes of Tired Tims and Weary Willies – alas! I must add manoeuvering Marthas'. Churchill contrasted relief payments financed by taxpayers with a true insurance programme financed by insurance premiums, which he claimed was exemplified by the National Insurance Act of 1911, for whose unemployment insurance provisions he had been responsible as President of the Board of Trade. This claim was incorrect as regards the 1911 Act, which Lloyd George had promoted as '9*d*. for 4*d*.' since the weekly insurance stamp was to be paid for by fourpence deducted from the employee's wages, threepence paid by the employer (which reduced wage offers) and twopence from the state.[63] Churchill's animosity to the dole was shared by *The Times*, which called attention to an instance, 'rightly described by Our Correspondent as sinister', in which a family of five received a total of 69 shillings a week unemployment benefit. This was clearly a case for action by the Attorney-General (fees, refreshers and other emoluments of £44,500 a year).[64]

Since unemployment benefits were both a cost to the taxpayers and an impediment to market-clearing wage reduction, they were a prime target of attempts to balance the budget. The May Committee, five businessmen and two labour representatives appointed by Snowden to advise how to cover a projected £120 million deficit (including £50 million as 'the usual provision for the redemption of debt'), recommended a tax increase and £96 million in expenditure cuts, of which £66.5 million was to come from reduced unemployment insurance benefits, £13.5 million from education, £8 million from reduced road-building, and the rest from pay cuts in the armed forces, with not a penny's reduction in the Sinking Fund contribution.[65] Although Snowden chose a more moderate course of reducing unemployment benefits by only £25 million and raising taxes by more than the May Report suggested, he fully supported nominal wage reduction, with the state to set an example with its military and civil pay lists. Naval lieutenants receiving £1 7*s.* a day lost a shilling a day, and able-bodied seamen getting 5*s.* a day also lost a shilling a day. The National Government subsequently decided to drop these provisions as a means of ending the naval mutiny.[66]

A recent study has offered an 'explanation of persistent unemployment in interwar Britain: the dole did it. Although aggregate demand was chiefly responsible for the high unemployment in 1921 and 1930–32, the million man armies of the unemployed of the late twenties and late thirties were for the most part volunteer armies', and described the dole as 'an extraordinarily generous poorly safeguarded system'.[67] This description has been questioned: nearly three million applications for unemployment benefits were rejected from 1921 to 1930 because the applicants were held not to be genuinely seeking work. Another 460,000 applications were refused in this period under a rule banning benefits to members of households with a weekly income of 13 shillings or more per person and allowing payment of unemployment benefits to members of households with incomes between 10 and 13 shillings a week only after an investigation of household means.[68] Similar views about unemployment insurance were expressed at the time. In the *Economic Journal*, arguments that subsidized unemployment benefits had raised the British unemployment rate were made by Professor Pigou in 'Wage Policy and Unemployment' in September 1927, by Sir Henry Clay in

'Unemployment and Wage Rates' in March 1928, and by Professor Cannan in 'The Problem of Unemployment' in March 1930. Continental economists advanced analyses. The prominent Swedish economist Gustav Cassel wrote an article in 1927 with the arresting title 'Self-criticism! The Senselessness of the German Unemployment Policy', condemning the policy of maintaining high wage rates and taxing the employed to pay for unemployment compensation, instead of encouraging the adjustment of wage rates so that all would be employed.[69]

Jacques Rueff, then teaching at the École Libre des Sciences Politiques but soon to return to the French Ministry of Finance, presented empirical and theoretical analysis to argue that unemployment insurance was responsible for British unemployment in his highly controversial article 'L'assurance-chômage, cause du chômage permanent' in the *Revue d'Economie Politique* (March–April 1931). Rueff's article was reprinted as a booklet with a strongly favourable foreward by Charles Rist, then Professor of Political Economy at the Law Faculty of the University of Paris but soon to be Governor of the Banque de France. Josiah Stamp summarized Rueff's argument, with large extracts from the original article, in two articles in *The Times* in June 1931, exposure which led to discussion of Rueff's views in the House of Commons.[70] Rueff and Rist were best known in the post-Second World War economics profession for their vigorous defence of the gold standard as the best possible international monetary system, in such forceful polemics as *The Age of Inflation* and *The Monetary Sin of the West*, both by Rueff, and *The Triumph of Gold*, by Rist.

J. Ronnie Davis has shown that not all American economists held what was known in England as the Treasury view. Jacob Viner, Paul Douglas, Henry Simons and several of their colleagues at the University of Chicago argued for a budget balanced over the length of the business cycle, instead of within each year, in a statement on *Balancing the Budget* issued by the University of Chicago Press in 1933 as the first of its series of Public Policy Pamphlets. The consensus at the round-table discussions following the Harris Foundation Lectures in Chicago in June and July 1931 was in favour of expansionist policy, and Keynes and Irving Fisher were in a minority at these discussions in stressing the importance of monetary policy to bring down interest rates, in addition to expansionary fiscal policy.[71] Gordon Tullock, in his foreward to Davis' *The New Economics and the Old Economists*, claims that Davis 'ably demonstrates that the point of view held by almost all leading economists in the United States during the period of the Great Depression was a view which most modern laymen would denominate "Keynesian". Indeed, after reading his book, one wonders where Presidents Hoover and Roosevelt were getting their economic advice.'[72]

One source of economic advice was the Brookings Institution, where Harold Moulton, Henry Seidemann and their associates spent the first months of 1933 providing President-elect Roosevelt and his new Budget Director, Lewis Douglas, with detailed plans for 'sweeping reductions in public expenditures, consolidation of bureaus, and elimination of government functions'.[73] A few years later, when the Roosevelt Administration had given up trying to balance the budget, one of Roosevelt's aides, Rexford Guy Tugwell, described the Brookings Institution as 'a kind of research organ for the conservatives'.[74] Another source of classical or 'Treasury view' opinions was Yale, where Fisher and James Harvey Rogers were the only economists to support expansionist measures. Four other Yale economists, three of them full professors, warned that 'A price rise promised almost entirely on increasing public expenditures and consequent deficit financing, in itself a depressant to productive private spending, is hardly the type of price rise which is symptomatic of a sound business recovery in a readjusted economy'.[75] Another Yale professor, Olin Glenn Saxon, held even more stridently classical views, which may be perused in his later pamphlet, *Keynes at Harvard: Economic Deception as a Political Credo*. This fascinating work was published anonymously, but the Veritas Foundation, which issued it, honoured Saxon as its author after his death in 1962. The tone and political paranoia of this pamphlet may be glimpsed by noting that Saxon described Joseph Schumpeter as 'one of the world's outstanding Marxists', observing darkly: 'Schumpeter taught at the London School of Economics, which was founded by Fabian socialists and generally reflected the Fabian view. He had a relationship of many years with Alfred Marshall (Fabian socialist economist).'[76] Such LSE professors as Edwin Cannan, Friedrich Hayek, Karl Popper and Lionel Robbins might have been surprised to learn that they reflected the Fabian view.

Professor Neil Carothers of Lehigh University expressed firmly classical views in a diatribe against New Deal monetary policy that appeared as a series of sixteen articles in the Sunday magazine of the

New York Herald Tribune, and was reprinted in other newspapers and as number 3 in the Farrar & Rinehart Pamphlets. With reference to attempts to restore the price level to its pre-Depression level by lowering the gold value of the dollar, Carothers wrote:

> Inflation is not a desperate remedy for a desperate situation. On the contrary, it is an arbitrary and unnecessary interference with a recovery already well begun. Its purpose is not to end depression, but to relieve certain groups of people of their obligations and to permit the government to spend money recklessly without balancing its budget. Peace-time inflation in all history is the device of a government unwilling to pay its debts but quite willing to dishonor its promises in order to give subsidies to clamoring elements in the population.
>
> The bloated prices of 1929 caused the collapse. The morbidly low prices of 1933 are the painful but necessary condition of restoration. They drain the water from such enterprises as Insull's. They deflate the swollen and unearned profits of industry and finance. They reduce the salaries and wages of certain parasitic groups. They wipe out the waste and the incompetence in business. Until this purging process is complete there can be no recovery. Four years of the Hoover administration proved the futility of attempts to stop the process.[77]

In the first of the Farrar & Rinehart Pamphlets, Walter Spahr, Chairman of the Department of Economics at New York University and Secretary-Treasurer of the Economists' National Committee on Monetary Policy, denounced the same proposal for monetary expansion as Carothers:

> [W]hen the price level rises as a result of currency inflation, the rise is due to an increased reluctance of sellers to sell except at the higher prices which they think will prevail in the future when they must replace their stocks; it is due, also, to fearful and hasty purchasing on the part of consumers who, although their incomes have not increased, wish to convert their savings and incomes into goods which they hope will appreciate in value. Under such conditions, purchasers buy because of *fear* and in an effort to save what they can from the despoiling effects of inflation. This rapid spending by consumers hastens the exhaustion of their incomes and sends them headlong toward poverty and disasters.
>
> In time, production ceases because producers cannot lay plans for future production; the nation is turned into a den of gamblers; unemployment becomes widespread; wages and salaries lag far behind the inflated prices; poverty, distress, and suffering became [*sic*] widespread; fear grips the masses; and the final result is disaster and the general impoverishment of the people.[78]

In Professor Spahr's view, currency inflation raises prices without increasing nominal incomes, and falling real wages not only fail to stimulate the demand for labour, but are accompanied by wide-spread unemployment.

The Economics of the Recovery Program, written by seven Harvard economists in 1934, displayed an absence of understanding of how stimulating effective demand could expand output. The list of authors includes several who were, either then or later, very well known: Douglass Brown, Edward Chamberlin, Seymour Harris, Wassily Leontief, Edward S. Mason, Joseph Schumpeter and Overton Taylor. Schumpeter, in his paper 'Depressions', argued that a depression was a necessary period of adjustment, and that government intervention would merely obstruct adjustment and lead to a severer crisis.[79] Other contributors, less averse to interventionist policy, lacked any theoretical basis for such policy. Edward Chamberlin, writing on 'Purchasing Power', held that saving was spending. Instead of treating spending out of wages by workers employed on public works projects as part of a multiplier process leading to increased output, he worried that such spending would drive up prices with constant output and so reduce the consumption of the rest of society.[80] Douglass Brown, in 'Helping Labor', warned sternly that 'Relief costs money',[81] and ignored the effect of spending by recipients of relief. Gottfried Haberler, who did not join Harvard until 1936, had previously expressed, in his Harris Foundation Lectures on 'Money and the Business Cycle' in 1932, views similar to those of Schumpeter on the need to let the Depression run its course.[82]

If almost all the leading American economists had grasped the income-expenditure theory before the publication of the *General Theory*, some trace of it should appear in *Stabilization of Employment* (1933), a volume of seventeen invited papers on that subject delivered to a joint session of the Econometric Society and the American Association for the Advancement of Science in Atlantic City in December 1932. Since the session was organized by Irving Fisher of Yale, as president of the Econometric Society, and Harold Hotelling of Columbia, as secretary of Section K (Economics, Sociology and Statistics) of the American Association, and the proceedings were edited by Charles F. Roos, author of the first two Cowles Commission monographs, the volume could draw on the greatest technical sophistication available in the American economics profession. Despite this, the only paper in the volume that could take a place in the later macroeconomic literature is Fisher's

'The Relation of Employment to the Price Level', in which he presented charts to support his contention that employment depended on a distributed lag of past changes in the price level, which he attributed to business receipts adjusting to price changes more quickly than business expenses did, because interest, rent, salary and wage rates would alter only as contracts expired.[83]

Three papers on public works, by Leo Wolman of Columbia, W. N. Loucks of the University of Pennsylvania, and John Lyle Harrington of the Reconstruction Finance Corporation, favouring the scheduling of public works projects which were to be undertaken any way for periods of cyclical unemployment, would not sanction any expansionary policy which would involve public works projects which would not have been otherwise approved. Another contributor approvingly summed up these papers:

> As pointed out by Dr Wolman, Dr Loucks and Mr Harrington, public works are as yet, untried for purposes of smothering out business cycles. The question of legislation coordinating national, state and municipal construction programs is much more within the realm of possibility than is the problem of financing a long range public works program. The billions of savings, credit or gold that would be necessary to finance a nation out of serious depressions would throw a burden on its credit structure that it would probably not be strong enough to bear.[84]

Royal Meeker, formerly of Princeton but then a close associate of Irving Fisher as president of the Index Number Institute in New Haven, warned that 'The rising tide of ordinary public squandering must be checked, but public expenditure for relief of unemployment must be increased until the emergency is past',[85] even though another paper in the book reported that public works spending in the United States was only half as large in 1932 as it had been in 1929.[86] Meeker also lamented:

> The term 'consumer purchasing power' is another economic aftermath of the war which is used with terrifying frequency and vagueness. This new dole theory assumes that the buying power of the donees will be increased while the buying power of the donors will remain unimpaired. The miraculous power attributed to 'consumer purchasing power' has as yet failed to lift us out of the ditch. ... Experience has shown, however, that the buying power added to the recipients is subtracted in almost equal amount from the donors – in the case of public doles, the taxpayers. Furthermore the policy of legally robbing industrious Peter to pay jobless Paul so discourages Peter that he lets down in his production, thus aggra-

vating and prolonging the depression. This was exemplified in Russia and the experiment is being repeated under our eyes at home.[87]

Meeker's paper, 'The Outlawry of Unemployment', called for an international treaty against unemployment, comparable to the Kellogg Pact outlawing war, as a symbol of determination to eliminate unemployment.

Leo Wolman observed:

> With reference, again, to the policy of heading off the depression by quickly expanding the volume of public construction, it is clear in retrospect that the use of government expenditure for this purpose was badly timed; that it had no effect in preventing the continuance of depression; and that, by delaying the processes of adjustment and at the same time adding to the already excessive outstanding capital charges, it contributed probably to the lengthening, and not to the shortening, of this depression. In this case, as well as in the proposal to borrow heavily for public improvements at the present time, increases in public spending are essentially of an inflationary character, although this fact is so frequently overlooked. Inflation has rules and principles of its own which, I suspect, do not cease to operate just because the proceeds of this inflation are employed directly in the stimulation of public improvements.[88]

James Angell of Columbia, writing on 'Monetary prerequisites for Employment Stabilization', urged that monetary policy be used to limit saving and investment, so that productive capacity would not grow faster than population. His worry was not that increased saving would reduce demand, but rather that investment increased potential output. He mentioned Keynes' concern in the *Treatise* with the difference between saving and investment in a footnote, but dismissed it as unimportant compared with the absolute level of saving and investment.[89] Angell made no distinction between a decision to save and a decision to invest.

Elmer J. Working insisted that 'The total demand for all commodities *is* the total production', which is Say's Law of Markets, ignoring the possibility that there could be an excess supply of all commodities because of an excess demand for the medium of exchange. Working supported this proposition by reference to Marshall's *Principles*, Book VI, chapter XIII, section 10, but failed to note Marshall's observation in that section that although an individual has a certain purchasing power, he may not choose to exercise it. Working proceeded to confuse matters by saying that '"demand" in the sense used here refers not to demand in markets, but to demand in a larger sense' and admitting that 'demand over short periods is subject to the influence of speculation, changes in stocks, etc., which are usually associated with changes in bank credit'.[90]

No writer in either *Stabilization of Employment* or *The Economics of the Recovery Program* made any reference to the multiplier, or paid any serious attention to the effect on purchasing power of successive rounds of spending resulting from an initial increase in government spending or in investment. The claim that the American economic profession was familiar with the Keynesian income-expenditure theory before Keynes published it cannot be supported from these volumes. The claim that 'the point of view held by almost all leading economists in the United States during the period of the Great Depression was a view which most modern laymen would denominate "Keynesian"' is not correct for Harvard, Yale, the Brookings Institution, the Econometric Society meetings, or the authors of the Farrar & Rinehart Pamphlets.

Although Keynes was not alone among economists in supporting public works and a managed currency, he offered a new theoretical justification for these policies as remedies for mass unemployment. The Treasury view had a substantial body of academic supporters, and those who were critical of it lacked a basis on which to construct an alternative. Both to believers in the conventional wisdom and to its critics, Keynes' theoretical argument in the *Treatise* for the use of open-market operations and bank rate policy to regulate the economy and his multiplier argument for public works in *Can Lloyd George Do It?*, which was refined in later works, seemed novel and striking.

'THE SOCIETY FOR THE PRESERVATION OF ANCIENT MONUMENTS'

Many economists in the 1920s and 1930s were quite prepared to support public works or interest rate reductions to reduce unemployment, but lacked theoretical justification for doing so. Their situation was similar to that of Churchill in 1925, when he had grave doubts about the advice that he was receiving but felt that he lacked respectable arguments with which to publicly defend a decision against returning to the prewar gold parity.

Professor A. C. Pigou of Cambridge was one leading economist who had great difficulty reconciling his views on policy with his classical principles. Pigou helped plan the return to gold as a member of the Cunliffe Committee in 1918 and of the Chamberlain-Bradbury Committee, whose report he drafted. Pigou later insisted that the political decision to restore the prewar parity had already been taken, so that his role was only to advise on timing and technique.[91] A critic of the Treasury view who felt confident of the economic principles underlying his criticism would hardly have been so active and diligent in assisting the Treasury and the Bank of England to do efficiently what should not have been done at all.

After reading Pigou's *Socialism versus Capitalism* (1937), Keynes wrote to Richard Kahn: 'Many thanks for sending me a copy of the Prof's new book. As in the case of Dennis [Robertson], when it comes to practice, there is extremely little between us. Why do they insist on maintaining theories from which their own practical conclusions cannot possibly follow? It is a sort of Society for the Preservation of Ancient Monuments.'[92] Keynes' reference suggested that the intellectual gymnastics of Pigou and Robertson were similar to those of Sir Josiah Stamp, who, having insisted that economics is concerned solely with material welfare, justified his railway company's decision not to level a sixteenth-century half-timbered building, Stratford House in Birmingham, to make room for railway sidings, by arguing that indifference to aesthetics would reduce output in the long run.[93]

T. W. Hutchison has exploded the myth that Pigou advocated nominal wage reductions as the remedy for mass unemployment, either as a witness before the Macmillan Committee or as a member of the Economic Advisory Council's Committee of Economists.[94] On the contrary, Pigou, like Robertson, agreed with Keynes on the need for public works, lower interest rates and even, before Britain went off the gold standard in September 1931, a protective tariff. A reviewer of Pigou's *Theory of Unemployment* (1933) noted that 'As short-run expedients Pigou admits the advisability of following many practices which his analysis condemns as permanent policies'.[95] Pigou's contributions to formal analysis of unemployment undermined his policy suggestions. His chapter on 'The Part Played by Rigidity in Wage-Rates' in his book *Industrial Fluctuations* (1927) argued that an all-round reduction in money wage rates could eliminate unemployment, because prices would fall by less than wages. His *Theory of Unemployment* reiterated the thesis that, apart from frictional obstructions, unemployment would be nonexistent if wage-earners did not habitually stipulate for a wage rate higher than the equilibrium level set by their productivity. His 1927 *Economic Journal* paper on 'Wages Policy and Unemployment' estimated that Britain's system of unemployment insurance added five percentage points to the unemployment rate.

J. R. Hicks, in his very widely reprinted 'Mr Keynes and the Classics', itself now a classic, held that Pigou's *Theory of Unemployment* presented 'doctrines ... quite as strange and novel as' the *General Theory* 'so that to be told that he has believed these things himself leaves the ordinary economist quite bewildered'.[96] This view is not supported by contemporary reviews of Pigou's book by Seymour Harris in the *Quarterly Journal of Economics*, Roy Harrod in the *Economic Journal*, Ralph Hawtrey in *Economica*, E. L. Bowers in the *American Economic Review*, and Paul Sweezy in the *Journal of Political Economy*. The length of the reviews indicates the importance attached to the book, with Harris writing thirty-nine pages, Harrod fourteen and Hawtrey twenty. Apart from Hawtrey's grumbling over the extent to which Pigou reasoned in real terms, arguing in terms of wage goods rather than money wages,[97] the reviewers treated the book as an extremely valuable exposition and elaboration of the traditional approach. They considered Pigou's book to be just what Keynes called it in the *General Theory*: 'the only attempt with which I am acquainted to write down the classical theory of unemployment precisely'.[98] It was the only full-length presentation in English of the analysis of unemployment underlying so many books and articles on the effects of unemployment benefits, trade unions and price deflation on unemployment. A comparable book, *The Causes of Unemployment*, had, however, been published in Swedish by Professor Gosta Bagge of the University of Lund in 1930. Bagge, a leader of the Swedish Conservative Party who was described in the later literature as 'the Swedish Pigou', considered all frictional aspects of unemployment at length, but gave scant attention to demand deficiency in his book, even though he was an advocate of higher public investment in slumps than in booms.[99]

Pigou was by no means the only economist to be sceptical of the Treasury view or inclined towards activist monetary and fiscal policy, but unable to break free from the attitudes and theories behind the Treasury view. G. D. H. Cole, Reader in Economics at Oxford and director of the New Fabian Research Bureau, urged, in his collected essays on *Gold, Credit and Employment* (1930), that the money supply should be based 'not on the stock of gold, but on the needs of industry and commerce'. This advice was negated by his belief that the pound sterling should remain convertible into gold at its existing parity, and that the Bank of England should sacrifice the stability of internal prices to stability of the exchange rate. Cole's solution for unemployment was a National Corps voluntarily recruited among the unemployed to keep the unemployed busy and out of mischief until the eventual revival of trade created jobs for them. For the revival of trade, he looked to rationalization of production through failure of inefficient forms and merger to exploit economies of scale.[100] Cole, who considered himself a daring socialist critic of establishment ideas, was concerned in his *Economic Tracts for the Times* and *British Trade and Industry* (both 1932) that public works spending to stimulate employment should be financed by current taxes, because of the need to balance the budget, and that the induced employment from public spending must not compete with the products of private enterprise.[101] He contributed a chapter to *What Everybody Wants to Know About Money* (1933), which he edited, about nationalization of the banking system, hardly a crucial plank in a programme for economic recovery.

Two young socialist economists from Oxford, Hugh Gaitskell (later leader of the Labour Party) and Evan F. M. Durbin, both then lecturing at University College, London, also wrote on money and employment. Durbin's *Purchasing Power and Trade Depression* (1932) and Gaitskell's 'Four Monetary Heretics' in *What Everybody Wants to Know About Money* were concerned to refute, not the Treasury view, but the underconsumptionist views of Major Douglas' Social Credit movement and other heretics who offered tinkering with the monetary system in place of a socialist transformation of society. Silvio Gesell, one of Gaitskell's four heretics, owes his notice in the *General Theory* to these critiques.[102]

Sidney Pollard has argued that:

> by the end of 1932 at the latest, all the bricks which went to make the Keynesian employment theory were available and could have been used by the unions, had they been minded to assemble them. Most of them are to be found in that remarkable publication, *What Everybody Wants to Know About Money*, written by nine Oxford economists under G. D. H. Cole's editorship in 1932 and published in 1933, in which authors of such diverse political views as Cole, Gaitskell, Colin Clark and Roy Harrod, dealt competently with the powers of the banks to create credit, the need

for Government deficit financing to cure unemployment, the employment multiplier, and the notion that when many resources are idle, additional purchasing power will serve to bring them into play rather than to raise prices.[103]

Not even the most generous reading of ambiguous passages can support a claim that the multiplier theory was generally understood by the authors of the Cole volume. Colin Clark, an Oxford graduate lecturing in statistics at Cambridge, came closest in his 'Investment, Savings and Public Finance'. There he explained that an increase in employment and wages producing consumable goods would produce no indirect employment, because the output of goods would rise by as much as purchasing power. If the initial employment was in building a road or school, products which would not be marketed, there could be additional employment as the wages were spent, but Clark gave no quantitative estimate of the multiplier, only remarking: 'It is only in special cases that these indirect repercussions will be considerable.'[104]

Evan Durbin, in the chapter on 'Money and Prices' in the Cole volume, considered the possibility that part of an increase in income would be saved, but instead of treating this as a leakage from spending, he considered this induced saving to be increased spending on investment goods.[105] The volume demonstrates that the Keynesian theory of effective demand was not understood in 1932 by the economists of the Labour Party. The political views of the authors of the volume was less diverse than Pollard supposes, for Colin Clark, although quite averse to socialism in later years, had stood as a Labour Party candidate for Parliament in 1929, and Roy Harrod's political views shifted to Conservatism only after the war.

American supporters of government action to relieve unemployment also suffered from the lack of an economic theory to support their proposals. In a proposal similar to Cole's National Corps, Frank Graham of Princeton urged, in his book *The Abolition of Unemployment* (1932), the creation of a National Emergency Employment Corporation which 'should arrange for the employment of all willing, and at present involuntarily idle, workers at jobs for which they are equipped, and should pay them, according to their choice, in the goods they themselves turn out'.[106] This plan showed no appreciation of the indirect multiplier effects of spending, or of the ability of monetary and fiscal policy to promote a general recovery of economic activity.

Such writers as Pigou, Cole and Graham at least supported increasing public works spending and opposed deflation as a remedy for unemployment in the Depression, however much these views might be tempered or undermined by concern for fixed exchange rates (until Britain went off gold in 1931) and budget balancing, and by a belief that in theory cutting money wage rates could eliminate mass unemployment. The great Swedish monetary theorist Knut Wicksell, reflecting on Swedish unemployment rates among trade unionists of 20 to 25 per cent in the 1921–2 recession in three articles in Swedish and a paper which Keynes firmly rejected for the *Economic Journal*, could offer no better policy response to unemployment than subsidized emigration in the short run and birth control as a long run solution.[107] Ernest Bevin, the general secretary of the Transport and General Workers Union and future Cabinet minister, was a critic of the Treasury view both on the Economic Advisory Council and the Macmillan Committee on Finance and Industry, on which he joined Keynes in signing an expansionist minority addendum to the report. Bevin's *My Plan for 2,000,000 Workless* (1933) called for a higher school-leaving age and for provision of adequate public pensions to encourage early retirement, measures which would merely redistribute jobs by contracting the supply of labour without increasing the demand for labour.[108] Dennis Robertson, testifying before the Macmillan Committee, held that mass unemployment was due to satiation of human wants, which, instead of reducing the working hours of all workers, somehow misallocated the reduced work so that some workers were thrown out of work entirely.[109] This stagnationist argument, which Robertson repeated in 1933 in a collection of essays in honour of the German business cycle theorist Arthur Spiethoff,[110] would support Bevin's proposals as well as limitation of the working week to forty hours or less.

The economics profession's perceived lack of a theory of the level of economic activity in the early 1930s is most tellingly shown by the amount of journal space devoted to the sunspot theory of business cycles, the theory developed in the previous century by William Stanley Jevons, based on a suggestion by the astronomer Herschel some decades earlier, that cyclical variations in solar activity affected weather conditions, which in turn influenced agricultural harvests and so the level of economic activity. The attempts of Jevons to demonstrate the link between sunspots and the trade cycle provoked amused and acerbic comment by, among others, Wesley Mitchell:

Jevons had an admirably candid mind; yet in 1875, when the sun-spot cycle was supposed to last 11.1 years, he was able to get from Thorold Rogers' *History of Agriculture and Prices in England* a period of 11 years in price fluctuations, and when the sun-spot cycle was revised to 10.45 years he was able to make the average interval between English crises 10.466 years. To get this later result, Jevons purposely left out from his list of crises 'a great commercial collapse in 1810–11 (which will not fit into the decennial series)'; he also omitted the crisis of 1873, and inserted a crisis in 1878, which other writers do not find.[111]

Despite such comments, when Professor Herbert Stanley Jevons revived his father's sunspot theory of business cycles in 1933, the *Journal of the Royal Statistical Society* gave forty-four pages to Jevons' paper and another seventeen pages to discussion of it. The *Quarterly Journal of Economics* gave the first fifty-one pages of its 1934–5 volume to a study of 'Solar and Economic Relationships'.[112]

CONCLUSION

Keynes' *Treatise on Money* was received as an innovative and import-ant contribution to a weak area of economic theory. Critics as well as admirers of the book stressed its signficance and the unsatisfactory state of the existing theory. Other economists had endorsed fiscal or monetary expansion to deal with unemployment. The novelty in Keynes' work was the theoretical underpinnings for such an analysis. Wage cutting could not halt a cumulative deflation in the *Treatise*, because spending would fall along with wage costs, leaving the disparity between investment and desired saving unchanged. Reduc-tion in interest rates or, if fixed exchange rates and the absence of international co-operation prevented monetary expansion, direct government investment could close the gap between investment and saving by stimulating investment. The lack of a theoretical expla-nation of how expansion could occur was evident in the expansionist proposals of other economists, who often combined support for public works and increasing the money supply during depression with contradictory injunctions to balance the budget (or even generate a surplus for the Sinking Fund), defend the existing exchange rate at the expense of domestic stabilization, or curtail the supply of labour, together with insistence that, in theory, reduction of money wage rates would eliminate unemployment.

Keynes' analysis of investment and saving in the *Treatise*, which drew upon Wicksell's distinction between market and natural rates of interest, was by no means universally accepted. In 1932, Gustav Cassel published several newspaper articles and a pamphlet in which he denied that public works or other means of increasing investment could stimulate employment, because the supply of savings was fixed.[113] Hayek's review of the *Treatise* and Keynes' reply to it sharply contrasted the *Treatise* with Hayek's *Prices and Production*, which presented the Austrian doctrine that the average period of production had been excessively extended during the boom, and that if any of the resulting malinvestments were to be preserved, saving would have to increase at the expense of consumption. In this view, 'the prime essential was the writing down of mistaken investments and the easing of capital markets by fostering the disposition to save and reducing the pressure on consumption'.[114] This approach to saving and spending was most succinctly presented by Lionel Robbins in 'Consumption and the Trade Cycle' in *Economica* (1932) and the young Swedish economist Johan Akerman in 'Saving in the Depression', in *Economic Essays in Honour of Gustav Cassel* (1933). Full-length treatments were given by Robbins in *The Great Depression* and by Akerman in three books, *Some Lessons of the World Depression* (1931), *Economic Progress and Economic Crises* (1932), and *Economic Forecast and Reality, 1928–1932* (1933). James Angell of Columbia felt that both saving and investment should be reduced in the Depression, lest productive capacity outrun purchasing power.

Robertson's review of the *Treatise* and Keynes' reply to the review stressed another area in which the *Treatise* made a major contribution: the demand for money as an asset. Where the earlier Cambridge cash balance approach of Marshall, Pigou, Lavington and the early works of Keynes had dealt with a transactions demand for money, dependent on the level of income, the *Treatise* considered money as one of several ways of holding wealth, so the demand for money would also depend on wealth and on the price of securities. Pigou's short review, which held that the *Treatise* offered only a more convenient presentation of Pigou's 'Equation of Exchange' and the Cambridge cash balance approach, missed this innovation.[115]

The reviews of the *Treatise* show that the disequilibrium analysis of the work was greeted as strikingly original, particularly as far as the English-language literature was concerned, and that the economics profession was receptive to new ideas. Several important points in the *Treatise* were brought out by reviewers, notably the distinction between profits as realization and as expectation, and the implicit assumptions of constant output and constant savings underlying such passages as the widow's cruse and the parable of the thrift campaign in the banana plantation. The evolution of Keynes' thought toward the *General Theory* was a struggle to repair the errors and omissions of the *Treatise* by developing an explicit theory of output.

In the preface to the *General Theory*, Keynes predicted: 'Those who are strongly wedded to what I shall call "the classical theory", will fluctuate, I expect, between a belief that I am quite wrong and a belief that I am saying nothing new.'[116] Examination of the reviews of the *Treatise* and of other relevant literature of the period contradicts recent myth-making which holds that Keynes was saying nothing new.

NOTES

1. Lekachman (1966); Stewart (1967).
2. Stein (1969), chapter 2; J. R. Davis (1971).
3. Stamp (1931), 242.
4. Hardy (1931a), 151.
5. Loria (1931).
6. Cabiati (1931).
7. Drucker (1979), 124–5.
8. Schumpeter to Keynes, 18 October 1930, in Keynes (1973), XIII, 176.
9. Schumpeter to Keynes, 29 November 1930, in Keynes (1973), XIII, 201.
10. See Jones (1964). Stamp was one of the few British economists of his time to hold a Ph.D. in economics.
11. Gunther (1938), 237.
12. Stamp (1931), 245.
13. *Ibid.*, 247.
14. *Ibid.*, 249.
15. Quoted by Stein (1969), 162. Keats should have put Balboa on the peak, not Cortez, and what Wordsworth actually wrote about the French Revolution was 'Bliss was it that dawn to be alive but to be young was very heaven.'
16. Williams (1931), 548.
17. *Ibid.*, 552.
18. *Ibid.*, 559. See also Stamp (1931), 243.
19. Williams (1931), 556–8.
20. *Ibid.*, 547.

21. Hardy (1931a), 150–2.
22. Robbins, introduction to Wicksell (1934–5), vii.
23. Hardy (1931b), 294n, referring to Keynes (1930), ıı, 202. See also Keynes (1930), ı, 197n.
24. H. Johnson in E. Johnson and H. Johnson (1978), 195, 245.
25. Hardy (1931b), 390; Samuelson (1947), 4.
26. Hardy (1931a), 153. Keynes was never a professor and, when addressed by the title, protested that he would not accept the indignity without the emoluments.
27. Hardy (1931b), 398.
28. E. G. Davis (1980). A later version of Hawtrey's critique of the *Treatise* was published as Chapter VI of Hawtrey (1932). Cf. Cain (1982).
29. Tarshis (1978), 49.
30. A. Hansen (1932); A. Hansen and Tout (1933).
31. A. Hansen and Tout (1933), 342.
32. Robertson (1931), 399; Keynes (1930), ı, 176–8.
33. Robertson (1931), 408–9; Keynes (1930), ı, 139.
34. Pigou (1931) and comments in Keynes (1973), xɪɪɪ, 217.
35. Schumpeter, in Harris (1947), 89n.
36. See Kaldor (1937).
37. Moggridge (1976), 30.
38. Keynes (1973), xɪɪɪ, 252.
39. *Ibid.*, xɪɪɪ, 265.
40. Keynes (1930), ı, 206–7, 271.
41. See Hardy (1942).
42. Patinkin (1982), 59.
43. J. O. B. Ferguson to Neville Chamberlain, 25 January 1935, quoted by Peden (1980), 5. In addition to Peden, Middleton (1982) discusses the conversion of the British Treasury to a more Keynesian approach in the course of the 1930s.
44. Blaug (1968), 656.
45. Hawtrey (1925).
46. Hawtrey (1933).
47. Hancock (1962), reprinted in Pollard (1970), 103.
48. Hancock (1962), reprinted in Pollard (1970), 119–20.
49. Winch (1969), 136.
50. Attributed by Robert Skidelsky to Tom Johnston and by A. J. P. Taylor to Sidney Webb, Lord Passfield. Moggridge (1969), 9, 98.
51. *Ibid.*, 53.
52. Stein (1969), 139, 483.
53. Moggridge (1969), 54–5.
54. James (1970), 194, 197.
55. Silk (1985); Stein (1969).
56. Stein (1969), 45, 474; Burns (1956), 231, 240–1.
57. Moggridge (1976), 14.
58. Gregory (1926), 18, 44–5, 93–4; Benham (1932), 30–1, 45; Robbins (1934), 77–8, 85, 97; Winch (1969), 159–60.
59. Pollard (1970), 21–2n.

60. Keynes (1936), 20n. Henderson, Keynes, Pigou, Robbins and Stamp comprised the Committee of Economists of the Economic Advisory Council. Keynes and Josiah Stamp were also members of the full Council, together with several bankers and businessmen, the trade unionist Ernest Bevin, the Oxford economist and political scientist G. D. H. Cole, the LSE economic historian (and sometime chairman of the Labour Party) R. H. Tawney, and two scientists, a physicist and a geneticist. Henderson was secretary of the Council. The full Council did not include Pigou, D. H. MacGregor and Robbins, the holders of the chairs of economics at Cambridge, Oxford and the LSE, respectively, or Beveridge, the Director of the LSE, or Robertson, the second-ranking economist at Cambridge. C. Clark (1977); Howson and Winch (1977).
61. Cannan (1932), 366–7, 370.
62. Cannan (1933), v.
63. James (1970), 383; Ensor (1936), 446.
64. Muggeridge (1940), 188–9.
65. Winch (1969), 137–8.
66. Muggeridge (1940), 119.
67. Benjamin and Kochin (1978), 315. Martin Feldstein, in his comments on this paper in Grubel and Walker (1978), 319, has pointed out that the ratio of unemployment benefit to wage rate was not exogenous, but was increased by the fall in the price level. He also suggested that the increase in the measured unemployment rate following from the rise of the benefit to wage ratio could be due to more complete registration of the unemployed, as the incentive to register rose, rather than a genuine increase in unemployment. See also Benjamin and Kochin (1979); Darby (1976).
68. Cross (1982). See also other comments in the same issue, together with a reply by Benjamin and Kochin.
69. Pigou (1927a); Clay (1928); Cannan (1930). Cassel, 'Selbstkritik! Die Sinnlosigkeit der deutschen Arbeitslosenpolitik' is cited in Hahn (1949), 239. On Pigou, Clay and Cannan, see Casson (1983), chs. 2, 3, 8.
70. Rueff (1931); Claasen and Lane (1978), 288–32. See Rueff (1951) for a restatement of his position.
71. J. R. Davis (1968, 1971).
72. Tullock, foreword to Davis (1971), x.
73. Saunders (1966), 53.
74. *Ibid.*, 57.
75. Fairchild, Furniss, Buck and Whelden (1935), 69.
76. Saxon (1962), 98, 96. The first seven printings of *Keynes at Harvard*, up to July 1962, amounted to 95,000 copies.
77. Carothers (1934), 16–17.
78. Spahr (1934), 11–12.
79. Schumpeter, in Brown *et al.* (1934), 16.
80. Chamberlin, in Brown *et al.* (1934), 27–8, 30.
81. Brown, in Brown *et al.* (1934), 68.
82. Haberler, in Wright (1932), 43–74. Haberler, previously of the Univer-

sity of Vienna, was appointed a Professor of Economics at Harvard in 1936, but had taught there earlier as a visitor.

83. Fisher, in Roos (1933), 152–9.
84. Everett Du Pay, in Roos (1933), 292.
85. Meeker, in Roos (1933), 270.
86. Wolman, in Roos (1933), 86.
87. Meeker, in Roos (1933), 260.
88. Wolman, in Roos (1933), 90.
89. Angell, in Roos (1933), 217.
90. Working, in Roos (1933), 178; Marshall (1920), 710–11.
91. Pigou, evidence to Macmillan Committee on Finance and Industry, quoted by Moggridge (1969), 68.
92. Keynes (1973), xiv, 259.
93. Robbins (1935), 28–30.
94. Hutchinson (1978). See also Casson (1983), 161.
95. Bowers (1934).
96. Hicks (1937), 53.
97. Hawtrey (1934).
98. Keynes (1936), 279.
99. See B. Hansen (1981); Winch (1966); and Ohlin, in Patinkin and Leith (1978).
100. Cole (1930); Wootton (1931).
101. Pollard (1969), reprinted in Pollard (1970), 157.
102. Cole (1933), chapters viii (by Gaitskell), xi (by Cole); Durbin (1932).
103. Pollard (1969), reprinted in Pollard (1970), 157.
104. C. Clark, in Cole (1933), 347–8.
105. Durbin, in Cole (1933), 264–5.
106. Graham (1932), quoted in Roos (1933), 282.
107. Jonung (1981).
108. Pollard (1969), reprinted in Pollard (1970).
109. H. Johnson, in E. Johnson and H. Johnson (1978), 187, 210.
110. Reprinted in Robertson (1940), 102–3.
111. Mitchell (1927), 384.
112. Jevons (1933); Garcia-Mata and Shaffner (1934).
113. Ohlin (1974), 890.
114. Robbins (1971), 154.
115. See Patinkin's Robertson Lecture for a comparison of the *Treatise* with earlier Cambridge treatments of money demand: Patinkin (1982), 165–88.
116. Keynes (1936), xxi.

4 From price adjustment to output adjustment

The *Treatise* was published in October 1930, and, as we have seen, was promptly hailed by such distinguished reviewers as Sir Josiah Stamp in the *Economic Journal* and John Williams in the *Quarterly Journal of Economics* as an important breakthrough in economic theory. At the moment when Stamp was acclaiming the *Treatise* as 'in many respects ... the most penetrating and epoch-making since Ricardo',[1] Keynes himself was already dissatisfied with the work's failure to make the leap from analysis of price fluctuations to determination of changes in output and employment. The arguments in Keynes' semi-popular essays, that increased public works spending would raise employment and national income, were not discussed in the *Treatise*, because Keynes had not yet succeeded in formalizing them. The *Treatise*'s implicit assumption of an exogenously-given level of output was brought forcefully to Keynes' attention by Ralph Hawtrey and Richard Kahn in the autumn of 1930, before the book's publication but after it was too late for Keynes to make any changes. The working out by Keynes and his close associates at Cambridge of the implications of Hawtrey's critique of the *Treatise* and of Kahn's analysis of the multiplier effects of government spending was the next significant step in the development of Keynes' economic thought after the *Treatise*.

At first, Kahn and other members of the 'Cambridge Circus' attempted to show that the multiplier was fully consistent with the theoretical framework of the *Treatise*. It soon became evident, however, that the multiplier process did not fit comfortably into the 'fundamental equations'. The post-publication debate over the *Treatise* led to recognition that, in addition to the rate of interest, output itself might serve as an equilibrating variable altering the level of saving. By the summer of 1931, Keynes and his associates at Cambridge had moved from the analysis of price fluctuations to efforts to construct a theory of employment and output. This theorizing pointed towards a reconciliation of the *Treatise*'s portfolio choice approach to interest rate determination and its analysis of expectations with the policy discussions collected in Keynes' *Essays in Persuasion* (1931). Why such a reconciliation was needed, and what it involved, can be discovered by examining Keynes' dissatisfaction with the *Treatise*, and by tracing the development of his thought on unemployment from his pre-*Treatise* pamphlets and journal articles up to the discussions in the 'Cambridge Circus' in 1930 and 1931.

'DOES UNEMPLOYMENT NEED A DRASTIC REMEDY?

The *Treatise on Money* emphasized interest rate reductions rather than expansionary fiscal policy as an appropriate response to slumps. This was partly due to a narrow interpretation of what topics belonged in a work on monetary theory. A more important cause of this emphasis was the difficulty Keynes had experienced in explaining how government spending affected the level of employment. The nature of this logical difficulty can be seen in Keynes' polemical writings on fiscal policy in the 1920s.

David Lloyd George first advocated a programme of public works spending during an economic slump in a letter to *The Nation and Athenaeum* in April 1924, just two years after he lost the Prime Ministership. The manner in which he stated his case now appears curious:

> A far-seeing manufacturer utilizes periods of slackness to repair his machinery, to reequip his workshop, and generally to put his factory in order, so that when prosperity comes he will be in as good a position as his keenest competitor to take advantage of the boom. I suggest that the nation ought to follow that wise example, and that this is the time to do so. Let us overhaul our national equipment in all directions – men and material – so as to be ready, when the moment arrives, to meet any rivals on equal or better terms in the markets of the world.[2]

What Lloyd George meant was that government projects (investment in social overhead capital), such as extension of the transport, health care and education systems, which were considered desirable on their own merits, should be undertaken during periods of cyclical unemployment. This would avoid diversion of labour from private enterprise, since the public works would employ workers who would otherwise be unemployed. In 1924, Lloyd George did not yet suggest that this programme would create an economic boom by generating secondary employment when workers on public projects spent their wages.

Lloyd George's proposal proved to be of little political advantage to the Liberal Party. As the uproar over the forged 'Zinoviev letter' polarized public opinion between the Conservative and Labour camps, the Liberals fell in the 1924 general election from 158 seats in the House of Commons to a mere 40 seats, a rump plagued by divisions dating back to Lloyd George's ouster of Asquith as Prime Minister of the wartime coalition in 1916. Lloyd George's letter, which was titled 'The Statesman's Task', provoked considerable debate in the columns of *The Nation and Athenaeum*, though it attracted more attention among economists than among voters. One correspondent, Walter Layton, a former Cambridge lecturer then editing *The Economist*, feared that fiscal expansion would delay necessary adjustments in wage rates. This response is interesting in view of Mark Blaug's recent attempt to show the conventional nature of Keynes' policy views by listing eight British economists who advocated expansionary fiscal policy as a remedy for unemployment, including Layton on the list together with four of Keynes' young followers: Roy Harrod, James Meade and Joan and Austin Robinson.[3]

Keynes entered the fray with a signed article 'Does Unemployment Need a Drastic Remedy?', in which he argued that public spending would have been more appropriate as a corrective to misguided monetary policy two years earlier, when unemployment had been double its 1924 level. At the lower level of unemployment, which still amounted to almost a million British workers without jobs, Keynes felt that 'a monetary policy which aimed at reducing the unemployed by more than (say) a further 100,000 would run dangerously near another inflation'. He went on to endorse a limited policy of fiscal expansion to achieve that reduction in unemployment, urging that 'The Treasury should not shrink from promoting expenditure up to (say) £100,000,000 a year on the construction of capital work at home', instead of devoting those resources to redemption of the war debt. Since the debt was being reduced out of a surplus, no budget deficit need be incurred.[4]

Keynes was concerned with using the rate of interest as well as public expenditure as means of stimulating employment. When the Bank of England raised the rediscount rate from 3 to 4 per cent in the summer of 1923 to protect the foreign exchange value of the pound, Keynes denounced the decision as 'one of the most misguided ... that has ever occurred'.[5] This contrasts sharply with the position Keynes took in February 1920, when he advised the Chancellor of the Exchequer, Austen Chamberlain, that a large increase in the bank rate was needed to burst a speculative bubble. 'K would go for a financial crisis (doesn't believe it would lead to unemployment). Would go to whatever rate is necessary – perhaps 10% – and keep it at that for three years', noted the Chancellor after the interview.[6] This advice was offered during a speculative boom in investment and in securities prices in a period of near-full employment. In both 1920 and 1923, Keynes emphasized the effect of bank rate changes on businessmen's expectations and thus on investment decisions, and urged that monetary policy be used to pursue domestic goals, not the defence of a fixed foreign exchange value of sterling.

In 'Does Unemployment Need a Drastic Remedy?' Keynes concluded that 'the ultimate cure of unemployment' would require both monetary policy to stabilize the price level and government-sponsored investment to divert British savings from foreign investment. The reason was that investment overseas generated less demand for domestic goods than an equal amount of investment at home. Debt-financed public expenditure was not seen in this analysis as creating additional demand through the multiplier, but only as a means of diverting demand from foreign countries by crowding out overseas investment. Such a beggar-thy-neighbour remedy for unemployment clearly provided an incentive for foreign governments to follow suit, in which case the policy would be ineffective.

Keynes estimated in 1924 that one-third to one-half of British saving was being invested abroad.[7] Given the small gold reserve held by the Bank of England, the British economy could adjust to the high rate of foreign investment either through depreciation of the pound or deflation of prices, which would stimulate British exports and reduce imports. Return to the gold standard at the prewar parity, already a declared goal of public policy, ruled out exchange depreciation, and Keynes was concerned about the social costs of forcing down sticky nominal wages and prices:

Our economic structure is far from elastic, and much time may elapse and indirect loss result from the strains set up and the breakages incurred. Meanwhile, resources may lie idle and labour be out of employment.[8]

The remaining means of restoring balance of payments equilibrium was diversion of foreign investment to domestic employment, which would at the same time solve the problem of idle resources. This effect of public investment on the balance of payments is not that stressed in later macroeconomic thought, which pointed out that expansionary fiscal policy would stimulate imports by increasing income. Despite this consideration, in 1924 Keynes endorsed a moderate programme of public works to reduce unemployment on the basis of an analysis of crowding out of foreign investment, rather than of the multiplier. At the time, Keynes' articles failed to explain how much income and employment would be generated by a given increment in state-sponsored investment, since they offered no analysis of successive rounds of spending or of leakages into saving, taxes and imports. Similarly, there was little consideration of how to ensure that government borrowing for public works would crowd out primarily foreign rather than domestic investment, at least not beyond the suggestion that lender's risk was lower on domestic securities and lowest on government debt, so that lenders would prefer to acquire domestic assets if more became available at the prevailing rate of return.

CAN LLOYD GEORGE DO IT?

Keynes' endorsement of expansionary fiscal policy in 1924 was tentative and restrained. He made it clear that in a closed economy he would prefer to stimulate investment by lowering interest rates. The strongest argument against a 'drastic remedy for unemployment' was that unemployment had declined by half in the previous two years. This suggested that wages and prices would move to new market-clearing levels in the wake of a shock and that labour would shift from declining to expanding industries without an intolerable time-lag. By 1929 such optimism about labour market-clearing was no longer tenable, however:

Except for a brief recovery in 1924 before the return to the gold standard, one-tenth or more of the working population of this country have been unemployed for eight years – a fact unprecedented in our history. The number of insured persons counted by the Ministry of Labour as out of work has never been less than one million since the initiation of their statistics in 1923. To-day (April 1929) 1,140,000 workers are unemployed.[9]

In the wake of the monetary contraction, price deflation and general strike association with Britain's return to the prewar exchange rate of \$4.86/£, British unemployment showed no signs of diminishing through the unaided action of market forces. Unemployment of such extent and duration could not easily be explained as the result of excessive wage demands based on misperceptions of the purchasing power of money or of the state of demand for labour. The subsidized system of unemployment insurance may have increased the time that workers were prepared to spend searching for the best available job and weakened their incentive to move to another region or industry in quest of work, particularly as price deflation raised the real value of unemployment benefits, but the expansion of government-sponsored employment exchanges should have worked to shorten search time. Moreover, the dole was far from being sufficiently lavish to make voluntary investment in search plausible as an explanation of eight years of mass unemployment.[10]

By 1929, Keynes was convinced that the government had a responsibility to stimulate demand rather than just tinker with the level of unemployment benefits or wait for unemployment to disappear unaided. Keynes and his former Cambridge colleague Hubert Henderson wrote a pamphlet, *Can Lloyd George Do It?*, in support of proposals put forward once again by Lloyd George to cure mass unemployment through public works. The pamphlet was published by *The Nation and Athenaeum* on 11 May, 1929, with one of its chapters appearing in the journal the next day as a signed statement of editorial policy. Thanks no doubt to the fame (or notoriety) Keynes had acquired by his denunciation of the Versailles Peace Treaty and its negotiator, David Lloyd George, the pamphlet attracted considerable attention in the 1929 general election campaign. Lloyd George's own attitude to economic theory resembled that of Ernest Wigforss, the Social Democratic Finance Minister in Sweden a few years later, who argued that, although no one understood why unemployment happened, this was no reason not to do something about it.[11] Keynes and Henderson took it upon themselves to provide academically respectable economic arguments for the effectiveness of the expansionary fiscal policy promised by Lloyd George and the Liberal Party, and to rebut Treasury criticism of the Liberal pledge to reduce unemployment. Although the periodical which they edited advertised for subscriptions with the slogan 'It matters what Liberals are thinking. Read the *Nation*', Keynes and Henderson produced arguments for the Liberal pledge of which the leading Liberal politicians were, at best, only dimly aware.

The concern in *Can Lloyd George Do It?* with fiscal policy and lasting unemployment contrasts with the emphasis on monetary policy and price stabilization in *A Treatise on Money*. Ever since the 1924 exchange in the pages of their weekly journal, Keynes and Henderson had been sympathetic to proposals to use public works to reduce unemployment. Their stand in favour of fiscal expansion in 1929 was much stronger than that taken by Keynes in 1924, however. In the earlier year, unemployment had been dropping, suggesting that falling wage rates and shifts of workers between industries and regions would restore full employment in the not-too-distant future. By 1929 this hope had vanished. Keynes and Henderson did not, however, commit themselves to the notion that the economy had necessarily come to rest in an equilibrium with involuntary unemployment. They noted that labour was moving out of the hardest-hit industries into other occupations, and attributed the decline of unemployment among coal miners from nearly 300,000 in August 1928 to 145,000 in April 1929 to workers leaving the industry.[12] In most cases, this would also mean leaving the district, given the dominance of coal mining in parts of Wales and the Midlands. Market adjustment, in this case adjustment to the shift of shipping to oil power and of railways to diesel, was occurring, even if only after much delay and suffering.

Keynes and Henderson mentioned repeated policy shocks to the economy, which impeded adjustment to previous shocks and could account for a protracted unemployment disequilibrium. Their concept of equilibrium was thus a position of rest with cleared markets, rather than one in which expectations are realized. The return to the gold standard at a parity that required a 10 per cent deflation of prices and nominal wages for British goods to remain competitive with foreign goods was the most severe shock. Another policy criticized by Keynes and Henderson was a reduction in the government housing subsidy, which cut the number of houses built under state sponsorship from 212,000 in the year ending September

1927 to 101,000 the following year. At the same time, road building was also cut back so severely that, according to Lord Montagu of Beaulieu, 'hardly a mile of new trunk road has been planned and constructed during the last two years'.[13] In sum, the evidence was not clear enough to enable Keynes and Henderson to state whether the British economy could have recovered from high unemployment without government intervention, because there had been repeated perverse interventions by the state choking off potential recovery.

In his review of Keynes' *Collected Writings*, Don Patinkin has noted that some of the most persuasive passages supporting expansionary fiscal policy in *Can Lloyd George Do It?* were left out of the abridged version of the pamphlet published in Keynes' *Essays in Persuasion* in 1931. He went on to speculate whether these passages were left out because they were by Henderson or because of ambivalence on Keynes' part about fiscal policy.[14] However, while seven of the pamphlet's first eight chapters were dropped from the reprint, the omitted chapters were no firmer in their endorsement of expansionary fiscal policy as a remedy for unemployment than the included ones. Much of the omitted material was highly topical, and of only limited interest to readers after the 1929 election campaign was over. Henderson was certainly not a stronger supporter of fiscal expansion than Keynes, as can be seen from a letter he wrote to Keynes in February 1931, when unemployment was more than double its 1929 level. In it he complained that Keynes was ignoring the danger of budget deficits in his advocacy of increased government spending: 'The effect is to convey the impression to all people, however intelligent and open-minded, who have some appreciation of the financial difficulties, that you have gone completely crazy, and impairing all the influence you have with them, while pleasing and encouraging only those who say that you mustn't lay a finger on the dole.'[15]

Keynes' *Treatise on Money* argues that the Bank of England could expand the level of aggregate demand and economic activity because of the existence of a fringe of unsatisfied borrowers who wished to undertake investment projects but were frustrated by credit-rationing.[16] Since they were willing to borrow at the prevailing interest rate, an injection of additional credit need not lower the rate of interest. In *Can Lloyd George Do It?* Keynes and Henderson accept monetary expansion as a necessary accompaniment to expansionary fiscal policy, since 'a deflationary policy aimed at preventing any expansion in bank-credit ... [would] ensure that the expenditure financed by the Treasury *was* at the expense of other business enterprises'. They add, however:

> But if we were simply to increase credit without providing a specific use for it at home, we should be nervous that too much of this extra credit would be lent to foreigners and taken away in gold. We conclude, therefore, that, whilst an increased volume of bank-credit is probably a *sine qua non* of increased employment, a programme of home investment which will absorb this increase is a *sine qua non* of the safe expansion of credit.[17]

Under fixed exchange rates, an increase in the money supply would be drained away by a capital outflow and balance of payments deficit, unless it was accompanied by expansionary fiscal policy.

In the *Treatise on Money*, profitability and output depend on price determination. If the ratio in which the earnings of the factors of production are divided between consumption expenditure and saving differs from the ratio between consumption goods and investment goods that entrepreneurs decided to produce in the previous period, realized prices will deviate from costs of production. By altering entrepreneurs' expectations of the future state of market demand, the resulting windfall profits or losses will affect investment decisions, and thus change both the level of productive capacity and the demand for investment goods in the next period. Stabilization of the price level, by manipulating the market rate of interest so that investment decisions are consistent with saving decisions, will stabilize entrepreneurs' investment and production plans by eliminating the windfall profits or losses which cause them to revise those plans. Consequently, monetary policy is of prime importance, and the *Treatise* urges the Bank of England and the Federal Reserve Board to respond to 'the slump of 1930' by reducing the bank rate, making open-market purchases of long-term securities, and pressuring their member banks to reduce the rate of interest on bank deposits, a reduction that would be in the interest of the banks, provided they all acted together.[18] Without joint action, expansion by one central bank under fixed exchange rates would cause a balance of payments crisis, but Keynes felt that the two central banks together were large enough relative to world financial markets to change the world market rate of interest.

In *Can Lloyd George Do It?*, the state can stimulate aggregate investment not only through reduction of the market rate of interest, but also directly through its own investment. Keynes and Henderson

point to roads, bridges, docks, harbours, land drainage and extension of the electrical and telephone systems as infrastructure projects
recognized in Britain as legitimate state activities, and as areas in
which additional spending was desirable, quite apart from its effect
on aggregate demand. To this list, they add financial support to the
railway companies for replacement of rolling stock, electrification of
some lines, and improvement of yards and terminals, so that road-
building would not discriminate against the railways by improving
the competitive position of haulage contractors. Housing was the
remaining item in the Liberal programme, which strictly excluded
the possibility of public investment in production in competition
with the private sector.[19]

The difference between the public works proposals in *Can Lloyd
George Do It?* and the emphasis on monetary policy in the *Treatise*
can be explained by the different nature of the two publications.
Lloyd George's election platform naturally concentrated on actions
which could be undertaken by the government, without requiring the
co-operation of foreign central banks or placing responsibility in the
hands of the Bank of England, which, despite strong semi-formal ties
to the state, was run by a strongly-entrenched and irascible Governor
and responsible to directors elected by shareholders of the Bank.
Like value theory, fiscal policy was excluded from the *Treatise* as not
being part of monetary theory. In fact, this narrow definition of
monetary theory was so strictly observed in the *Treatise* that the
natural rate of interest was discussed without explicit reference to the
concept of marginal productivity of capital. Such stringent compartmentalization was broken down in the *General Theory*, which turned
from the theory of money to the theory of a monetary economy.

Can Lloyd George Do It? and the brief passages on unemployment
in the *Treatise* attribute widespread unemployment to the slow downward adjustment of nominal wage rates after a shock such as the
return to gold. Harry Johnson suggested that 'Had the exchange
value of the pound been fixed realistically in the 1920s – a prescrip-
tion fully in accord with orthodox economic theory – there would
have been no need for mass unemployment, hence no need for a
revolutionary new theory to explain it, and no triggering force for
much subsequent British political and economic history'.[20] However,
an explanation is still needed for the failure, lasting over several
years, of wages and prices to adjust to an arbitrary exchange rate.

Once an increase in the pegged exchange rate leads to a fall in the price level, so that domestic goods remain competitive with foreign goods, market clearing can be restored in the labour market in one or more of three ways. Money wage rates could be reduced, as with the reduction of coal miners' wages which sparked the 1926 General Strike, but labour resistance was recognized as stiff. The *Treatise*, in an argument given greater emphasis in the *General Theory*, holds that trade unions behave rationally when they resist nominal wage cuts in a setting of decentralized collective bargaining and staggered wage contracts fixed in money terms, with uncertainty as to how general the wage cuts would be and to what extent lower wages would be passed on as lower prices. Trade unions bargain for relative wages, but cannot determine their real wages through nominal wage bargains. Members of a union which accept a lower money wage rate would receive lower earnings relative to workers whose contracts had not yet expired.[21]

If nominal wages could be forced down only through the pressure of prolonged, massive unemployment accompanied by strikes and industrial unrest, devaluation of the pound and higher prices would appear the obvious alternatives in restoring labour market equilibrium. An increase in the price level would affect the real value of all wages equally and simultaneously. Unfortunately, abandonment of the gold parity of the pound was obstructed by a political and intellectual consensus that the City of London could be restored to its prewar position as a world financial centre only if Britain kept faith with foreign investors who had purchased sterling-denominated assets at the prewar parity, which had been unchanged for nearly a century. Keynes' letter to *The Times* on 28 September 1931, withdrawing his proposal for a protective tariff as soon as a balance of payments crisis had forced Britain off the gold standard, made it clear that he considered his suggestion for reducing unemployment as no more than a second-best solution, advanced only because of the immobilization of monetary policy by the fixed gold parity of sterling.[22]

The remaining course of action would be to stimulate the demand for labour by increasing aggregate demand. The task of Keynes and Henderson was to explain how the government could do this, despite Treasury claims to the contrary. Some of the Treasury's objections were easily disposed of: 'If we build houses to cover our heads, construct transport systems to carry our goods, drain our lands, protect our coasts, what will there be left for our children to do? No, cries Mr. Baldwin, it would be most unjust. The more work we do now, the less there will be to do hereafter.'[23] Keynes and Henderson dealt with this argument simply by pointing out that improved transportation and communications facilitate the expansion of other activities, and that new employment opportunities would be created as the economy grew. They dismissed Treasury fears that increased spending on public works would just divert labour from private employment as misguided when a large pool of unemployment labour was available.

The most important criticism of expansionary fiscal policy was that, even if an increase in aggregate demand could increase employment, government borrowing would crowd out borrowing by private entrepreneurs, with the interest rate rising to ration the limited supply of loanable funds. Fiscal policy would then fail to increase aggregate demand. This point was formulated by Ralph Hawtrey of the Treasury in response to Lloyd George's 1924 proposal, and was reiterated by other Treasury officials in the 1929 Treasury memorandum.[24] The *Treatise* seemed to provide an explanation for the stimulative effect of state borrowing and spending during periods of profit deflation. If entrepreneurs were suffering windfall losses, saving would be greater than investment, on the *Treatise* definitions.[25] This suggested that there existed savings which would run to waste unless the government borrowed and used them. The government could borrow these savings and carry out investment spending, closing the gap between investment and saving without reducing private investment.[26] Indeed, private investment would be higher in later periods because the state investment would eliminate the losses which discouraged investment. In Keynes' later work, this argument was replaced by the consumption function and multiplier analysis, showing how the additional income generated by increased government spending would lead to additional saving and taxes, so that the quantity of savings was not fixed after all. *Can Lloyd George Do It?*, however, does not directly reply to the argument that crowding out would be caused by a fixed supply of savings available for borrowing, either by reference to the *Treatise* analysis or the saving function.

Keynes and Henderson emphasized instead that a 'source of the funds required for the Liberal policy will be found by a net reduction of foreign lending'.[27] Foreign governments and municipalities, which traditionally had borrowed heavily in the London market, would be among the borrowers crowded out by British government borrowing and spending, so that a larger proportion of domestic saving would be going to finance domestic spending. Debt-financed government spending would ease the foreign exchange situation by improving the capital account, and, according to Keynes and Henderson, might have made unnecessary a recent increase in the bank rate, which had strengthened the pegged exchange rate at the cost of discouraging investment. This reduction in net foreign lending would finance increased imports: 'For the new schemes will require a certain amount of imported raw materials, whilst those who are now unemployed will consume more imported food when they are once again earning decent wages.'[28] This optimistic treatment of balance of payments difficulties of expansionary policy matched the assurance that 'Inflation only results when we endeavour, as we did in the War and afterwards, to expand our activities still further after everyone is already employed and our savings are being used up to the hilt'.[29]

Keynes and Henderson discussed the attitude of the economics profession to their rejection of complete crowding out in two interesting paragraphs which were left out of the abridgement of their pamphlet in *Essays in Persuasion*:

> This conclusion is not peculiar to ourselves or to Mr Lloyd George and his advisors. The theoretical question involved is not a new one. The general problem of whether capital developments financed by the Government are capable of increasing employment has been carefully debated by economists in recent years. The result has been to establish the conclusions of this chapter as sound and orthodox and the Treasury's dogma as fallacious. For example – to quote authorities of diverse gifts and experience – our preceding argument has closely followed Professor Pigou's reasoning in his recent volume 'Industrial Fluctuations' (Part II, Chapter x), where he quotes a statement of the Treasury dogma and declares it to be fallacious; this conclusion is endorsed by Sir Josiah Stamp; and it has been ardently advocated by Mr McKenna (see, in particular, his 1927 Address to his shareholders, reprinted in 'Post-War Banking Policy', p. 118) who, speaking as the Chairman of the greatest bank in the world, maintains, without hesitation, that an increase in the volume of money investible in business activity is possible without inflationary consequences.
>
> Indeed, we have not been able to discover any recent pronouncement to the contrary, outside the ranks of the Treasury, by an economist of weight or reputation. It is an error to believe that Mr Baldwin and Mr Churchill and Sir Laming Worthington-Evans are talking impeccable economic orthodoxy when they maintain that Government borrowing necessarily attracts to itself resources which would otherwise have been

employed in private enterprise, and that Mr Lloyd George is offering no better than a specious dodge when he maintains the contrary. Precisely the opposite is true. The theory underlying the Liberal Party's policy is the theory which is supported by the weight of expert opinion.[30]

This view of Keynes sharing the standpoint of Pigou and of the weight of expert opinion is in sharp contrast to the rejection of Pigou's theoretical writings in the *General Theory*, but it was generally valid as far as issues of policy were concerned. The only major emendation required in the statement by Keynes and Henderson would be to note, after the remark about Treasury officials (including the economist Hawtrey), that Professors Cannan, Gregory and Plant of the London School of Economics also shared much of the Treasury view, as did Lionel Robbins and Friedrich Hayek, who obtained chairs at LSE within the next two years.[31] The myth that Pigou advocated wage-cutting rather than public works has been demolished by T. W. Hutchinson's analysis of Pigou's testimony before the Macmillan Committee in 1930.[32] As early as his *Wealth and Welfare* (1912), Pigou had given reserved support to the counter-cyclical public works policy advocated in the Minority Report of the Poor Law Commission, written by Beatrice Webb with the collaboration of Sidney Webb and the statistician A. L. Bowley, although Pigou questioned some of the report's assumptions and statistics.[33] What Keynes objected to was that Pigou held theoretical positions from which his policy views could not follow.

Ralph Hawtrey offered a succint summary of the Treasury view in reply to the report: 'The writers of the Minority Report appear to have overlooked the fact that the Government by the very act of borrowing for this expenditure is withdrawing from the investment market savings which would otherwise be applied to the creation of capital.'[34] Dennis Robertson, in a thesis supervised by Keynes which gave 'cordial support' to the Minority Report's proposal on public works, declared: 'Mr. Hawtrey's attack upon the proposal scarcely deserves formal refutation.'[35] Here is where Keynes, in *Can Lloyd George Do It?* and in his later work leading up to the *General Theory*, parted company with Pigou and Robertson. Endorsement of countercyclical public works was insufficient by itself. The Treasury view did require formal refutation, and it was the responsibility of the economists advocating expansionary fiscal policy to explain, on the basis of rigorous economic theory, how such policy would stimulate employment and production.

THE MULTIPLIER

Keynes and Henderson argued that the number of jobs created by the public works programme would be considerably greater than the number of workers directly employed on the projects. Much of their attention was devoted to rebutting ministerial attempts to minimize the number of workers who would be employed by ignoring jobs producing and transporting construction materials, and instead counting only labourers employed on the construction site itself.[36] However, they went beyond this to make the crucial point that 'The fact that many workpeople who are now unemployed would be receiving wages instead of unemployment pay would mean an increase in effective purchasing power which would give a general stimulus to trade'. The Liberal pamphlet, while dealing extensively with the indirect employment resulting from the increased demand for construction materials, devoted only a single paragraph to a rather off-hand recognition that secondary employment could result when newly employed workers spent their wages. Henderson and Keynes drew attention to this secondary round of spending, and linked its influence to the effect of rising demand on business confidence. They noted that:

> It is not possible to measure effects of this character with any sort of precision, and little or no account is, therefore, taken in 'We Can Conquer Unemployment'. But, in our opinion, these effects are of immense importance. For this reason we believe that the effects on employment of a given capital expenditure would be far larger than the Liberal pamphlet assumes.[37]

This passage shows that in 1929 Keynes and Henderson grasped the importance of secondary employment resulting from successive rounds of consumption spending out of wages. What they did not know was how to calculate its magnitude. They did not even treat the effect of successive rounds of spending as being easier to quantify than the effect on entrepreneurs' confidence. An estimate of five thousand man-years of employment per million pounds of expenditure was quoted by Keynes and Henderson from the Liberal Party pamphlet, and defended by them solely on the basis of how many skilled and unskilled workers would be required directly in road-building and how many in producing and transporting supplies for the road. A line which they cited from the Liberal pamphlet – 'Expert opinion is that some 80 per cent of total expenditure represents the amounts paid directly or indirectly in wages' – neglected all but the initial round of spending.[28]

Another indication that Keynes and Henderson had only imperfectly worked out the concept of the multiplier came in their discussion of the cost of the Lloyd George programme:

> Mr Lloyd George has given a pledge that the execution of his programme will not mean an addition to taxation. He has added that, of course, this does not mean that it will cost nothing, but that the cost will be less than the money which it will save in other directions *plus* the buoyancy of the revenue attributable to it *plus* economies on such things as armaments.[39]

While it was appropriate to observe that the increase in income resulting from increased government spending would cause higher tax revenues, increased spending on public works would fail to increase aggregate demand or employment if it was matched by economies on other government expenses, such as armaments and the dole.

The stumbling block in developing the multiplier theory was the lack of any explanation of how an increase in income would be divided among spending on domestic goods and services, imported goods and saving. A passing remark by Keynes and Henderson about increased consumption of imported food by the newly employed does not constitute recognition of the functional relationship, especially since this leakage was not used to estimate the ratio of secondary to primary employment. In the absence of recognition that the level of income influenced the rate of saving, it could not be argued that the creation of additional savings would alleviate the crowding out of private borrowers by debt-financed government borrowing. Furthermore, if savings did not depend on income, it was not clear why hiring one worker to dig a ditch would not produce full employment, if only he spent all his wages on domestic goods and services, and if the suppliers of these goods and services did the same. If he (or she) purchased imported goods as well, worldwide full employment would be the result. This was described in later multiplier terminology as a marginal propensity to consume equal to one. The parable of the banana plantation in the *Treatise* illustrated a cumulative process which exploded because of an implicit assumption that the amount of saving did not depend on the level of income.[40]

The notion that public works would lead to a second round of spending as the workers spent their wages was not new in 1929, although Lloyd George and his advisors treated it gingerly in a single paragraph in *We Can Conquer Unemployment* as an unfamiliar and possibly unsound speculation. Richard Kahn recalls, in his Raffaele Mattioli Lectures, learning from his father, an avid amateur economist, about the successive rounds of spending, when he was eight years old.[41] Such early versions of the multiplier had two crucial weaknesses, because they lacked leakages into saving from each round of income. Without reference to such leakages, there was no explanation of how public investment created additional saving, so that it did not simply crowd out private investment. Without leakages, the infinite series of successive rounds of spending implied an infinite multiplier, which conflicted with the observed results of government spending.

The unrealistically high estimates of the expenditure multiplier which could be derived from the Keynes and Henderson discussion, in the absence of a theory of leakages into saving, are illustrated by a speech given in October 1929 by the Japanese statesman Korekiyo Takahashi. Takahashi, a former Governor of the Bank of Japan who had been Minister of Finance in four Cabinets (one of which he had led as Prime Minister) and who was to hold that post in three more before his murder in 1936, was a sober, respected financial authority, not given to extravagant statements, yet he followed an incisive discussion of the paradox of thrift with a suggestion that the spending multiplier might be between twenty and thirty. Since Takahashi was known to be an avid reader of *The Times* of London and of Western books and periodicals on economics, as shown by his references to Irving Fisher and to a University of Chicago seminar in a 1933 speech on countercyclical fiscal policy, two recent writers on Takahashi have suggested that his 1929 speech was based on the pamphlet by Keynes and Henderson, which had appeared a few months earlier.[42]

The very high estimates of the multiplier which seemed to be implied by the infinite series of successive rounds of spending caused uneasiness among economists. In April 1930, Colin Clark, a statistician on the staff of the Economic Advisory Council, and A. W. Flux, who had held the chair of economics at McGill University but was then at the Board of Trade, prepared a note on the employment effects of increased exports. They included no estimate of the secondary effects of increased employment in the export industries because:

> It will be seen at once that any crude calculation ... would lead to assuming an infinite series of beneficial repercussions. This clearly cannot represent the case, nor on the other hand can we categorically deny the possibility of beneficial repercussions. The limiting factors, however, are obscure and economic theory cannot state the possibilities with precision.[43]

The unsatisfactory state of economic analysis of the effects of government spending can be seen in Pigou's article on 'The Monetary Theory of the Trade Cycle', which appeared in the *Economic Journal* in 1929. As a paper by the occupant of the foremost chair of economics in Britain, published in a journal edited by Keynes at about the same time as *Can Lloyd George Do It?* came out, this article can be taken as representative of the orthodox theory available to Keynes at that time. Pigou tackles 'the question how far in a regime of stable prices, i.e., apart from inflation, it is possible by means of Government expenditure to diminish the volume of unemployment',[44] yet produces nothing that would have eased the qualms of Clark and Flux.

Pigou considers an island of wheat-growers, with a wage rate of one bushel of wheat a week. If the government spent an additional R bushels hiring labour in a particular week and used the labour in building roads or bridges, employment would rise by R for one week. There would be no secondary employment from the workers spending their wages, since presumably they consumed the wheat wages themselves. Pigou does not discuss whether the government spending diverts a fixed pool of saving away from private borrowing and investment. If the workers were employed producing consumable goods (wheat in the example) instead of building bridges and roads, the government would get the proceeds of their labour to be used to hire more workers. Only a declining marginal product of labour in wheat-growing, that is, an increasing cost of producing wheat, would keep this additional employment from being infinite.[45] Pigou forgets that the R workers hired in the first week would lose their jobs at the end of the week without new spending, so that the ratio of the total employment generated by the additional government spending to the primary employment is one in his model, not infinite, even with a constant cost of producing wheat. Where Pigou incorrectly generates an infinite series of additional employment, he relies on price changes rather than leakages to make the sum of additional employment finite.

Macroeconomics was rescued from the perplexity of Clark and Flux and the muddle of Pigou's analysis by the derivation of a finite multiplier from an infinite series of rounds of spending with leakages from each round, and with the level of output rather than the interest rate as the variable which equilibrates investment and saving. Versions of this multiplier theory were independently developed at about the same time by four economists: L. F. Giblin in Australia, Ralph G. Hawtrey at the British Treasury, Richard F. Kahn at Cambridge University, and Jens Warming in Denmark. These multiple independent discoveries indicate that the multiplier theory was an idea whose time had come, as a logical extension of earlier literature, particularly including the *Treatise on Money* and *Can Lloyd George Do It?*, with its emphasis on secondary employment.

The first to publish was Lyndhurst Falkiner Giblin, who had gone from King's College, Cambridge, to occupy the chair of economics at Melbourne University. In his book *Australia, 1930*, published by the Melbourne University Press in 1930, Giblin uses the multiplier, with leakages into imports, to analyse the effects of a decline in exports:

> Consider the following argument. A woolgrower receives £900 less income than his average. He has, therefore, £900 less to spend. He will reduce his expenditure on those goods and services he can spare. One-third of his total consumption is on imports and exportable goods, and we may assume that one-third of his reduction in expenditure, £300, will be for such goods, so that the balance of trade will improve to that extent. The remainder will be for non-exportable goods and services. Let us suppose that he puts off a fencer engaged in improving his property at a cost of £200 per annum; saves £200 on clothing, putting a tailor out of work; and saves another £200 in pleasure travelling, putting a motor mechanic or driver out of work who was previously earning that sum. There is no other income available for employing the fencer, tailor or motor mechanic, and there is, therefore, a further loss of income of £600, two-thirds of the original £900. This £600 of income was also being spent by the fencer, tailor and motor mechanic, one-third, or £200, on imports and exportable goods and two-thirds, or £400, on the landlord, the butcher and the boot-maker and other Australian workmen. So that there will be an improvement in the balance of trade by £200, and a further loss of Australian income by £400. And so on, until, in the end, there has been a reduction in the consumption of imports and exportable goods of £900 in all, and a reduction in Australian income of £2,700, or three times the direct shortage of income of the wool-grower.[46]

This passage shows a clear and explicit use of the multiplier, but there are problems with Giblin's multiplier. His concern was the balance of trade, in connection with the extensive journal discussions of the Australian case for protection, rather than with the equilibrium level of income. With imports as the sole leakage from spending, Giblin is forced to accept that an increase in Australian exports would fail to provide any easing whatsoever of Australia's debt-service problem, because imports would increase by just as much as exports.[47] Furthermore, Giblin neglects the fact that Australian imports are exports of the rest of the world. If there are no domestic leakages into saving and taxes, the fall in Australian exports which causes Australian income and imports to decline will also reduce the exports and income level of the rest of the world, and so reduce Australian exports still further. With leakages into imports, but not of spending, the multiplier will be infinite, and Giblin's example should, on his assumption, lead to zero world income. With no effect of income on saving and taxes, Giblin's analysis cannot explain how increased government spending can generate additional saving and taxes instead of just crowding out private borrowing of existing savings.

Australia, 1930 was delivered by Giblin on 30 April 1930 as his inaugural lecture as the first Ritchie Research Professor of Economics at the University of Melbourne. His appointment caused some surprise, because Giblin, who had been Government Statistician of Tasmania for nearly ten years, had no formal background in economics.[48] He had been led to the multiplier as an indirect result of the desire of the Development and Mining Commission of the Victoria government to justify the building of the Nowingi railway to open up new wheatlands. The railway would not earn enough revenue to pay for construction, but the Commission's economic advisor, Douglas Copland, Dean of Commerce at the University of Melbourne, felt that construction would be justified if the increased wheat exports led to a sufficient increase in national income. 'Copland was aware of these considerations, but was unable to state the problem precisely in terms of the effect on national income as a whole. He took this problem to Giblin who produced the first formula of the multiplier.'[49]

Giblin, who was ten years older than Keynes, was a graduate of King's College, Cambridge, with which he retained sufficiently close ties for King's to make him an Honorary Fellow in 1938 and establish a Giblin Studentship open to Australian graduates. Although Giblin did not meet Keynes until 1918, long after Giblin left

Cambridge, they became friendly enough so that, during Giblin's trip to England in 1938, he stayed in Keynes' rooms at King's and visited Keynes at his country home, Tilton.[50] There is no evidence that either Keynes or Kahn knew of either Giblin's analysis in his inaugural lecture of the multiplier effects of a £900 drop in exports, or his 1928 analysis for the railway proposal of the effects of a £900 increase in wheat exports. Giblin's correspondence with Keynes in 1933 about the multiplier theory of Keynes' pamphlet *The Means to Prosperity* neither mentions Giblin's earlier work, nor indicates that Giblin had then any clear understanding of how the multiplier was calculated.[51]

Giblin and his colleagues at Melbourne do not seem to have appreciated the importance of Giblin's contribution until many years later. An article by Copland, Giblin and G. L. Wood on 'The Restoration of Economic Equilibrium' in the *Economic Record* in November 1930 makes no use of the multiplier. In the autumn of 1933, Douglas Copland delivered eight Alfred Marshall Memorial Lectures at Cambridge on *Australia and the World Crisis, 1929–33*. In the book based on these lectures, published the following year, Copland refers to other parts of Giblin's *Australia, 1930*, but not the multiplier.[52] One Cambridge economist did recognize Giblin's achievement, however. E. Ronald Walker of St John's College, Cambridge, writing a doctoral dissertation on *Australia in the Great Depression* (1933) under the supervision of Dennis Robertson before returning to a lectureship at the University of Sydney, devoted two pages of that book to discussing Giblin's multiplier and comparing it with Kahn's version.[53] A search of the journal literature by A. L. Wright revealed only one reference to Giblin's multiplier, a single sentence in a footnote in an article by Walker in the Australian journal *Economic Record*.[54] Giblin's contribution, although honoured in Australia by the Giblin Library at the University of Melbourne and the annual Giblin Memorial Lecture to the Australia and New Zealand Association for the Advancement of Science, passed unknown and unremarked outside Australia.

Ralph Hawtrey's first excursion into multiplier theory was in a Treasury memorandum on German reparations and the transfer problem in August 1928, the same year that Copland turned to Giblin for an estimate of the effect of a change in exports on national income. Hawtrey's 1928 memorandum is strikingly similar to Giblin's multiplier, with imports as the only leakage and no recognition that a fall in one country's imports will reduce income in the rest of the world and so feed back as a reduction in the exports and income of the home country. The crucial section of this previously unpublished memorandum, which Eric Davis of Carleton University has discovered, argues:

> The theory is best illustrated by a numerical example. Assume a country with a consumers' income (total national income measured in money units) of 100,000,000 currency units per annum. Suppose that it produces and consumes (at the existing price levels) 40,000,000 units' worth of home trade products and 60,000,000 of foreign trade products. Let the country become liable to make an annual external payment of 5,000,000. The first step is to impose taxation calculated to yield 5,000,000 a year. If there is nothing in this measure to affect the proportions in which consumers divide their outlay between home trade products and foreign trade products, the consumption of each will be reduced by 5 per cent, and will become 38,000,000 and 57,000,000 respectively.
>
> There results a loss of equilibrium in two directions. The demand for home trade products is 2,000,000 short of the output of 40,000,000 and the excess of production over consumption of foreign trade products is only 3,000,000 and is 2,000,000 short of the external liability.
>
> Production of home trade products must fall to 38,000,000 (either through a reduction of price or a reduction of output). But there will then be a further decline of 2,000,000 in the demand for both classes of products, say, 800,000 home trade products and 1,200,000 foreign trade products.
>
> Equilibrium is only regained when the mutual influence of the consumption and output of home trade products has persisted up to the point at which they balance once more at 36 2/3 millions. (The reduction is the sum of the series, $2,000,000 + 800,000 + 320,000 + 128,000 + \ldots\ldots$ or $2,000,000 \times [1 + 2/5 + (2/5)^2 + (2/5)^3 + \ldots\ldots]$. The sum of the series is $2,000,000 \times \dfrac{1}{1 - 2/5}$ or 3 1/3 millions).[55]

Hawtrey's 1928 memorandum has the same weaknesses as Giblin's analysis, because imports are the only leakage. Despite these weaknesses, it compares favourably with Keynes' paper on 'The German Transfer Problem' in the *Economic Journal* in June 1929. Despite observing that 'If £1 is taken from you and given to me and I choose to increase my consumption of precisely the same goods as those of which you are compelled to diminish yours, there is no Transfer Problem', Keynes proceeded to neglect income effects and to conclude that the improvement in the German current account needed for the capital transfer could be achieved only by a deterioration of the German terms of trade. Bertil Ohlin, writing in the next issue of the journal, quoted the sentence from Keynes above, and noted that the country receiving the transfer would demand more imported goods.[56] Hawtrey could not have been criticized for ignoring the income effects of reparations transfers, although he examined them only for the country paying the reparations, not for both, as Ohlin did.

Hawtrey went beyond his 1928 analysis in his comments on proof-sheets of the *Treatise on Money*. These comments, stressing the equilibrating role of changes in output and criticizing the *Treatise* for implicitly assuming constant output, reached Keynes at about the same time as the first draft of Richard Kahn's article on the multiplier. Keynes sent proofs of roughly a third of the *Treatise* to Hawtrey on 23 April 1930, followed by 'a good batch' of Volume II on 24 June, and Chapter 30, the historical illustrations of Keynes' theory, on 7 July.[57] Hawtrey's comments were delayed by his responsibilities at the Treasury, and, while comments were in Keynes' hands before the publication of the *Treatise*, Keynes did not reply to them until 28 November, nearly a month after publication.

Hawtrey's critique of the *Treatise* proofs,[58] which was published in revised form in 1932 as a chapter of Hawtrey's *The Art of Central Banking*, raised the 'possibility of a reduction in output being caused directly by a contraction of demand without an intervening fall of price'.[59] He argued that the short-run response of retailers to a slump in demand, perceived as being possibly only temporary, would be to reduce their orders from wholesalers, not to cut prices. The shift in demand would initially be reflected in inventories rather than prices. Hawtrey stressed the importance of stocks held by traders who finance them through the banking system, so that on questions of monetary policy he was concerned primarily with the short-term interest rate which affected inventory-holding decisions, as opposed to Keynes' emphasis on the effect of the long-term rate on investment in fixed capital.[60]

Keynes' rearguard action in defence of the *Treatise* reveals the direction in which Hawtrey's criticism prodded him:

> I repeat that I am not dealing with the complete set of causes which determine the level of output. For this would have led me an endlessly long journey into the theory of short-period supply and a long way from monetary theory; – though I agree that it will probably be difficult in the future to prevent monetary theory and the theory of short-period supply from running together. If I were to write the book again, I should

probably attempt to probe further into the difficulties of the latter; but I have already probed far enough to know what a complicated affair it is.[61]

Hawtrey's sharpest criticism was of Keynes' parable of the thrift campaign on a banana plantation, in which the implicit assumption that consumption spending would change by as much as income changed while saving would be unaffected led to the result that an initial windfall loss would generate deflation without limit. Keynes replied that:

> It would lead me too far afield to examine the causes which prevent output from declining to zero. Amongst other things one must not neglect the effect of all these events on the volume of saving.
>   The question *how much* reduction of output is caused, whether by a realised fall of price or an anticipated fall of price, is important, but not strictly a monetary problem. I have not attempted to deal with it in my book, though I have done a good deal of work at it. I am primarily concerned with what governs *prices*, though of course every conceivable factor in the situation comes in somewhere into a complete picture.[62]

Hawtrey proved a numerical example of the multiplier, with leakages into saving and income changing to equate saving to a new level of investment, in his comments on the proofs. He elaborated this example in January 1931 in working paper no. 66 for the Macmillan Committee, and presented an algebraic model as a section of his 1932 chapter on the *Treatise*. In his 1932 analysis, Hawtrey examined the effect on income of an initial change in consumption spending of amount b'. The income of producers is initially reduced by b'. They then reduce their consumption by a fixed proportion k of the fall in their income, and reduce their saving by the proportion $(1-k)$ of the fall in their income. The initial price level P will fall by p, and the available output A will decline by a. The condition for the accumulation of unsold goods to cease is that the total change in income and expenditure, $Pa + pA - pa$, be equal to $\dfrac{b'}{1-k}$.

Despite Hawtrey's contribution to the development of the multiplier, his own subsequent writings on fiscal policy ignored his own demonstration that increased investment, by increasing income, generates the saving to finance it, and he was distinctly cool toward Keynes' *General Theory*. Hawtrey's paper on 'Public Expenditure and Trade Depression' in the *Journal of the Royal Statistical Society* in 1933 was just as emphatic as his paper on 'Public Expenditure and the Demand for Labour' in *Economica* in 1925 had been in insisting that an increase in government spending would simply crowd out an exactly equal amount of private investment through higher interest rates. He did not rest this conclusion on the later monetarist argument for crowding out, a completely interest-inelastic demand for money, which implies that, with a given money supply, increased government spending simply causes the interest rate to rise by enough to keep income, and hence the transactions demand for money, unchanged. He also did not believe that the supply of output was unresponsive to changes in demand, since he held that monetary expansion, by increasing the supply of funds available for borrowing, could stimulate output. Rather, Hawtrey argued that the public and private sectors competed for a fixed pool of available saving, forgetting his own demonstration that increased public investment could create additional saving by increasing income. Hawtrey did not, however, wish to associate himself with the 1929 Treasury reply to Lloyd George, pointing out to Colin Clark that he had been on vacation when it was drafted.[64]

The contrast between Hawtrey and Keynes on policy has drawn more attention than Keynes' acclaim of Hawtrey as 'my grandparent ... in the paths of errancy',[65] or his 1930 letter to Hawtrey that 'I feel that ultimately I am joined in common agreement with you as against most of the rest of the world'.[66] Paul Samuelson, in his memorial article on Keynes, suggested: 'Young economists who disbelieve in the novelty of the Keynesian analysis, on the ground that no sensible person could ever have thought differently, might with profit read Hawtrey's testimony before the Macmillan Committee, contrasting it with the Kahn article.'[67] In fact, it was in a working paper for that very committee that Hawtrey provided a multiplier analysis comparable to that of Kahn, and identified unintended changes in inventories as the difference between saving and planned investment. Hawtrey and Keynes were much closer on matters of theory than of policy, the reverse of the relationship between Pigou and Keynes.

THE RELATION OF HOME INVESTMENT TO UNEMPLOYMENT

In July 1930, Richard Kahn, one of Keynes' younger colleagues at King's College, was appointed one of the two joint secretaries of the

Committee of Economists of the Economic Advisory Council, a committee chaired by Keynes. Kahn, who was then twenty-five years old, had written a fellowship dissertation on the Marshallian short period and was lecturing on that topic at King's, but had not yet been appointed to any university position.[68] With assistance from Colin Clark in drafting as well as with the statistical material, Kahn produced what he later described as a primitive draft of part of his article 'The Relation of Home Investment to Unemployment'.[69] In September 1930, this draft was circulated to the members of the Committee of Economists: Keynes, Henderson, Pigou, Robbins and Stamp.

> Keynes ... attempted to incorporate the early results of Kahn's work on primary and secondary employment ... to give some idea of the magnitudes involved in an expansionary programme, and to emphasise that the 'inflationary' effects on domestic prices of increases in employment would arise out of any scheme for increasing employment. Even so, Kahn's findings gave rise to controversy between Kahn, Pigou and Keynes on the validity of the exercise.[70]

Pigou and Henderson resisted Keynes' attempt to advance a multiplier argument for public works, based on Kahn's ratio of primary to secondary employment. Unlike Robbins, however, Pigou and Henderson joined Keynes in a majority report supporting public works, together with tariffs and export subsidies to offset the overvaluation of sterling. The report thus endorsed increased spending on public works, without explaining why. Henderson's position was a particular disappointment for Keynes, since it was a retreat from the cruder multiplier arguments of *Can Lloyd George Do It?*, which Keynes had drafted from Henderson's leading articles in *The Nation and Athenaeum*.

Keynes was also the only member of the committee to take an interest in calculations circulated among the committee by Colin Clark, which showed that industrial output per man-year had risen in Britain in the 1920s, so that rising real wages were in part a reflection of rising productivity. 'Keynes was very interested in these results. The other members of the Committee, the leading economists of the day, without examining the evidence, refused to believe them.'[71] Lionel Robbins insisted that unemployment was caused by excessive wages and could be cured by cutting wages. He forcefully drew the committee's attention to the work of Jacques Rueff, who in a 1925 article had obtained a high positive correlation between Britain's unemployment rate and wage/price ratio for 1919–25. Rueff obtained a similar result for 1919–30 in a paper published in 1931, but apparently available to Robbins the previous year. Stamp's role was quieter than that of Robbins, but he had discussed Rueff's first paper in *The Financial Times* in March 1926, and went on to present Rueff's second paper in two articles in *The Times* in June 1931. Colin Clark was disdainful of Rueff's statistical analysis: a simple correlation between two short series of annual data, it ignored the increasing productivity of labour, and 'nearly the whole weight of the correlation came from the data for the single year 1921'. Furthermore, Rueff had deflated wages by the wholesale price index in the belief that this represented the price of manufactured output, so that he and Robbins thought that he had shown industrial wages to be too high in terms of final product. In fact, the index represented almost entirely the prices of food and raw materials.[72]

Stymied at the Committee of Economists by colleagues who found Rueff's correlations more promising, Keynes promoted Kahn's multiplier theory elsewhere. He arranged for Kahn to present his paper in the autumn of 1930 to the Political Economy Club, a select group of Cambridge undergraduates with good examination results which met in Keynes' rooms. Keynes also accepted a revised version of the paper for publication in the *Economic Journal*, where it appeared the following June.[73] The article analysed the effect of increased government investment on employment under the assumptions that the central bank would pursue an accommodative monetary policy and that money wages would not rise, but promised that an article in a later issue of the *Economic Journal* would show that there would still be some increase in employment even if real wages were unchanged.[74] This second article was never published, and its concerns were dropped by Keynes and the Cambridge 'Circus' in favour of emphasis on the inability of workers to determine their real wages through nominal wage bargains, an argument foreshadowed in the *Treatise*. Similarly, Giblin admitted in his inaugural lecture that he did 'not see his way clearly through the tangle of price reactions that must follow the loss of income'.[75]

Kahn noted that secondary employment was often invoked by advocates of public works, but that little had been done to evaluate these repercussions in concrete terms. He examined an economy which was initially at rest and then displaced from equilibrium by an 'aggravation' such as increased road building. The economy was assumed to have unused productive capacity, without discussion of how this could exist in an equilibrium. Employment of one additional worker would entail payment of W in wages, receipt by capitalists of an amount of profits P, and payment of R for imported raw materials. Out of this income, $mW+nP$ would be spent on domestic consumption goods, creating a further derived demand for labour to produce those goods. Kahn neglected the multiplier effect of imports on foreign income, which would cause the rest of the world to increase its imports from the home country. The ratio of the second round of employment to the first round would thus be k, where

$$k = \frac{mW+nP}{W+P+R}.$$

This ratio is clearly less than one, so each round of spending and employment is smaller than the preceding one. Unlike Giblin's inaugural lecture and Hawtrey's 1928 Treasury memorandum, Kahn's article presented a process in which each round of spending would be smaller than the preceding one even if the multiplier effect of imports on foreign income and hence on imports were included, because not all the leakages were into imports. The secondary employment of k man-years for each man-year of first-round employment would lead in turn to k^2 man-years of employment as the result of the next round of spending on domestic consumption goods and services: 'some time will, of course, elapse before the point when the secondary employment reaches its full dimensions, because wages and profits are not spent quite as soon as they are earned'. The geometric series k, k^2, k^3, ... sums to $k/(1-k)$, which is the ratio of secondary to primary employment.[76]

Kahn showed that the process of expansion would peter out when the 'alleviation' or leakages equalled the 'aggravation', the initial injection of government spending into the economy. He presented this finding as 'Mr Meade's relation' which held that the cost of investment was equal to the saving on the dole plus the increase in the excess of imports over exports plus the increase in unspent profits minus the diminution in the rate of saving due to the increase in prices. Two important leakages were omitted: the increase in tax revenue because of the increased income, and the increase in personal saving. Although the increase in unspent (and presumably undistributed) profits was an increase in saving, the only reference to personal saving was to a reduction in saving due to higher prices, not to an increase due to higher income.

'Mr Meade's relation' was added when Kahn revised the paper during the 1930–1 academic year, which the young Oxford economist James Meade spent at Cambridge. Kahn observed that:

> This relation should bring immediate relief and consolation to those who are worried about the monetary sources that are available to meet the cost of roads. The increase in the excess of imports over exports is equal, if gold is not flowing at an appreciable rate, to the reduction in foreign lending. So that if one is looking for sources *outside* the banking system, they are available to precisely the right extent. The cost of the roads is equal to the saving on the dole *plus* the reduction in foreign lending *plus* the increase in unspent profits *minus* the reduction in the rate of saving.[77]

Writing to Don Patinkin in 1974, Lord Kahn identified the main importance of his 1931 article as being less the estimate of the multiplier than the refutation of the Treasury view of crowding out by showing that alleviations equal aggravations.[78] Since 'Mr Meade's relation' omitted the increase in tax revenues and personal saving resulting from increased income, and since it is not clear why a trade deficit under fixed exchange rates should lead to reduced foreign lending instead of a gold outflow (unless the interest rate at home rises, which would reduce investment), it seems more appropriate to stress the demonstration that the spending multiplier is finite. Earlier multiplier discussions, with imports as the only leakage, did not provide a valid demonstration of a finite multiplier. Kahn's estimate of a multiplier of about two was more plausible than Takahashi's suggestion that the multiplier might be twenty or thirty. The estimates of the ratio of secondary to primary employment which Kahn derived in the early part of his article from data supplied by Colin Clark relied on leakages into imports and saving on the dole (that is, reduced government payment of unemployment benefits), neglecting the increase in unspent profits. Although Kahn insisted that 'it is clear that Mr Meade's relation is merely a special statement of Mr. Keynes' general proposition that "profits" are equal to the difference between investment and savings',[79] Kahn's article made an important advance beyond the *Treatise* by deriving a finite ratio of secondary to primary employment and by showing how changes in the level of output equalized aggravation and alleviation.

A year later, Jens Warming, a professor of statistics at the University of Copenhagen, extended Kahn's analysis in a paper on 'International Difficulties Arising Out of the Financing of Public Works During Depression' in the June 1932 issue of the *Economic Journal*. Warming criticized Kahn's optimistic assumption that leakages into imports ·from expansionary fiscal policy would simply displace foreign lending without raising the interest rate. Kahn's discussion of this point had ignored Chapter 21 of the *Treatise*, which analysed foreign lending (the capital account of the balance of payments) as a function of relative interest rates, and the *Treatise's* general concern with the effect of interest rates on investment. Warming argued that, given the balance of payments constraints placed on policy by fixed exchange rates, public works could be used as a remedy for un-employment only through international co-operation, not by one country alone. He expressed concern about the extent to which the increase in nominal income would reflect higher prices rather than higher output, the issue which was to have been treated in the promised, but never published, companion piece to Kahn's article. Most importantly, he linked saving to income:

> It is here that I have something to add, as the saving from this income is a very important byproduct to the secondary employment, and it is just as capable of financing the activity. The sum of this saving can be calculated by aid of the same mathematical formula which Mr Kahn employs.[80]

Warming used an example with a marginal propensity to save 0.25, an initial investment of 100 and an implicitly fixed price level to show that 'the secondary employment must continue until the total created income causes so much saving that the original investment can be paid'.[81]

Kahn replied to Warming in 'The Financing of Public Works – a Note' in the next issue of the journal. He denied that he assumed that the propensity to save out of increased personal income was zero, and, more convincingly, pointed to his references to increases in unspent profits as leakages into corporate saving. Looking back in his Raffaele Mattioli Lectures half a century later, Kahn credited Warming only with 'an extremely important linguistic breakthrough. [...] But Warming had failed to realise that the equality of the increase in saving with the increase in investment insured him against what he called "inflation"'.[82] While equality of investment and saving, as defined in the *Treatise*, would prevent what the *Treatise* termed 'profit inflation', this is not a valid criticism of Warming, since there is nothing in the multiplier process to keep an increase in aggregate demand from raising the price level.

Warming drew on an earlier Danish tradition of multiplier analysis. Julius Wulff, a member of the Danish Parliament, had derived a multiplier, with imports as the only leakage, in 1896, and his work was discussed by Fr. Johannsen, Director of the Copenhagen Telephone Company, in articles in 1925 and 1927. Wulff and Johannsen failed to note that, if the increased exports of the rest of the world also have a multiplier effect with imports as the only leakage, public works spending would have an unbounded multiplier effect. They also combined the finding that imports would increase by as much as the public works spending with the incompatible notion that the worldwide total of employment is fixed, so that public works spending amounts to exporting unemployment. Warming's analysis was thus a decisive improvement on these earlier, cruder writings. According to Hugo Hegeland:

> Fr. Johannsen's writings were studied particularly by his fellow country-man Jens Warming, professor of statistics. Warming objects to Johannsen's view according to which the total amount of employment of the whole world seems to be treated as a given figure. He suggests the idea, often recurring in his later articles, of creating employment by producing goods and services which the re-employed are going to purchase themselves. This is said to mean a real solution of the problem of unemployment and not merely throwing the problem away on some other country. Savings are estimated as 12 to 15 per cent of individual income and Warming correctly perceives their weakening effect on the total increase in production. This is still more evident in a later article published in October 1931, where Warming by means of a hypothetical example demonstrates how new streams of saving will finally amount to the same figure as the original spending, but how, during the process, (desired) investment and (desired) saving do not co-incide. No reference appears in this article to Kahn's analysis, which was published in June 1931, and it may be that Warming had no knowledge of Kahn's contribution when writing his article.[83]

Alfred de Lissa, writing in Australia in the 1890s, has been suggested as a possible anticipator of Giblin, comparable to his contemporary, Wulff, as an anticipator of Warming. This identification cannot be accepted, because, while de Lissa summed an infinite geometric series, he discussed a process in which each round of income was entirely spent on domestic output. De Lissa classed agriculture, mining, forestry and fisheries as primary activities which were income-generating, of exogenous magnitude, and fundamental to the health of the economy. The amount of primary production determined the size of the secondary sector: trade and commerce, construction and entertainment. Starting with output of primary products, and hence the first round of income, of 100, de Lissa assumed three-quarters of each round of income would be spent on secondary goods and services, generating another round of income and spending, but that the one-quarter of each round of income spent on domestically-produced primary products acted as a leakage. He found equilibrium income of 400 in this example by a calculation resembling the multiplier,[84] but the economic process involved is utterly unlike the later multiplier analysis of Giblin, Hawtrey, Kahn and Warming.

N. A. J. L. Johannsen, a German (subsequently American) contemporary of Wulff and de Lissa, developed a multiplier theory similar to Wulff's, but with leakages into 'impair savings', which were not turned into investment. N. Johannsen is of interest because Keynes wrote a footnote on him in the *Treatise on Money*, but it appears that Keynes' knowledge of him came entirely from a single paragraph in Wesley Mitchell's *Business Cycles*, which mentioned the concept of impair savings without any hint whatsoever of the multiplier process.[85]

TOWARD A THEORY OF OUTPUT

In his journalistic and political writing in the 1920s, collected in his *Essays in Persuasion*, Keynes strongly supported Lloyd George's proposals to cure unemployment through public works. When addressing an audience of professional economists in his *Treatise on Money*, Keynes omitted this stand and the arguments for successive rounds of spending with which he had supported it. He did so because he was then unable to explain why the multiplier was finite (since an infinite multiplier was implausible) or to explain why increased government spending did not simply crowd out an equal amount of private borrowing of a fixed pool of savings. Thus, although his analysis of monetary theory was motivated by his conviction that Britain was suffering prolonged unemployment and reduced output because of a mistaken monetary policy of returning to the prewar gold parity of sterling, his work on monetary theory and policy lacked a theory of output and employment. The multiplier theory which he received from Hawtrey, Kahn and, shortly afterwards, Warming resolved these difficulties, and enabled Keynes to build a theory of output and employment for a monetary economy.

The advance was in the economic theory which supported Keynes' policy recommendations, not in the policy recommendations themselves. This point has been too often misunderstood, and commentators have sometimes denied that Keynesian economics made any contribution because Keynes was not the first person to say a kind word for public works. Thus George Garvy opens his article on 'Keynes and the Economic Activists of Pre-Hitler Germany' by observing: 'One of the perplexing riddles in the history of social science is how a man of the intellect of Keynes could have labored for years on what he considered to be a revelation without becoming aware of its multifarious antecedents, and how such a large segment of the English-speaking community of economists could have accepted his analysis and policy conclusions as such.' Remarking that 'This note focuses on economic policy guides which have entered history as "Keynesian," rather than the theoretical underpinnings for these prescriptions', Garvy goes on to deny the novelty and originality of Keynesian economics on the grounds that there were in Germany in 1931, five years before the publication of the *General Theory*, economists who favoured monetary and fiscal expansion as a response to mass unemployment. Not a shred of evidence is offered that the policy prescriptions or theoretical arguments of these economists were the tiniest step beyond the activist monetary policy of the *Treatise*, the attack on an overvalued exchange rate of the *Economic Consequences of Mr Churchill* (1925) or the secondary employment case for public works of *Can Lloyd George Do It?* (1929) – works familiar to this group of economic activists, since Garvy mentions W. S. Woytinsky as quoting Keynes' writings several times, and Jacob Marshak as giving a seminar on Keynes at Heidelberg University in the summer of 1931. The only reference to theory is an admission that 'Kindleberger errs, however, in saying that Woytinsky had presented a multiplier-mechanism analysis'.[86]

The important advance was in the theoretical case for activist policy. Keynes signed the preface to the *Treatise* on 14 September 1930, and the book was published – to a response more enthusiastic than lasting – on the last day of October. Keynes had been working on the book for six years, ever since his *Tract on Monetary Reform* came out, and an advertisement in *Can Lloyd George Do It?* had announced the *Treatise* as due to appear in October 1929. Keynes waited until very late in the production of the *Treatise* to circulate it for comments, so it was only in the last weeks before he signed the preface that he received Hawtrey's comments and the first draft of Kahn's article. These two papers spotlighted the *Treatise*'s implicit assumption of constant output and pointed to the multiplier as the cornerstone of a theory of the level of output. A cornerstone is not a complete building, so that even once the multiplier was rounded out with a personal saving function in the exchange between Warming and Kahn in 1932, the multiplier theory of aggregate demand still needed to be joined to a theory of aggregate supply. Already when the *Treatise* was published, Keynes knew that it required major reworking. This reworking did not imply any abandonment of what Keynes had already achieved in the *Treatise*, whose bearishness theory of money demand and asset market equilibrium formed the basis of the liquidity preference theory of the interest rate, even though the particular forms of the 'fundamental equations' were dropped. Keynes and his young colleagues in the Cambridge 'Circus' set out to synthesize the *Treatise*'s theory of a monetary economy with an improved and more rigorous version of the multiplier analysis of *Can Lloyd George Do It?*

Kahn insisted gamely in his multiplier article that his analysis could be fitted neatly in the *Treatise* framework: 'But this conclusion – that under certain circumstances employment can be increased without any significant alteration in the difference between savings and investment – does not in the slighest degree invalidate the causal force of Mr Keynes' argument',[87] but his very attempts to do so, emphasized the *Treatise*'s implicit assumptions of constant output and full employment as clearly as Hawtrey's comments had:

> But simplest of all is the case where it is not the supply of consumption-goods that is completely inelastic but *total* employment that is fixed, so that if investment increases, the production of consumption-goods must diminish by an equal amount. Then there is no alleviation, since there is no change in employment, and if in addition the aggravation is negligible, the rise in the price-level of consumption-goods is simply equal to the cost of the new investments divided by their volume. This is the case to which Mr Keynes' equations apply in their full simplicity. It occurs when the whole of the factors of production are employed, and continue to be employed, in producing either for consumption or for investment.[88]

Faced with knowledge of the limitations of the theoretical structure of the *Treatise*, while reviewers were still acclaiming it or fussing over index number problems of the 'fundamental equations', Keynes turned to the development of a monetary theory of production, which led him on to the *General Theory*.

NOTES

1. Stamp (1931), 242.
2. Lloyd George (1924); Stein (1969), 137.
3. Blaug (1978), 686. The others were Stamp, Pigou and Robertson.
4. Keynes (1924a); Stein (1969), 137.
5. Garraty (1978), 156.
6. Moggridge (1976), 63; Howson (1973).
7. Keynes (1924c), 587.
8. Keynes (1924b), 312; Harrod (1951), 346–8.
9. Keynes and Henderson, in Keynes (1931), 118.
10. See Benjamin and Kochin (1978).
11. *The Times*, 13 January 1937, cited by Robert Skidelsky in Milo Keynes (1975), 90n.
12. Keynes and Henderson (1929), 27.
13. *Ibid.*, 21. Lord Montagu was a contributor to the 1924 debate.
14. Patinkin (1976), 136.
15. Henderson to Keynes, 14 February 1931, quoted by Middleton (1982), 55. Cf. Keynes (1979), xxix, 218–20, for Henderson's denunciation of Keynes (1936) before the Marshall Society at Cambridge.
16. Keynes (1930), i, 263, and ii, 364–7.
17. Keynes and Henderson (1929), 37.
18. Keynes (1930), ii, 386–7.
19. Keynes and Henderson (1929), 14–18.
20. H. Johnson, in E. Johnson and H. Johnson (1978), 206.
21. Keynes (1930), i, 271; Keynes (1936), 14–15.
22. Keynes (1931), 286–7.
23. Keynes and Henderson (1929), 10.
24. Hawtrey (1925). Cf. Hawtrey (1933).
25. Keynes (1930), ii, 364–7.
26. Keynes and Henderson (1929), 35–6.
27. *Ibid.*, 37.
28. *Ibid.*, 38.
29. *Ibid.*, 36.
30. *Ibid.*, 39.
31. Winch (1969), 159–60, 375–6.
32. Hutchison (1978), 175–99. For a statement that Pigou urged wage cuts in his Macmillan Committee testimony, see Klein (1947), 46.
33. Hutchison (1953), 402.
34. Hawtrey (1913), 260, quoted by Hutchison (1953), 417.

35. Robertson (1915), 253, quoted by Hutchison (1953), 403.
36. Keynes and Henderson (1929), 22-5.
37. *Ibid.,* 25.
38. *Ibid.,* 22.
39. *Ibid.,* 30.
40. Keynes (1930), I, 178.
41. Kahn (1984), 101.
42. Nanto and Tagaki (1985).
43. Howson and Winch (1977), 36n. Flux was then President of the Royal Statistical Society.
44. Pigou (1929), 188.
45. *Ibid.,* 189.
46. Giblin (1930), 10-11, quoted by A. Wright (1956), 189-90. Cf. Copland (1958); Karmel (1960).
47. Cain (1979), 112.
48. Copland (1951), 69.
49. Copland *et al.* (1952), 194.
50. Giblin (1946), 2.
51. Keynes (1973), XIII, 414-17.
52. Copland (1934).
53. Walker (1933), 162-4.
54. A. Wright (1956), 190n. Walker (1935), including the sentence on Giblin and the multiplier, is reprinted in Walker (1936).
55. Hawtrey, memorandum quoted in E. G. Davis (1983), Appendix.
56. See Keynes (1929) and Ohlin (1929), reprinted in Ellis and Metzler (1949).
57. Keynes (1973), XIII, 130, 132.
58. *Ibid.,* 150-64. Hawtrey also wrote a brief review of Keynes (1930) in the *Journal of the Royal Statistical Society* (1931), 618-21.
59. Keynes (1973), XIII, 152.
60. See E. G. Davis (1980); Cain (1982).
61. Keynes (1973), XIII, 146.
62. *Ibid.,* 143-5.
63. Hawtrey (1932), 350-1.The Macmillan Committee working paper no. 66 is in the Public Records Office, London (PRO T208/153). See E. G. Davis (1983), 17-20.
64. C. Clark (1977), 84.
65. Keynes (1973), XIV, 202n.
66. *Ibid.,* XIII, 132.
67. Samuelson, in Harris (1947), 160n.
68. E. A. G. Robinson, in Patinkin and Leith (1978), 26.
69. Kahn (1984), 95-6.
70. Howson and Winch (1977), 59.
71. C. Clark (1977), 88.
72. Claasen and Lane (1978), 228-32; C. Clark (1977), 88.
73. Kahn (1972), vii. On the Political Economy Club, see E. Johnson and H. Johnson (1978), 91-2, 131-3.
74. Kahn (1931), 175.

75. Giblin (1930), 11, quoted by A. Wright (1956), 190.
76. Kahn (1931), 183–4.
77. *Ibid.*, 189.
78. Kahn to Patinkin, 19 March 1974, in Patinkin and Leith (1978), 147.
79. Kahn (1931), 188.
80. Warming (1932), 214. See Andersen (1983) for Warming's 1911 analysis of fisheries as a common-property resource.
81. Warming (1932), 215–16.
82. Kahn (1932); Kahn (1984), 100–1.
83. Hegeland (1954), 17–19; Cain (1979), 113–14; Topp (1981); Shackle (1967), 193–7.
84. Goodwin (1962).
85. Keynes (1930), ii, 100n; Mitchell (1927), 25n. Hegeland (1954) and Shackle (1967) discuss N. Johannsen.
86. Garvy (1975), 391, 397, 399. Garvy omits to mention L. Albert Hahn, the one German economist who claimed to have anticipated Keynes' theory (as distinct from his policies). See Hahn (1949), Chapter 16; Heimann (1945), 232–4.
87. Kahn (1931), 187.
88. *Ibid.*, 186–7.

5 The monetary theory of production

After the publication of his *Treatise on Money*, Keynes strove to remedy its deficiencies by developing a theory of output to add to its analysis of asset markets, money demand and Wicksellian price movements resulting from a market rate of interest not equal to the natural rate. His attention was drawn from price changes to the equilibrating role of changes in output by Kahn's celebrated article on the multiplier, by Hawtrey's commentary on the *Treatise*, and by Keynes' exchange with Ohlin on reparations. Keynes wrote to Hawtrey to thank him for his 'tremendously useful' Macmillan Committee working paper in February 1931,[1] and on 5 January, replying to a letter from Ohlin about the *Treatise*, wrote: 'As to your point that reparations cause a shift in the demand curve of the receiving country irrespective of any rise in the price level of that country, I do not think I disagree with you.'[2] This was a concession which Keynes had resisted in 1929 in his reply to Ohlin's article, in his rejoinder to Ohlin's rejoinder, and in discussion with Ohlin at a London dinner party.[3]

Although Keynes was one of the editors of the *Economic Journal*, he did not present preliminary versions of his theory of output and employment in journal articles for the rest of the economics profession to offer criticism and suggestions. Apart from his controversies with Hayek and Robertson, his contribution to journal reworking of the *Treatise* was limited to a couple of single-page notes in the *American Economic Review*, one in 1932 accepting Alvin Hansen's point that the 'fundamental equations' needed correction if the rates of technical progress in the consumption and capital goods sectors differed, and another in 1933 marvelling that E. C. Simmons could have supposed that Keynes wished monetary policy to be concerned with the short-term interest rate rather than the long-term. In those instances where Keynes had chosen to present preliminary versions of his books and pamphlets, these had been his less technical works and were presented in the newspapers: *A Tract on Monetary Reform* in the supplements to the *Manchester Guardian Commercial* and 'The Economic Consequences of Mr Churchill' in the *Evening Standard*, as later *The Means to Prosperity* and *How to Pay For the War* came out in *The Times*. Consequently, the stages of Keynes' thought as he moved from the *Treatise* to the *General Theory* must be sought in his discussions with colleagues at Cambridge and in the lectures from 1932 to 1935, in which each year Keynes presented the latest version of his projected book on 'The Monetary Theory of Production'. The surviving material on Keynes' interactions with his colleagues, including the 'Cambridge Circus' of 1930–1, was made available in 1973 with the publication of Volume xiii of Keynes' *Complete Writings*, supplemented by Volume xxix in 1979, after the discovery of a laundry hamper full of additional correspondence and papers. In 1976, three former Cambridge students, Robert Bryce, Walter Salant and Lorie Tarshis, addressed a conference on *Keynes, Cambridge and the General Theory* at the University of Western Ontario, and revealed that they had preserved their notes from Keynes' lectures, Bryce for three years of lectures, Salant for 1933, and Tarshis for four years.[4] These sets of lecture notes, together with others discovered later, provide an extraordinary opportunity to observe Keynes' progress toward the *General Theory* year by year.

Keynes' discussions and lectures at Cambridge, reworking the *Treatise* and attempting to construct a theory of output, came as his influence outside academic circles was diminishing. The majority of the Macmillan Committee agreed with Professor Gregory rather than with Keynes. Keynes persuaded the Committee of Economists, over Robbins' objections, to recommend expansionist measures, but without recourse to the multiplier to explain why. Lord Robbins later recalled, however: 'I was recruited for another secret committee, this time under Stamp's chairmanship, with Keynes absent; and I signed a report whose anti-expansionist recommendations I had certainly played a due part in shaping.'[5]

The May Report, which warned that there would be a substantial budget deficit (much inflated by treating reduction of the National Debt as an expenditure) unless unemployment benefits were cut, led to the break-up of the Labour Cabinet, and the formation of a

National Government under Ramsay MacDonald to defend the fixed exchange rate. Despite being forced to devalue, MacDonald won the subsequent election, waving handfuls of German banknotes from the hyperinflation and predicting that a postage stamp would cost a million pounds sterling if his former colleagues in the Labour Party regained office. Keynes' Liberal Party split into three rival parties over the National Government. Sir Herbert Samuel led the official Liberal Party into the coalition in 1931 and then out of it the next year in defence of free trade, losing his own seat and those of most of his followers in the next election. However, 'other Liberals, led by Sir John Simon, had made it clear that there was no conceivable issue which might be expected to lead to their resignation. Like Charles II, they had been on their travels, and now, unexpectedly restored to office, were determined to travel no more.'[6] Keynes observed acidly: 'Not all my Free Trade friends proved to be so prejudiced as I had thought. For after a Tariff was no longer necessary, many of them were found voting for it.'[7]

Lloyd George declined to join the National Government when it was formed, and sat in the Commons with a group of his relatives as 'independent Liberals', organized around his Council of Action. 'Mr Lloyd George's Council of Action was mostly inactive, and when active, ineffectual. "We Can Conquer Unemployment" gave place to "We Can Conquer Germany", and that, surprisingly, to "We Can Make Peace With Germany", without much evident result.'[8] Keynes included in his *Essays in Biography* (1933) a character sketch of Lloyd George which had been excised from *The Economic Consequences of the Peace* as too offensive, and Lloyd George found ample opportunity for retaliation in *The Truth About the Peace Treaties*, *The Truth About War Debts and Reparations*, and many volumes of *War Memoirs*. *The Nation and Athenaeum*, which had advertised itself in *Can Lloyd George Do It?* with the slogan 'It matters what Liberals are thinking. Read the *Nation*', faded when it no longer mattered what any of the three Liberal parties thought, and was absorbed by its Labour rival, the *New Statesman*. Keynes retained a seat on the editorial board of the merged journal, but was very much out of sympathy with its editorial policies.

Keynes commended Sir Oswald Mosley, a former Conservative MP turned Labour junior minister, for presenting a plan for public works, tariffs and government purchases of commodities to the Labour Party conference in October 1930, and the following April, after Mosley's expulsion from the Labour Party, Harold Nicolson found that 'Keynes is very helpful about the economics of the New Party'.[9] However, Nicolson recorded that at a dinner a week later with Keynes, Mosley and J. L. Garvin of *The Observer*, 'Both Keynes and Garvin are very sympathetic to Tom's [Mosley] programme but object deeply to his methods',[10] and Keynes gave no public encouragement to the New Party. In Whitehall and in the political parties, Keynes' influence was at a low ebb.

THE NATURE OF THE PROBLEM

The discussions of the 'Cambridge Circus' and Keynes' lectures at Cambridge offer insights into two controversial aspects of the evolution of Keynes' thought from the *Treatise* to the *General Theory*. First of all, there is a question of timing: at what point had Keynes formulated a theory of effective demand that is today recognizable as the *General Theory*? James Meade, who returned to Oxford from Cambridge in the autumn of 1931, is 'cautiously confident that he took with him back to Oxford most of the essential ingredients of the subsequent system of the *General Theory*',[11] while Richard Kahn points to the change in emphasis between Keynes' lectures on 'The Pure Theory of Money' in the spring of 1932 and on 'The Monetary Theory of Production' that autumn,[12] and Lawrence Klein places the 'Keynesian Revolution' in the summer of 1933, based on differences between two articles by John Robinson in that year.[13]

The question of timing can be settled only after dealing with the more important question of what constitutes the important innovation or innovations in Keynes' thought. Discovery of one element in the Keynesian theory of employment and output is not the same as possessing the complete theory. The development of Keynes' macroeconomic theories in the years following publication of the *Treatise* was a process of synthesis and integration fully as important as the discovery of any one element of the synthesis. Although I argue for a late date for Keynes' theory of unemployment equilibrium, finding it in his lectures in autumn 1933 but not in those which he delivered in autumn 1932, this delay does not represent simply a failure of Keynes and his colleagues to grasp the multiplier analysis of Kahn's 1931 article on home investment and unemployment, and of Hawtrey's critique of the *Treatise*. The consumption function, from which the multiplier is derived, is only one of four crucial building blocks of Keynes' theory of output, the others being liquidity preference, the marginal efficiency of capital, and aggregate supply. The multiplier analysis of the effect of changes in government spending (public investment) on real output is valid only if there are unemployed resources, and if government spending does not simply displace an equal volume of private investment. Keynes' argument that the labour market may fail to clear in a monetary economy, because of the inability of workers to adjust their real wages by bargaining for nominal wage rates, is an important part of his theory which is separate from the discovery of the multiplier. The same is true of his analysis of the effect of uncertain expectations on investment and the demand for money as contributing to instability in the absence of government intervention. The liquidity preference theory that money is held as an asset as well as to be used as a means of payment, and that therefore the demand for money is a function of the rates of return on other assets, served to refute claims that, even with unemployed resources, government spending increases would just drive up the interest rate until private investment had fallen by the same amount. Keynes' analysis of demand for money as an asset in the *Treatise* was already a decisive step beyond the earlier Cambridge cash balance approach.

There was important work to be done after 1931 on the multiplier analysis itself. The basis of the multiplier, as subsequently presented, is the consumption function, which holds that a fraction of increase in income will be saved and the remainder spent. This implies that changes in the level of income can equilibrate investment and saving, eliminating undesired changes in the level of inventories. This consumption function is now so familiar that there is a danger of reading it into earlier works in which it has no place. Sir John Hicks, in 'A Note on the *Treatise*', writes down the consumption function as part of the model of the *Treatise*, and then complains: 'Keynes (rather irritatingly) does not give this form of the Fundamental Equation explicitly; he leaves it to be inferred from the rhetorical passage about the Danaid Jar (p. 139) and from many other references.'[14] Keynes, however, was not merely being roundabout and obscure in exposition; he did not yet know the consumption function, and passing remarks about the possibility that increasing poverty might cause the thrift campaign in the banana plantation to peter out before the whole population starved to death are no grounds for attributing an understanding of the marginal propensities to consume and to save to the *Treatise*.

The same danger exists for early presentations of the multiplier. Don Patinkin argues that 'if the General Theory is the proposition that an increase in investment generates an equal amount of saving, then ... this theory was first presented in an imprecise form by Keynes in his 1929 *Can Lloyd George Do It?* and was then rigorously developed by Richard Kahn in his celebrated 1931 multiplier article. (Or, if one prefers to say so, by the earlier Danish writer Julius Wulff.)'[15] Wulff, like Giblin and like Hawtrey's 1928 memorandum, had imports as the only leakage, so that a penny of additional spending would generate worldwide full employment. Kahn's 1931 article did not consider leakages into increased tax revenues or personal saving. Kahn mentioned an increase in unspent profits in the context of 'Mr Meade's relation', but neglected it when calculating the possible value of the multiplier, where he treated increased imports and reduced payment of unemployment benefits as the relevant leakages. The reference to unspent profits resembles the *Treatise*, where unanticipated profits are treated as unplanned saving, and Kalecki's later assumption that only capitalists save, rather than the aggregate saving function of the *General Theory*. The only reference to personal saving in Kahn's 1931 paper is to a *decrease* in the rate of saving due to higher prices, an element of 'Mr Meade's relation' omitted from Patinkin's quotation of the relation.[16]

Patinkin has pointed out that Kahn, like Giblin and Hawtrey, calculated the value of the multiplier, and demonstrated that this value was finite, by summing a geometric series of successive rounds of spending, rather than by calculating and comparing the equilibrium levels of income before and after the injection of additional investment. Similarly, when Kahn used 'Mr Meade's relation' for an alternative demonstration that the withdrawals equalled the cost of additional investment, he did so without working out the new level of income at which this would hold true. While accepting Paul Samuelson's argument that the multiplier formula is logically equivalent to the equation for the equilibrium level of income, Patinkin points out that this was not understood at the time. Furthermore, Kahn's multiplier analysis, unlike that of Hawtrey, did not show that when income diverged from its equilibrium level, undesired changes in inventories would result, causing output to be altered towards equilibrium.[17]

The distinction between logical equivalence and chronological equivalence is important. Hawtrey's development of the multiplier was published in 1932 as part of his critique of the *Treatise* in Chapter 6 of *The Art of Central Banking*. This book was discussed at length by A. L. Macfie in *Theories of the Trade Cycle* (1934), Gott-fried Haberler in *Prosperity and Depression* (1937), and Raymond Saulnier in *Contemporary Monetary Theory* (1938), yet none of these writers noticed the multiplier in Hawtrey's work. Similarly, Giblin's multiplier analysis was entirely ignored, along with expansionary fiscal policy, by Copland, Giblin and G. L. Wood in their article on 'The Restoration of Economic Equilibrium' in the *Economic Record* in November 1930, and in a report to the Australian Government by Giblin, Copland and J. Dyason that September, only a few months after Giblin's inaugural lecture. The Melbourne economists recommended a 10 per cent reduction in real government expenditure, a 10 per cent supertax on property income, and a 'depreciation of the currency sufficient to restore real income in export industries to 10 per cent of its former level'.[18] Giblin's multiplier was so thoroughly forgotten that in 1938 Giblin reviewed a book by Colin Clark on Australian national income accounts, which included a chapter on the value of the multiplier in Australia, without mentioning that in 1930 he had estimated the multiplier as three. In 1939, the *Economic Record* published notes by J. Dyason and F. B. Horner on 'The Multiplier in Australia' and a note by James Plimsoll on 'An Australian Anticipator of Mr Keynes', but Dyason and Horner were only discussing Clark's estimates and Plimsoll referred to Keynes' proposal for government storage of foodstuffs. The logical equivalence of a contribution with the multiplier was no guarantee that its implications would be noticed or developed.

The importance of the multiplier was recognized at Cambridge, where its implications, together with those of the *Treatise*, were developed. The evolution of Keynes' thought beyond the *Treatise* is to be found in his discussions with his younger colleagues at Cambridge and in his Cambridge lectures, but he was aware of what economists were doing elsewhere. While Keynes did not choose to present preliminary studies in journals, economists around the world submitted their work to his *Economic Journal*, so that, for example, the multiplier analysis of Jens Warming, Professor of Statistics at the University of Copenhagen, reached Keynes even though it was unknown to Bertil Ohlin, Professor of Economics at Copenhagen from 1925 to 1929.

CAMBRIDGE AND THE 'CIRCUS'

One of the most striking aspects of the Faculty of Economics at Cambridge in 1931 was how small it was, particularly when only those dons concerned with economic theory are considered. The graduate staff of the Faculty of Economics and Politics comprised one professor, one reader, ten lecturers, and one assistant lecturer who soon left to join the Bank of England. Two lecturers, Evans and Burns, taught economic history, and, like Sir John Clapham, the Professor of Economic History (not a member of the Faculty of Economics), had little contact with economic theory. In the words of Austin Robinson, 'two others (Alston and Thatcher) were wholly engaged in pass degree teaching and were (I hope I may be forgiven for saying) survivals, recognised by themselves as such, from the teaching of an earlier pass degree system'.[19] Cambridge's position in mathematical economics had been weakened the previous year by the death at an early age of Frank Ramsey, who, although a logician rather than a member of the Faculty of Economics, had been coaxed by his friend Keynes into publishing two papers in the *Economic Journal*, the first establishing what is now known as Ramsey-optimal pricing and the other the foundation stone of optimal growth theory. Claude Guillebaud, a lecturer who was Alfred Marshall's nephew and eventually edited the variorum edition of Marshall's *Principles*, was 'too modest, too self-effacing' to make a mark among the strong personalities who dominated economic theory at Cambridge.[20] Guillebaud did important work outside economic theory, however, writing pioneering books on *The Economic Recovery of Germany, 1933-38* (1939) and *The Social Policy of Nazi Germany* (1941), as well as *Economic Journal* articles on such topics as 'The Economics of the Dawes Plan' (1924) and 'Hitler's New Economic Order for Europe' (1940).

Although Arthur Cecil Pigou, 'the Prof', had held the chair of economics at Cambridge since 1908, he was still only fifty-four years old in 1931, just six years older than Keynes. Pigou was willing to converse at length on any subject except economics, about which he claimed that he could think only with a pencil in his hand. 'As new ideas or new topics in economics came to the surface Pigou in a curious way digested them by writing a book about them himself, and in an equally curious way it was through his books or articles rather than through discussion that most of us in Cambridge discovered what he was thinking. But because we could never discuss, we could misunderstand him and he could misunderstand us.'[21] Pigou rarely attended the Political Economy Club, which met in Keynes' rooms on Monday evenings, though he did present a paper to the club in November 1929.[22] He was unenthusiastic about Kahn's multiplier paper in the Committee of Economists, and dismissed the *Treatise* in a brief review which neglected the *Treatise*'s analysis of the demand for money as an asset. Keynes sent Pigou a set of proofs of the *Treatise* in autumn 1929. Pigou's marginal notes on the proofs[23] have now been supplemented in Volume xxix of Keynes' *Collected Writings* with a fragment of more detailed comments, in which Pigou observed that the Fundamental Equations showed the effect of windfall profits on price levels on the implicit assumption of constant output.[24]

Dennis Holme Robertson, Reader in Economics and Fellow of Trinity College, played a much larger role in the discussion of Keynes' work, but not a more constructive one. Robertson had Keynes as his director of studies as an undergraduate and later worked closely with him, but they drew apart in the years of the *Treatise* and *General Theory*. Robertson's reverence for the Marshallian tradition led him to stress continuity rather than revolution in economics, and he was irritated by Keynes' continued insistence that Robertson really agreed with the substance of Keynes' message.[25] Much of the extensive correspondence between Keynes and Robertson concerning and following Robertson's review of the *Treatise* and Keynes' rejoinder[26] was about the differences and similarities of various definitions of lacking in Robertson's *Banking Policy and the Price Level* (1926) and of saving in the *Treatise*. This hair-splitting led to a note by Robertson on 'Saving and Hoarding' in the *Economic Journal* in September 1933, with replies by Keynes and Hawtrey and rejoinder by Robertson in the December issue, and to renewed debate when Keynes defined realized saving and investment as equal in the *General Theory*, instead of defining profits as their difference. Keynes opened his series of lectures in the spring of 1932 with the complaint that 'Critics often argue as if *logical* points were involved in definitions where in fact none such are present. Provided definitions are used *consistently* in a given context, each set will lead to perfectly accurate Fundamental Equations',[27] but the arguments continued.

The other principal subject of controversy between Keynes and

Robertson was the start of their long disagreement whether the interest rate is determined in the money market by liquidity preference and the supply of money, or in the bond market by the supply of and demand for loanable funds. Keynes showed in the *Treatise* that because money is a store of value, demand for money will depend on wealth and on 'bearishness', that is, on expectations about the rate of interest on securities and about securities prices. This contrasted with the work of, for example, Pigou, who related the demand for money simply to the level of income and discussed changes in the velocity of circulation in *Industrial Fluctuations* (1927) without linking them to changes in the rate of interest. Keynes and Robertson interpreted Keynes' new theory of money demand as a denial that thrift and the productivity of capital influence the rate of interest. However, as Hicks pointed out in his review of the *General Theory*, each individual faces a budget constraint such that the value of that person's excess demands in all markets must add to zero, since every demand is an offer of payment of equal value. If the value of excess demands must add to zero for each individual, it must do so for the whole economy. Because of this adding-up condition, the excess demand equation for any one market may be dropped as redundant. Dropping the equation for the bond market gives a liquidity preference model, dropping the equation for the money market yields Robertson's loanable funds model, yet these are simply two ways of representing exactly the same model.[28] The rate of interest, like other variables, is determined by the entire set of equations of a model. Meaningful differences in the dynamics implied by the two approaches, and determination of the interest rate in a particular market, can be obtained by specifying that one of the two markets, money and bonds, clears at every moment in time while the other does not, but this is not what Keynes and Robertson did in their arguments in the 1930s.

Worsening personal relations between Robertson and Keynes contributed to Robertson's acceptance of a chair at the London School of Economics in 1938, which turned out to be less of a change than anticipated, since the LSE spent the war in Cambridge. Relations improved during the war, when they collaborated closely and amicably in the Treasury and at the Bretton Woods conference. Harry Johnson's view that Robertson 'had been prevented from receiving what he (and many others) considered was the final reward of a serious academic career, namely the professorship at Cambridge'[29] must be qualified by the fact that Robertson could not be elected to the chair until Pigou vacated it. Robertson succeeded Pigou in 1944, after Keynes declined the chair for reasons of health in a letter urging the appointment of Robertson.[30] One can imagine worse indignities than being second choice after Lord Keynes at that stage of Keynes' career. This later reconciliation does not alter the fact that the discussions between Keynes and Robertson of definitions of saving and determination of the interest rate in the 1930s became increasingly bitter and unfruitful.

The senior members and many lecturers of the Cambridge Faculty of Economics thus were not involved in the reworking and discussion of Keynes' theories by the 'Cambridge Circus'. This small group of young lecturers and researchers served, together with Hawtrey at the Treasury and Roy Harrod at Oxford, as the sounding board for Keynes' developing views on economic stabilization. The 'Circus', organized at the suggestion of Piero Sraffa, held formal meetings from January to May 1931, at first in Richard Kahn's rooms in the Gibbs Building of King's College and later, as more people attended, in the Old Combination Room at Trinity College, followed by informal sessions in the summer. Keynes did not attend these discussions of the *Treatise*, but received an oral report from Kahn after each session.[31] In his memorial article on Keynes, Austin Robinson, one of the participants in the 'Circus', recalled:

> It so happened that the publication of the *Treatise* coincided in time with a remarkable younger generation in Cambridge. R. F. Kahn had just been made a Fellow of King's; J. E. Meade was spending a year in Trinity before returning to Oxford; they with P. Sraffa, C. H. P. Gifford, A. F. W. Plumptre, L. Tarshis, Joan Robinson and several others of us formed a 'circus' which met weekly for discussions of the *Treatise*, and R. F. Kahn retailed to Keynes the results of our deliberations.[32]

This recollection of who was involved, which was cited both by Sir Roy Harrod in his *Life of Keynes* and by Donald Winch in his *Economics and Policy*,[33] requires some correction. Wynne Plumptre completed two years of study with Keynes, Pigou and Gerald Shove at King's in May 1930, and returned to Canada at the end of that summer with a trunk full of proof copies of the *Treatise* for his students at the University of Toronto. Lorie Tarshis studied the *Treatise* under Plumptre in Toronto and did not arrive in Cambridge until the autumn of 1932, after the formal meetings of the 'Circus'.[34] In the autumn of 1931, after Meade's return to Oxford, the group of younger Cambridge economists interested in Keynes' ideas was joined by Colin Clark from the Economic Advisory Council as a lecturer in statistics and by E. Ronald Walker from the University of Sydney as a doctoral candidate. A few undergraduates were allowed to attend 'Circus' meetings after satisfying an interviewing board of Austin Robinson, Richard Kahn and Piero Sraffa.[35] One of these undergraduates, Charles Gifford of Magdalene College, provides the least familiar name in the 'Circus', because he left economics for the family business after graduation. Apart from participating in the 'Circus', he published articles on capital theory and the period of production in the *Economic Journal* and *Econometrica*, and a note on the effect of a protective tariff on the price level in the *Economic Record*. In the foreword to her *Economics of Imperfect Competition*, Joan Robinson wrote that she first learned of the marginal revenue curve from Gifford, who was one of several independent discoverers of the concept. With such an undergraduate career, Gifford's decision to give up economics must be counted as a sad loss to the economics profession.

Piero Sraffa, an Italian Marxist economist, was brought to Cambridge by Keynes in 1927, after such earlier contacts as translating Keynes' *Tract on Monetary Reform* into Italian, writing the *Economic Journal* obituary of Pantaleoni and contributing his celebrated 1926 paper in the *Economic Journal* on the incompatability of increasing returns to scale and the Marshallian representative firm. In 1930, Sraffa, then aged thirty-two, gave up lecturing to become Marshall Librarian and an Assistant Director of Research, in charge of the few graduate students in economics, devoting the bulk of his time to editing the works of Ricardo for the Royal Economic Society. Keynes, writing on Malthus in his *Essays in Biography* (1933), anticipated publication of Sraffa's edition of Ricardo within the year, but, partly because of the discovery of additional material, the first volumes did not appear until 1951.[36] Austin Robinson lectured on industrial organization, and was writing *The Structure of Competitive Industry* (1931) for the Cambridge Economic Handbooks edited by Keynes.[37] His wife, Joan Robinson, taught at a Cambridge women's college, Newnham, receiving a university appointment as assistant lecturer in the 1931–2 academic year. Her belated promotion to lecturer in 1938, five years after her *Economics of Imperfect Competition* and a year after her collected *Essays in the Theory of Employment*, can be attributed only to Cambridge's attitude toward women. Although Cambridge had tolerated two colleges for women, Girton and Newnham, since the 1870s, it did not permit women to hold university teaching posts until 1926 or to take degrees until 1947, even (or perhaps especially) in such cases as when a woman received the highest marks in the Mathematics Tripos in 1890.[38] Richard Kahn, a graduate in mathematics and physics, lectured on the Marshallian short period, the topic of his fellowship dissertation, and was translating Wicksell's *Interest and Prices*, a project begun in 1929 in response to a suggestion by Ohlin to Keynes, although the translation did not appear until 1936.

James Meade's contributions to Cambridge discussion can be discerned in Kahn's article on home investment, where 'Mr Meade's relation' shows that leakages from spending will equal the increase in investment, and in Robertson's review of the *Treatise*, where Meade is thanked for pointing out that several important passages in the *Treatise* rest on the implicit assumption of constant output.[39] Austin Robinson is credited by other members of the 'Circus' with spotting what they termed 'the widow's cruse fallacy'. In the *Treatise*, profits are a widow's cruse which cannot be exhausted, because if entrepreneurs spend out of profits, prices will rise so that profits rise by as much as entrepreneurs' spending did. If entrepreneurs reduce their consumption to save more, 'the cruse becomes a Danaid jar which can never be filled up'.[40] This assumed an inelastic output of consumption goods, when changes in entrepreneurs' consumption was considered, and of investment goods, for changes in investment, and was inappropriate when there was unemployment of labour and productive capacity.[41] In place of this assumption, Kahn's article had a supply curve for output as a whole, with both the money wage rate and productive capacity given in the short period, so that each state of demand corresponded to a particular amount of employment and price level. (The second part of Kahn's paper, which was to dispense with an arbitrarily fixed money wage rate, never appeared.)

The members of the 'Circus' were not aware of Hawtrey's memorandum to Keynes on the Treatise.[42] In addition to noting the implicit constant output in the *Treatise*, Hawtrey argued that a decline in consumers' outlay would cause an increase in unsold stocks, inducing firms to reduce their output, and that the resulting drop in income would reduce saving, leading to restored equilibrium.[43] Although Keynes' letter to Hawtrey on 28 November 1930 was defensive about Hawtrey's criticisms and suggestions, Lorie Tarshis has suggested that 'the *General Theory* would probably have taken a different shape had Hawtrey's "Comments" not been written'.[44] Keynes was much more receptive to Hawtrey's Macmillan Committee working paper, in which he extended his multiplier analysis after reading Keynes' Macmillan Committee evidence. On 16 February 1931 Keynes wrote to Hawtrey,

> I feel enormously honoured by the final version of your opus on me and the trouble you have taken. It is very seldom indeed than an author can expect to get as a criticism anything so tremendously useful to himself. I made a good many notes on points which I should like to discuss with you, though, particularly in the first 12 pages, there is comparatively little from which I dissent.... I only wanted to say before too much time had elapsed how grateful to you I am for it.[45]

This letter contrasts sharply with Keynes' reaction to critiques of the *Treatise* by Hayek and Robertson.

Keynes lent a copy of Hawtrey's working paper to Kahn, whose comments, in a letter to Keynes on 25 March 1931, included the remark: 'On the possibility of output altering as a result of a change in savings or investment you could, of course, admit the justice of H.'s contribution.'[46] Kahn's letter did not refer to the functional dependence of saving on income in Hawtrey's paper, or the equilibrating role of changes in income. These are also missing from Keynes' reply to Kahn's letter on 17 April, which shows Keynes groping for the connection between output and saving (O is the level of output measured in physical terms):

> Not only is the *total* income of entrepreneurs as defined by me a function of their output, but also their *rate* of income per unit of output. For as output falls the reward per unit of output which leaves them under no incentive to *change* their output falls also (assuming the supply schedule is upward).
> Thus as output falls, the income of entrepreneurs falls *faster* than output. Thus when O is falling, unless entrepreneurs' expenditure on consumption falls faster than O, there is a *reduction* of saving.[47]

The earliest surviving recognition by Keynes of a functional dependence of saving on income appears in a letter to Kahn on 20 September 1931, in which Keynes offers the following formula for S/E, the ratio of saving to the earnings of the factors of production:[48]

$$\frac{S}{E} = f_1\left(\frac{E}{P}\right) + f_2\left(\frac{Q}{P}\right) . \frac{S}{E} = f_1\left(\frac{E}{P}\right) + f_2\left(\frac{Q}{P}\right) .$$

In subsequent versions of the saving function, S/P, the real volume of saving, would take the place of S/E, the ratio of saving to income. Kahn's reply to Keynes on 24 September makes the crucial observation: 'As it appears to me at the moment, the *only* condition necessary for reaching a new position of equilibrium is that S increases as E increases. But this is not quite accurate, because on top of that there is some condition necessary for equilibrium to have been possible at all.' Kahn was ill at the time: 'my mind is not too clear at the moment ... would you return me the document in a few days, when I hope I shall feel competent to deal with it?', which accounts for his admission that 'I feel sure that this new method is the right one and that the conclusions are correct, but I have not quite been able to follow the steps.... I am sorry to be so useless.'[49] This correspondence makes it clear that Kahn encountered the saving function as a 'new method' after Meade's return to Oxford, and that the functional relationship of the fraction of income saved to the levels of earnings and windfall profits was presented by Keynes to Kahn, not the other way around.

Lawrence Klein, following up a suggestion of his thesis adviser, Paul Samuelson, argued that comparisons of two articles by Joan Robinson showed a major shift of outlook in Cambridge economics in the summer of 1933. 'A Parable on Savings and Investment', which appeared in *Economica* in February 1933, was simply a clear exposition of the *Treatise* for 'the simple-minded reader', while 'The Theory of Money and the Analysis of Output', in the inaugural issue of the *Review of Economic Studies* that October, again purported to be an exposition of difficulties in the *Treatise* but was in fact 'one of the first expositions, in which she is so lucid, of the really essential parts of the *General Theory*'.[50] However, the first article was written in the summer of 1931 and submitted to *Economica* in April 1932, but publication was held up by a backlog of accepted articles which a new journal like the *Review of Economic Studies* did not have.[51] The second article was written two years after the first one, not just a few months.

'A Parable on Savings and Investment' is thus evidence for Cambridge macroeconomic thinking at an earlier stage. In it, Joan Robinson singled out what her husband had named 'the widow's cruse fallacy', the claim that spending out of profits would simply increase windfall profits by an equal amount:

Mr Keynes has now admitted that in that passage (p. 139) he was tacitly assuming that output was unchanged although the price level was falling. Evidently he, like the rest of us, had been misled by his upbringing into keeping his eye on Demand and forgetting Supply.[52]

Keynes commented on this paper in a letter to Mrs Robinson on 14 April 1932:

> I think you are a little hard on me as regards the assumption of constant output. It is quite true that I have not followed out the consequences of changes in output in the earlier theoretical part. I admit that this wants doing, and I shall be doing it in my lectures; though that does not absolve me from being criticised for not having done it in my *Treatise*. But in my *Treatise* itself, I have long discussions with [? of] the effects of changes in output; it is only at a particular point in the preliminary theoretical argument that I assume constant output, and I am at pains to make this absolutely clear. Surely one must be allowed at a particular stage of one's argument to make simplifying assumptions of this kind; particularly when, as you agree, the assumption in question does not make a very vital difference to the whole character of the argument. All the same, I do not ask you to make any change in what you have written.[53]

The assumption of constant output in Book III and most of Book IV of the *Treatise* does, however, make a vital difference to the whole character of the argument. Chapter 20 of Book IV, 'An Exercise in the Pure Theory of the Credit Cycle', was intended by Keynes as

> an essay in the internal mechanics of the price-wage-employment structure during the course of a cycle which represents a recovery in the volume of employment from a preceding slump which has reached an equilibrium between prices and costs of production, but is still character-ised by unemployment.[54]

This attempt failed because the chapter offered no theory of the level of output and employment, nor, since it lacked any recognition of the effect of changes in output on saving, any explanation of how equilibrium could be achieved except by accident. Windfall profits caused changes in entrepreneurs' offers to the factors of production, which was assumed, without adequate explanation, to affect the volume of employment, not just prices and wages. However, the determination of the level of profits, developed in earlier chapters, still assumed constant output.

Hawtrey's comments on the *Treatise* and the 'Circus' discussion of the widow's cruse fallacy, identified by Austin Robinson and pre-sented in Joan Robinson's 'Parable', drove home to Keynes the inappropriateness of the *Treatise*'s implicit assumption of constant output. Kahn's 1931 article, with assistance from Colin Clark and James Meade, presented a rising short-period supply curve for output as a whole, given a fixed money wage rate, and demonstrated that the multiplier was finite, with leakages into unspent profits and reduced dole payments as well as imports. However, Kahn's 1974 view of his 1931 article as 'finally disposing of the "Treasury view" that in a time of unemployment, an increase in one kind of investment will be at the expense of another kind. I demonstrated how the whole of the necessary finance is provided in the form of an increase in saving'[55] telescopes the contributions of three of his articles into one. What the 1931 article opposes to the Treasury view is that the increase in imports will reduce foreign lending without an increase in the domestic interest rate which would reduce investment. The only reference to personal saving is to a possible fall in saving because of higher prices, while the increase in unspent profits is neglected in the calculations of the possible value of the multiplier. It was in 'Financing Public Works: a Note', his 1932 reply to Jens Warming, that Kahn stated the *ex post* identity of investment and saving, and explicitly recognized leakage into saving by making the increase in unspent profits a fraction of the increase in profits, arguing, contrary to Warming, that this was implicit in his earlier paper. Kahn finally presented a multiplier derived from marginal propensities to save and to import in his paper on 'Public Works and Inflation', delivered to the American Statistical Association annual meeting in Cincinnati in December 1932.[56] Hawtrey's Macmillan Committee working paper in January 1931, which Keynes warmly welcomed and lent to Kahn, derived a finite multiplier from a propensity of save out of changes in income, calculated the equilibrium level of income before and after a change in expenditure, and identified undesired increases in inventories as the channel by which a fall in expenditure caused a fall in output.

This interpretation of developments after the publication of the *Treatise* stressed recognition of the equilibrating role of changes of the level of output because of the effect of changes in output on saving. This reflects Keynes' acceptance that the *Treatise* was flawed because crucial parts of it assumed constant output, and because it did not make saving a function of income. Some recent writers have denied that the *Treatise* has either of these flaws. Roy Rotheim observes:

Through the nagging of his disciples in what was then known as the 'Circus,' Keynes agreed that in developing his Fundamental Equations, he had posited all variations in price with none in output. And yet, the Fundamental Equations implied variability in both.[57]

Rotheim offers no further discussion of this rejection of Keynes' reading of the Fundamental Equations. Even Lord Kahn himself, after citing the announced intention of Chapter 20 of the *Treatise* in his Mattioli Lectures, wonders:

> I do not see how we – the members of the Circus – could have attributed to Keynes the assumption of inelastic supply, and I am completely mysti-fied by the questions:
> (a) why we did not see this for ourselves;
> (b) why it did not come out in the course of the discussions between Keynes and me, on one of the occasions when I reported on difficulties which had arisen in discussions at the Circus – the upshot of which I would have reported back to the other members of the Circus.[58]

The discussions in the *Treatise* of cumulative inflation and deflation, and of windfall profits and losses as a widow's cruse or Danaid jar support, however, the simple explanation that Hawtrey and the members of the 'Circus' saw a fallacy in these passages due to an implicit assumption of constant output, and that Keynes accepted this view, because the fallacy and the hidden assumption were in fact present in those passages.

Ghanshyam Mehta goes further to argue that Keynes already recognized in the *Treatise* that output variations bring about saving-investment equality by changing saving. He cites Keynes' passing remark that the thrift campaign in the banana plantation might peter out because of increasing poverty before all production stopped and the entire population starved to death, as evidence for understanding this equilibrating mechanism, rather than as evidence against.[59] Mehta stresses another passage in the *Treatise*:

> There is another matter which deserves a word in passing. When for any reason an entrepreneur feels discouraged about the prospects, one or both of two courses may be open to him – he can reduce his output or he can reduce his costs by lowering his offers to the factors of production. Neither course, if adopted by entrepreneurs as a whole, will relieve in the least their losses as a whole, except in so far as they have the indirect effect of reducing savings or of allowing (or causing) the banking system to relax the terms of credit and so increase investment (neither of which is what the entrepreneurs themselves have in mind); whilst, on the other

hand, both courses are likely to aggravate their losses by reducing the cost of investment.... A discussion of the precise circumstances which determine the degree in which a class of entrepreneurs or an individual entrepreneur pursues the one course or the other over the short-period would, however, lead me too far into the intricate theory of the economics of the short-period.... Nor do any of the qualifications of this section affect in any way the rigour or the validity of our conclusions as to the quantitative effect of divergences between saving and investment on the price-levels ruling in the market.[60]

In this passage, Keynes gave only slight emphasis to the equilibrating effect on saving as compared to the aggravation of losses by reducing spending on investment,[61] and he refused to be drawn into discussion of the extent to which entrepreneurs chose one course rather than the other, or of how and by how much saving was affected. There is no indication in this passage that, at the time he wrote the *Treatise*, Keynes felt that he had an explanation of short-period changes in output and their effect on saving, or that such changes required significant modification of his price-level analysis.

I conclude that when Hawtrey and the members of the Circus criticized the widow's cruse fallacy and offered in its place an analysis of the equilibrating role of changes in the level of output, and when Keynes accepted these contributions as advances beyond the *Treatise*, they were correct, because the *Treatise* did not contain a theory of output or a saving function. Similarly, when Kahn and others at Cambridge were slow to formulate the saving function, they were not failing to perceive that the multiplier analysis of Kahn's 1931 article was logically equivalent to the saving function. The multiplier analysis of Kahn's 1931 article, unlike his 1933 paper on 'Public Works and Inflation' or Hawtrey's Macmillan Committee working paper, did not rely on leakages into personal saving, and, while mentioning leakage into unspent profits, did not use this leakage in calculating the multiplier.[62] The formulation of the saving function, under the prodding and illumination first of Hawtrey's numerical example and then of Warming's paper, was not a recognition of something that was already in Kahn's first multiplier article, but was an important step beyond that article. The contributions of Kahn's 1931 article, in which Meade and other members of the Circus had a share, were the supply curve for output as a whole and the demonstration, independent of and at about the same time as Hawtrey's comments on the *Treatise*, that the multiplier was finite, which earlier models with leakages only into imports had failed to demonstrate validly.

In May 1931, the Macmillan Committee on Finance and Industry wound up its activities, and the Cambridge 'Circus' ended its formal sessions for the examination period. Keynes went to the United States to deliver three lectures on 'An Economic Analysis of Unemployment' at a Harris Foundation conference at the University of Chicago in June. The expansionist tone of Keynes' lectures contrasted with those given by Karl Pribram of the University of Frankfurt. Pribram was sceptical about public works, and could recommend only restricting output of some raw materials and removing barriers to free international trade.[63] Although Kahn writes of Keynes' Chicago lectures that 'The members of the Circus were entitled to feel that Keynes was responding to their criticisms with remarkable speed and lucidity',[64] the argument was still largely that of the *Treatise*, with no mention of Kahn's relation between primary and secondary employment:

> I find the explanation of the current business losses, of the reduction of output, and of the unemployment which necessarily ensues on this not in the high level of investment which was proceeding up to the spring of 1929, but in the subsequent cessation of this investment. I see no hope of a recovery except in a revival of the high level of investment. And I do not understand how universal bankruptcy can do any good or bring us any nearer to prosperity, except in so far as it may, by some lucky chance, clear the boards for the recovery of investment.[65]

> Thus the costs of the entrepreneurs are equal to what the public spend plus what they save; while the receipts of the entrepreneurs are equal to what the public spend plus the value of current investment. It follows, if you have been able to catch what I am saying, that when the value of current investment is greater than the savings of the public, the receipts of the entrepreneurs are greater than their costs, so that they make a profit; and when, on the other hand, the value of current investment is less than the savings of the public, the receipts of the entrepreneurs will be less than their costs, so that they make a loss.
>   That is my secret, the clue to the scientific explanation of booms and slumps (and of much else, as I should claim) which I offer you.[66]

> In the past it has been usual to believe that there was some preordained harmony by which saving and investment were necessarily equal. If we intrusted [sic] our savings to a bank, it used to be said, the bank will of course make use of them, and they will duly find their way into industry and investment. But unfortunately this is not so. I venture to say with certainty that it is not so. And it is out of the disequilibriums of savings

and investment, and out of nothing else, that the fluctuations of profits, of output, and of employment are generated.[67]

Keynes attributed the decline in investment in the United States, to which he attributed the subsequent fall in profits, to Federal Reserve policy in raising interest rates to curb the Wall Street boom at a time when a fall in the interest rate would have been needed to maintain equilibrium because the best investment opportunities had already been taken up.[68]

Up to this point, Keynes' Harris Foundation Lectures offered the doctrine of the *Treatise*, plus a foreshadowing of a declining marginal efficiency of capital schedule. Keynes went on, however, to suggest two reasons 'for expecting an equilibrium point of decline to be reached'. His first reason, that a given deficiency of investment would cause only a given decline in profits, neglected the further drop in investment that the decline in profits would cause. Keynes went on to observe that:

> There is also another reason for expecting the decline to reach a stopping-point. For I must now qualify my simplifying assumption that only the rate of investment changes and that the rate of saving remains constant. At first, as I have said, the nervousness engendered by the slump may actually tend to increase saving. For saving is often effected as a safeguard against insecurity. Thus savings may decrease when stock markets are soaring and increase when they are slumping. Moreover, for the salaried and fixed-income class of the community the fall of prices will increase their margin available for saving. But as soon as output has declined heavily, strong forces will be brought into play in the direction of reducing the net volume of saving.
>
> For one thing the unemployed will, in their effort not to allow too great a decline in their established standard of life, not only cease to save but will probably be responsible for much negative saving by living on their previous savings and those of their friends and relations. Much more important, however, than this is likely to be the emergence of negative saving on the part of the government, whether by diminished payments to sinking funds or by actual borrowing, as is now the case in the United States.[69]

Although Keynes considered the changes in personal saving as probably less important than the change in government saving, he recognized the change in saving induced by the change in output as an equilibrating force. Although Lord Kahn has recalled that 'Keynes made a great deal of my multiplier article, for example, in the Harris lectures', Keynes made no use in those lectures of either the demonstration that the multiplier can be calculated and has a finite value, or of the other contribution of Kahn's paper, the supply curve for output as a whole. The point that Keynes did use, the output-induced change in saving balancing the initial change in investment, was, as Kahn told the Centennial Keynes Seminar at Canterbury, not clear to Kahn before he read Jens Warming's 1932 note: 'Although Warming's article contains a misunderstanding, it was he who really brought out the fact which, as I said in my contribution earlier today, was not clear to James Meade and me, that if you define income and saving in a commonsense way so that abnormal or subnormal profits *are* included in income you get an identity between aggregate saving and aggregate investment.'[70]

The argument that a decline in investment, by reducing income, would cause an equilibrating drop in saving was made by Hawtrey in his comments on the *Treatise* in September 1930, and extended with a numerical example in his Macmillan Committee working paper and an algebraic statement in *The Art of Central Banking*. Keynes accepted this point as early as his Harris Lectures. Paradoxically, Hawtrey subsequently neglected this process in his 1933 paper, when he insisted that an increase in government spending would simply crowd out an equal amount of investment, because the volume of saving would remain constant.

KEYNES' LECTURES, 1932

An exceptional opportunity to track the development of Keynes' thought is provided by the lectures he gave at Cambridge. Once, Keynes had carried a full teaching load and lectured on the standard set subjects. Harrod recounts of Keynes' busiest teaching years, 1911–12 and 1913–14, that 'In the Michaelmas Term he lectured twice a week on Principles, twice a week on the Theory of Money and once a week on Company Finance and the Stock Exchange; in the Easter (Summer) Term, he lectured twice a week on Principles, twice a week on Currency and Banking and once a week on the Money Market and the Foreign Exchanges. Earlier in 1911 he gave a course once a week on the currency and finance of India' in which he presented his forthcoming book, *Indian Currency and Finance*.[71] This was in addition to tutoring, for which he had twenty-four private pupils in 1909, a year before he extended his activities beyond

King's College by becoming Director of Studies for undergraduates reading economics at Trinity College, one of whom was Dennis Robertson.[72] All this changed when Keynes returned from Versailles and the Treasury in June 1919. Keynes informed King's College that he wished to tutor fewer students and told the University that he would lecture only once a week for a single term on 'Economic Aspects of the Peace Treaty', the topic of his *Economic Consequences of the Peace*. He resigned the Girdler Lectureship the following May and gave up his fellowship dividend from King's, becoming a Supernumerary Fellow.[73]

From 1919, Keynes gave only eight lectures a year, on Monday mornings in Michaelmas Term (October and November), and lectured only on the subject of whatever book he was writing at the time. The Political Economy Club met in his rooms Monday evenings, and he spent Tuesday to Friday in London, attending to such matters as the chairmanship of *The Nation and Athenaeum*, the National Mutual Life Assurance Society and the Committee of Economists. By 1928, Keynes supervised only eight pupils, meeting them in two groups of four on alternate Saturday afternoons to discuss their essays on topics chosen by Keynes, such as the Treasury doctrine that public borrowing and spending cannot expand employment (April 1929, while he was writing *Can Lloyd George Do It?*) or the distinction between the budgetary problem and the transfer problem in German reparations payments (early 1929, while Keynes was writing his paper on the transfer problem).[74]

Keynes' 1922 lectures on Money, attended by Roy Harrod, were a preliminary version of his *Tract on Monetary Reform*. 'There was a footnote to the notice of his lecture, stating that only those who had obtained a first class in Part I or were specially recommended could come.' Keynes' lectures on the Pure Theory of Money during the Michaelmas Term of 1929, the only lectures he gave during Wynne Plumptre's two years at Cambridge, were delivered from galley-proofs of the first volume of the *Treatise*. These lectures were attended not only by students reading for degrees, but also by dons and research students, including the mathematician Frank Ramsey in 1922, and Dennis Robertson at least once in 1929.[75] It was through such lectures, rather than journal articles, that Keynes shared his work-in-progress with economists at Cambridge, and visitors from Oxford and London. John Kenneth Galbraith, who was at Trinity in 1937-8, records being told of one way in which Keynes' lectures affected his books:

> At Cambridge when Keynes was completing his masterwork *The General Theory of Employment Interest and Money*, he read to his lecture audiences from the printer's proofs. On occasion a proof would slip from the sequence to the floor. It was said he never noticed.[76]

Because he cancelled his lectures announced for the Michaelmas Term of 1931, Keynes lectured in April and May of 1932, as well as in October and November. In 1979, a supplementary volume to Keynes' *Complete Writings* came out, containing material discovered in 1976 in a laundry hamper at Keynes' country house, Tilton. This material included notes from which Keynes appeared to have lectured on 25 April, 2 May, 10 October and 14 November 1932. The first two lectures were dated from the correspondence found with them, including a 'manifesto' from Kahn and the Robinsons to Keynes about the lecture on 2 May, while the two later lectures were dated by comparing them with notes taken by two students, Robert Bryce and Lorie Tarshis.

Bryce and Tarshis arrived in Cambridge in the autumn of 1932 from the University of Toronto, where Tarshis had studied the *Treatise* under Wynne Plumptre. At Plumptre's recommendation, they were admitted to Keynes' Political Economy Club and attended his lectures each year for as long as they were in Cambridge. Bryce acquired sufficient command of Keynes' theory so that in 1935 he presented an 'Introduction to a Monetary Theory of Employment',[77] which Keynes had read and approved, to four sessions of Hayek's seminar at LSE, and then went on to Harvard, where Schumpeter observed that 'Keynes is Allah, and Bryce is his prophet'.[78] Tarshis achieved early professional renown by differing from the *General Theory* on the relative movement of real and nominal wages over the trade cycle, and having the correction promptly accepted by Keynes.[79] Bryce and Tarshis preserved their notes on Keynes' lectures, Bryce for the years 1932 to 1934 and Tarshis for 1932 to 1935. Bryce, Plumptre and Tarshis remained linked: Plumptre succeeded Bryce as an Assistant Deputy Minister of Finance in 1954, when Bryce became Clerk of the Privy Council and Secretary to the Cabinet, and, after Plumptre left the Canadian Government to become the first Principal of Scarborough College, University of Toronto, he brought Tarshis back to Canada from Stanford as chairman of Scarborough's Division of Social Sciences. After Bryce's retirement as Deputy Minister of Finance, he donated his lecture notes to the MacOdrum Library at Carleton University. In addition to the Bryce and Tarshis notes, T. K. Rymes of Carleton has collected students' notes of Keynes' lectures in 1933 or later taken by Walter Salant (for 1933), D. G. Champernowne, A. K. Cairncross and Marvin Fallgatter, the last of whom was a physics student taking notes in 1933 on behalf of James Earley, an economist at the University of Wisconsin.

While there are several independent sets of notes on the 1933 lectures, the Michaelmas 1932 lectures were covered only by Bryce and Tarshis, whose notes are not independent, since if one of them missed a lecture, he would copy the other's notes. Sir Austin Robinson, speaking to the Centennial Keynes Seminar at the University of Kent at Canterbury, expressed concern about the reliability of Bryce's notes for the first year, since Bryce was new to economics, with an undergraduate degree in mining engineering.[80] However, Tarshis had studied economics, and the *Treatise* in particular, and the survival of Keynes' notes for two of the lectures provides a check on the accuracy of the students' notes, a test which they pass quite well.

While the discovery of the laundry hamper of Keynes' correspondence and notes at Tilton has been compared to the discovery in 1943 of an iron box containing Ricardo's side of his correspondence with James Mill,[81] the recovery of the students' notes of Keynes' lectures recalls Edwin Cannan's discovery of a set of student's notes of Adam Smith's lectures, since supplemented by another set.[82] Smith's lectures, going back fourteen years before the *Wealth of Nations*, enabled historians of economics to establish Smith's priority with respect to the work of the Physiocrats, and to study Smith's treatment of such topics as Hume's specie-flow mechanism, which he discussed in his lectures but omitted from his book. Similarly, the notes on Keynes' lectures not only illuminate questions of timing, but also show Keynes tentatively expounding approaches which he later revised or abandoned.

The outline for the first of Keynes' lectures on the Pure Theory of Money, delivered on 25 April 1932, is headed 'Notes on Fundamental Terminology'. It contains his plea for an end to quibbling over definitions, provided that the definitions are used consistently, and expresses his 'hope that in these lectures I shall show that I am not obstinate and can take advantage of criticism on substantial points of argument and exposition'. A section of the outline which was crossed out, and presumably not given as part of that lecture, defines Income, E', as the gross receipts of entrepreneurs in nominal terms, and states that this is a return to the usage of most economists from the terminology of the *Treatise*.[83]

Keynes' lecture on 2 May, attended by Piero Sraffa, Richard Kahn and Austin and Joan Robinson, was concerned to demonstrate that investment and output vary together. This lecture was followed by a 'manifesto' from Kahn and the Robinsons to Keynes, arguing that the conditions imposed by Keynes to obtain this result were needlessly restrictive, and by further correspondence on the subject between Keynes and Joan Robinson.[84]

The centrepiece of Keynes' argument is the dependence of investment, I, and the normal earnings of factors of production, E, on profits, Q. Profits are defined, as in the *Treatise*, as $I-S$, except that saving, S, is replaced by $E-F$, where F is presumably consumption spending, although no explicit definition of F survives. The lecture, although presented in terms of tautologies similar to those of the *Treatise*, comes close to stating the saving function, without quite doing so:

> Since *cet. par.* I and E are both likely to fall with Q, and F to fall with $E - Q$, it follows that any given position of O is one of unstable equilibrium, in the sense that any movement away from O in either direction will tend to aggravate itself by stimulating a further movement in the same direction, until a point is reached where the fall in E is sufficiently in excess of the fall in F to offset the fall in I (and similarly *mut. mut.* with an upward movement). Thus if we preach and practise open-handedness when I is rising and economy when I is falling, (as unfortunately we generally do) we run the risk of aggravating the upward and downward movement as the case may be.
>
> These examples illustrate how, if we introduce a few simple assumptions based on general knowledge of the outside world, we can galvanise our truisms into being generalisations of far-reaching practical importance. Indeed, I believe, that any man who has thoroughly grasped the truism
>
> $$\Delta Q = \Delta I + \Delta F - \Delta E$$
>
> and has allowed this colourless and in itself inoperative liquid to enter his marrowbones, will never be, in his outlook on the practical world, quite the same man again![85]

This truism is simply the *Treatise* definition of profits, which holds that profits are equal to investment minus saving, so that the change in profits will be the change in investment minus the change in saving. The advance beyond the *Treatise* in this lecture is the recognition that a new equilibrium will be reached when E has changed by sufficiently more than F (that is, when saving has changed) to offset the change in I. In the *Treatise*, a windfall loss (Q less than zero) would lead entrepreneurs to cut back on their investment plans and on their offers to the factors of production, further reducing Q by the amount that investment was reduced, since consumption spending (F) was implicitly assumed to change by as much as the earnings of the factors of production, E. If, however, a decline in Q and E also reduces $E-F$, the cumulative deflation would eventually come to a halt at a lower level of investment and saving. This process deals with investment and saving in nominal terms. To have the new equilibrium at a position of lower output and employment, Keynes made the additional assumption that the volume of investment and the volume of output vary in the same direction.[86]

Kahn and the Robinsons began their 'manifesto' by presenting Keynes' formal proof from his lecture that an increase in I increases O:

Conditions laid down
    (a) $\Delta E'$ and ΔO have the same sign.
    (b) $\Delta E' - \Delta F$ and $\Delta E'$ have the same sign.
Proof
    $\Delta E' - \Delta F = \Delta I$
    $\therefore$ ΔI and ΔO have the same sign.

We first criticise condition (b)
    This condition means that if income increases, expenditure will not increase by as much. Now it is surely obvious that if this condition is not fulfilled, i.e. if expenditure increases by more than income increases, the presumption in favour of your assertion that I and O move together is actually strengthened.
    The fact of the matter is that condition (b) is necessary, not to show that I and O move together but to ensure that there shall be a stable equilibrium. If expenditure were to increase by more than income, equilibrium would be unstable and any small increment in investment would cause output to rise either to infinity or to the point where condition (b) came into operation, whichever happened first.[87]

After this brilliant demonstration that a positive marginal propensity to save is a stability condition, Kahn and the Robinsons proceeded in the rest of the manifesto to discuss alternative proofs that I and O vary together, without quite recognizing that condition (b) corresponds to a saving function and, like Keynes in his lecture, without using the multiplier to derive the ratio $\Delta O/\Delta I$. On condition (a), the assertion that nominal income and real output vary together, Kahn and the Robinsons wrote:

> Let us grant for the sake of argument that an increase in O will be accompanied by an increase in E. It does not follow that an increase in E will be necessarily accompanied by an increase in O, for an increase in E may (as in your exceptional case) be accompanied by such a large increase in cost of production that O declines.[88]

They failed to note that condition (a) could be replaced by the supply curve for output as a whole given a fixed money wage rate, a relation between output and the price level which Kahn had used in his 1931 article.

Neither Keynes in his lecture nor Kahn, Joan Robinson and Austin Robinson in their manifesto and related correspondence suggest that they can show more than that the change in output and the change in investment have the same sign, and that an equilibrium will exist. The proposition that a change in spending will cause output to change in the same, rather than the opposite, direction was then controversial, and contrary views were held at LSE. This was made clear in January 1931 when Hayek, on his way from Vienna to LSE to deliver four lectures on *Prices and Production*, summarized this book to the Marshall Society at Cambridge. Joan Robinson later recalled:

> I very well remember Hayek's visit to Cambridge on his way to the London School. He expounded his theory and covered a blackboard with his triangles. The whole argument, as we could see later, consisted in confusing the current rate of investment with the total stock of capital goods, but we could not make it out at the time. The general tendency seemed to be to show that the slump was caused by consumption. R. F. Kahn, who was at that time involved in explaining that the multiplier guaranteed that saving equals investment, asked in a puzzled tone, 'Is it your view that if I went out tomorrow and bought a new overcoat, that would increase unemployment?' 'Yes,' said Hayek. 'But,' pointing to his triangles on the board, 'it would take a very long mathematical argument to explain why.'[89]

It is surprising that Kahn and the Robinsons did not go beyond refuting this argument in their 'manifesto' to show how large a change in output would result from a given change in investment, since, according to Joan Robinson's reminiscences, it was at about the same time that Kahn, Meade and the Robinsons spent a week-end with Abba Lerner and three other LSE students at an inn half-way between London and Cambridge. Meade and Kahn explained the multiplier to the LSE students. Lerner was persuaded of the validity of the multiplier analysis, and came to Cambridge for a term.[90]

When Brian Reddaway wrote his first paper as a pupil of Keynes in October 1932, Keynes pointed out to him that while the *Treatise*, which Reddaway was then reading, dealt with price movements, Keynes now considered output movements more important.[91] Keynes began his series of lectures that month by stressing the significance of the change in title from 'The Pure Theory of Money', which had been the title of the first volume of the *Treatise*, to 'The Monetary Theory of Production'. Although the opening remark of Keynes' lecture on 10 October was that he would examine 'the influence of monetary manipulation on production rather than on prices',[92] he made no use of the saving function or multiplier to present a theory of effective demand, and the lectures were largely concerned with monetary theory narrowly defined. Four of the eight lectures, those from 31 October to 21 November, discussed the interaction of liquidity preference and expected quasi-rents in determining the rate of interest, with the treatment of liquidity preference drawing on the *Treatise*'s analysis of bearishness.

Keynes told his audience that his lectures were the beginning of a new book on the functioning of a monetary economy.[93] By a monetary economy, he did not mean simply a money economy, where money was used as a medium of exchange but was neutral. Instead, he proposed to examine an economy in which 'The monetary disturbances don't wash out over the long period. The introduction of money leads to a different long period conclusion'. In contrast,

> Professor Pigou is essentially dealing with a neutral economy – e.g. his supply curve of labour is independent of changes in the value of money. Pigou's 'neutral' economy is a 'real wage' economy – he measures in terms of real wages and the supply of labour.[94]

> We do now live in Monetary Economy as shown in sticky wages, old debts. Marshall and Pigou were well aware of this but did not base their analysis on this.[95]

Although the change in tone from the *Treatise* was enough to startle and dismay Lorie Tarshis, who had arrived in Cambridge as a firm believer in the *Treatise*, Keynes' lecture on 10 October showed an affinity to the *Treatise* on an important point:

> So long as there is an excess of S over I – entrepreneurs will incur a loss at whatever level E/O is fixed – though in case of a system not closed this is not true. But if it is closed the level of E/O will not affect the excess 'S' over 'I'.[96]

In this passage, Keynes recognized the possibility of leakages into imports, but not the equilibrating influence of a change in saving caused by a change in earnings.

On 14 November Keynes summarized the parameters of a monetary economy as the quantity of money, the state of liquidity preference, expectation of quasi-rent, state of time-preference, and 'the supply schedule – the response of supply ... to state of profits etc.' In his next lecture, he presented the equations of his theory. The rate of interest, P, is determined in the money market as

$$P = A(M)$$

where M is the quantity of money, and the function A represents the state of liquidity preference. P_2, the price of capital assets, depends on B, the state of expectations of quasi-rents, and on the interest rate, by which the stream of expected quasi-rents is discounted to get the present value of the assets:

$$P_2 = B(p).$$

P_2 in turn determines

$$I' = C(P_2)$$

where 'I' equals amount of investment where C is the [flow] supply function of capital assets in regard to their price complex'.[97] Keynes remarks that the 'State of time preference can only affect price level of assets unless [?if] it either acts on B or p. Now there seems to be no particularly good reason why it should react on p except via policy of monetary system – but it probably will affect B via change in price level of consumables – and will affect of course state of liquidity preferences and so on – but we'll neglect this'.[98] The role of time preference is to determine the price of consumables by influencing the choice between current and future consumption:

$$P_1 = G(I,H)$$

where P_1, the price of consumables, depends on investment, I, and the state of supply of consumables, H, given the state of time preference, G. The output of consumables, R, is

$$R = H(P_1).$$

Keynes then introduces profits, Q, and restates the supply functions, without discussing how these relate to his previous presentation, as

$$R = H(Q_1) \text{ and } I' = C(Q_2).$$

Combining the supply functions for R and I' gives output

$$O = J(Q).$$

Keynes notes that the earnings of the factors of production, which are the costs of production, can respond to profits and output:

$$E = L(O,Q).$$

Profits are the difference between investment and saving, as in the *Treatise*:

Usually $\Delta Q = \Delta I - \Delta S$
or $\quad \Delta Q = \Delta I + \Delta F - \Delta E$
ΔQ or $\Delta O = \Delta D - \Delta E$ (also change in costs).[99]

The word 'usually' seems to indicate that these expressions are intended as more than a mere definition of Q, while it is surprising to see the change in profits and the change in output used interchangeably as the change in disbursements (total spending) minus the change in earnings.

Keynes concludes his lecture:

Output increases when disbursement increases faster than costs. Generally safe to assume that changes in investment (ΔI) are the same in sign as changes in disbursement relatively to changes in costs. Generalizing then whether or not Output is increasing depends on whether or not Investment is increasing. ('Problem of curing unemployment is a problem in monetary economics').[100]

The model which Keynes presents in his Michaelmas 1932 lectures is clearly not that of the *General Theory*. The supply functions for the output of capital and consumer goods are not derived from any explicit assumptions, nor is it clear whether supply depends on prices or on profits. The labour market is not even mentioned, apart from a passing criticism of Pigou in the first lecture for assuming that wage bargaining is in terms of real wages. There is no saving function, and Keynes' recognition in his Harris Foundation lectures of the equilibrating effect on saving of changes in output is not repeated. The multiplier is never mentioned, even though Kahn's article was published more than a year before. Instead, Keynes limits himself to the assertion that changes in output have the same sign as changes in investment. In his lecture on 7 November, Keynes has investment dependent on the ratio of the discounted present value of the anticipated stream of quasi-rents from a capital asset to the cost of production of that capital asset, but does not develop the marginal efficiency of capital or even distinguish marginal and average conditions. The treatment of liquidity preference is closer to its final form, with the possibility of a liquidity trap discussed on 31 October, but there is not yet a statement of a money demand function depending on both income and the interest rate.

Windfall profits or losses, investment minus saving, are at the centre of the analysis of the Michaelmas 1932 lectures on 'The Monetary Theory of Production', just as in the *Treatise*. Similarly, in Keynes' correspondence with Colin Clark in January 1933 about Clark's book on British national income, Keynes applied Kahn's estimate of a multiplier of two to the excess of saving over investment, as defined in the *Treatise*, instead of comparing changes in national income with changes in investment.[101]

The eighth and final lecture of the series, delivered on 28 November, bears a striking resemblance to Chapter 23 of the *General Theory*, but is only a presentation of the window-dressing of the *General Theory*, not its essential elements. In this lecture, Keynes discussed Jeremy Bentham's criticism of Adam Smith's defence of the Usury Laws, and spoke of Bernard Mandeville's *Fable of the Bees*, which argued that the extravagant man benefits his neighbours

in a society where saving tends to outrun investment. As in his proposal for a protective tariff, which he had withdrawn as soon as
Britain left the gold standard, Keynes held that a favourable balance
of trade had the same effect on domestic demand as investment, and
that the mercantilist concern with improving the trade balance was
thus rational when there was unemployment due to insufficient
demand. Furthermore, with a metallic currency, as under the gold
standard, mercantilist policy to achieve a trade surplus would be the
only way to increase the quantity of money and so hold down the
rate of interest when liquidity preference increased. Keynes' defence
of the rational basis for mercantilism is shown by this lecture to
predate his reading of Eli Heckscher's *Mercantilism*, which, although
first published in Swedish in 1931, did not appear in an English
translation until 1935. Keynes' complaint that 'the free trader
assumes that all factors are fully occupied' was very likely a rebuttal
to *Tariffs: the Case Examined* (1931), in which a group of LSE
economists, including Sir William Beveridge, A. L. Bowley,
Theodore Gregory, J. R. Hicks, Walter Layton and Lionel Robbins,
had attacked Keynes' tariff proposal on the basis of the classical
principle of comparative advantage. This book, later described by
Joan Robinson as 'marking the low ebb of neoclassical thought',[102]
did not consider that expansion of employment in import-substituting
industries which used previously unemployed resources differed in its
consequences for economic welfare from the case where the resources
had to be withdrawn from employment in other industries. In fair-
ness to Lionel Robbins, it should be noted that he was on sounder
ground when he objected to Keynes' implicit assumption that other
countries would not retaliate against British tariff protection.[103]

In his 28 November lecture, Keynes repeated his hope, first
expressed in 'Economic Possibilities for Our Grandchildren' (1930),
that capital accumulation would eventually resolve class conflict by
driving down the return on capital: '*K*. wants to see this gradual
reduction of the minimum profitable rate of interest – hence get rid
of troubles of capitalist system'. He suggested that in the current
situation 'marginal productivity is knocking hard against the minimum rate of interest', that is, capital accumulation and investment
were held back because a liquidity trap kept the rate of interest from
falling.[104]

Keynes' lectures for 1932 finished with peripheral topics that will
be familiar to readers of the *General Theory*, notably mercantilism,

the Usury Laws, the *Fable of the Bees*, and the liquidity trap. What was missing was the analysis of effective demand, output and employment which is at the heart of the *General Theory*.

THE MONETARY THEORY OF PRODUCTION, 1933

In October 1933, Joan Robinson announced in the inaugural issue of the *Review of Economic Studies* that 'the Theory of Money has recently undergone a violent revolution. It has ceased to be the Theory of Money, and become the Analysis of Output.... Now, once Mr Keynes has shown us how to crack the egg, it appears the most natural thing in the world to attack the interesting part of the problem directly, instead of through the devious route of the Quantity Theory of Money. If we are interested in the volume of output, why should we not try what progress can be made by thinking in terms of the demand for output as a whole, and its cost of production, just as we have been taught to think of the demand and cost of a single commodity?'[105] She did not, however, present a theory of output in her paper. Instead, she used a Quantity Equation for hairpins, suggested by Richard Kahn, to show that the comparable equation for money is a tautology without causal force, since the velocity of circulation need not be constant, and then demonstrated that the widow's cruse of profits in the *Treatise* depended on the assumption of a perfectly inelastic supply of consumption goods.

Another passage in the *Treatise* attracted Mrs Robinson's criticism, the parable of the thrift campaign in the banana plantation:

> He points out that if savings exceed investment, consumption goods can only be sold at a loss. Their output will consequently decline until the real income of the population is reduced to such a low level that savings are perforce reduced to equality with investment. But he completely overlooks the significance of this discovery, and throws it out in the most casual way without pausing to remark that he has proved that output may be in equilibrium at any number of different levels, and that while there is a natural tendency towards equilibrium between savings and investment (in a very long run), there is no natural tendency towards full employment of the factors of production.[106]

This insight, which Keynes had previously offered in his Harris Foundation lectures, was the basis for the theory of effective demand elaborated by Keynes and his associates in 1933. The first of Keynes' circle to publish a multiplier analysis incorporating personal saving was James Meade, in a Fabian Society pamphlet on *Public Works in their International Aspect* in January 1933,[107] followed closely by Richard Kahn in his paper to the American Statistical Association on 'Public Works and Inflation', which was published in March. Meade examined the multiplier effect of a sustained increase in public works spending, given leakages into personal saving as well as imports, and concluded that, because of balance of payments problems, international expansionary measures were preferable to national ones.

Keynes first presented a multiplier analysis in print in four articles on 'The Means to Prosperity' in *The Times* in March 1933, which were promptly reprinted in a pamphlet which sold 12,000 copies in two weeks.[108] Another article, entitled 'The Multiplier' in the *New Statesman* on April Fools Day, was incorporated in the American edition of the pamphlet as a chapter on 'The Relief to the Budget'. The term 'multiplier' was coined by Keynes in these articles for what Kahn had described as the ratio of secondary to primary employment. After directing the reader's attention to Kahn's 1931 article in the *Economic Journal*, Keynes derived the multiplier for public works spending, on the assumption that 30 per cent of expenditure would not increase income, because it would simply replace unemployment benefits or draw resources out of other employment, and that 30 per cent of the increase in income would be saved instead of spent. The second round of spending would then be roughly half as large as the first round, and, by summing an infinite series of geometrically decreasing terms, the multiplier would be two. 'The amount of time which it takes for current income to be spent will separate each repercussion from the next one. But it will be seen that seven-eighths of the total effects come from the primary expenditure and the first two repercussions, so that the time-lags involved are not unduly serious.'[109] Keynes pointed out that loan-financed increases in government spending would lead to increased tax revenue at existing tax rates as well as reduced payment of unemployment benefits. He proposed that the forthcoming World Economic Conference consider an international note issue, since monetary expansion would not cause balance of payments difficulties if undertaken by all countries at the same time, and cautioned against schemes to raise price levels by restricting supply.

In *The Means to Prosperity*, Keynes did not complement his exposition of the multiplier by discussing the determination of the equilibrium level of income, nor did he explain that the dependence of saving on income meant that equilibrium would be restored at a new level of income after a change in investment. The pamphlet did not present supply and demand curves for output as a whole, nor did it explain the existence of involuntary unemployment by the inability of workers to adjust their real wages by bargaining for money wages. A chapter on 'The Raising of Prices' argued that the price level should be raised by expansion of demand rather than restricting output of selected commodities, but did not present the argument in terms of the effect on the real wage rate and employment of moving along the aggregate supply curve. The chapter on raising prices did not go beyond the analysis that Keynes presented in June 1931 to the New School of Social Research in New York in two lectures entitled 'Do We Want Prices to Rise?' and 'What Can We Do to Make Prices Rise?'. In these lectures, Keynes urged restoration of the price level to its previous, higher level because of the existence of nominal debts incurred before the deflation and because of labour resistance to lowering nominal wage rates.[110]

In 1933, Keynes published a brief paper on 'A Monetary Theory of Production' in a collection of essays in honour of the German business cycle theorist, Arthur Spiethoff. This article closely followed his first lecture under that title, given on 10 October 1932. Keynes distinguished a 'real exchange economy', where money is merely a neutral link between transactions in real things and real assets, from a monetary economy, where 'the course of events cannot be predicted, either in long period or short, without a knowledge of the behaviour of money between the first state and the last'. He criticized Pigou for assuming a supply schedule for labour independent of changes in the value of money, and noted that the conditions for 'neutrality' of money in the sense of Marshall's *Principles* were those which would ensure that crises do not occur.

> This is not the same thing as to say that the problem of booms and depressions is a purely monetary phenomenon. For this statement is generally meant to imply that a complete solution is to be found in banking policy. I am saying that booms and depressions are phenomena peculiar to an economy in which – in some significant sense which I am not attempting to define precisely in this place – money is not neutral.[111]

Like the 1932 lectures, this paper argued for the construction of a theory of a monetary economy, but did not provide such a theory. Keynes presented a theory of a monetary economy in his lectures in the Michaelmas Term of 1933. These lectures contrast sharply with those given by Keynes a year earlier, and represent a major advance beyond *The Means to Prosperity*.

On 16 October, Keynes told his audience that the *Treatise* had been primarily interested in prices, and had assumed a monetary position of the economy, even while claiming to provide a clue to movements of output. Now Keynes would be concerned with the volume of output and employment. He began by presenting the two fundamental postulates of the classical theory, as exemplified by Pigou's *Theory of Unemployment*:

(1) The wage is equal to the marginal product. The wage of an employed person is in equilibrium equal to reduction in value occasioned by reducing employment by one unit. The amount of marginal product differs according to what period of time we have in view – is capital adjustable or not? The question too regarding perfection of competition and markets.

(2) In equilibrium the utility of wage when a given volume of labour employed is equal to marginal disutility of that amount of employment.[112]

The first postulate gives the demand for labour by profit-maximizing competitive firms. Keynes' remark about competition and markets indicates his recognition that, if competition is imperfect, the wage rate offered at each level of employment would be lower because of the difference between price and marginal revenue. The second postulate gives the labour supply schedule for utility-maximizing households. If both conditions hold, there can be no excess supply of labour. Keynes went on to discuss types of unemployment that were compatible with the classical theory, such as seasonal unemployment, transitional unemployment as workers change jobs in response to temporary maladjustments, and voluntary unemployment, where a worker prefers leisure to a wage equal to the marginal product of labour.

While accepting the first classical postulate, Keynes rejected the second one, so that involuntary unemployment was possible in his theory:

Men are involuntarily unemployed if the supply of labour willing to work for a money wage worth less in terms of product than the existing money wage is greater than the existing volume of employment.[113]

Keynes accepts correlation between real wage and unemployment but *not that between real wages and money wages*. Real wages determined by other forces. High real wages of the slump not due to labour *standing out* for them but to other factors.[114]

Keynes pointed to the example of the United States in 1932 as evidence that labour had accepted money wage reduction in the Depression, but had not been able to adjust real wages to clear the labour market. In that year, according to later studies, average hourly earnings in the United States fell by 12.9 per cent, while the consumer price index fell by 10.3 per cent.[115] In his next lecture, on 23 October, Keynes returned to criticism of the classical theory of employment, objecting that

The classical theory assumed that a refusal to accept lower money wage was tantamount of refusal to accept lower real wage. And that labour as a whole can bring down its real wages if only it will cut its money wages sufficiently.

Pigou's argument based on assumption that at outset nothing happened to non-wage earners income. . . . *But* – there is a pressure through competition for prices to fall from above marginal cost towards marginal costs. Therefore the non-wage receipts fall off.

The Classical argument really presupposing that factors are rewarded in terms of a predetermined share of total product of industry and not seen in terms of money – a Co-operative Economy.[116]

According to Keynes, 'Struggle over money wages is really over distribution of the total wages among earners'. This was a recognition of the significance of a passing remark in the *Treatise* that nominal wages could be sticky because overlapping contracts meant that not all nominal incomes could be reduced by the same proportion at the same time.[117] Consequently, Keynes held,

Trade Unions have shown themselves to be more rational than the classical economists, in that they have consistently opposed all small reductions in money wages, but they have not opposed all small rises in the cost of living.[118]

Money wage rates may be slow to fall both because of workers' concern with relative wages in a world of decentralized collective bargaining and overlapping contracts, and because trade unions perceive the futility of trying to adjust real wage rates by cutting money wages. In an economy where bargaining is in terms of money wages rather than real wages, changes in money wages would affect prices. Keynes' acceptance of the first classical postulate implied that involuntary unemployment was due to too high a real wage, but, in a money wage economy, the way to deal with this problem was to raise the price level by stimulating aggregate demand. This advice contrasted with the reliance of Cannan, Robbins and Rueff on reducing money wage rates. Referring to the controversy between Malthus and Ricardo over effective demand, which he discussed in the paper on Malthus in his *Essays in Biography* published that year, Keynes suggested that Say's Law of Markets – that 'Supply creates its own demand' – should be replaced by 'Expenditure creates its own income'.

On 6 November 1933 Keynes redefined Q as expected quasi-rents, the excess of expected sales proceeds over E, 'the cost to which the entrepreneur commits himself when he makes a short period decision to employ people'. This definition follows from the one passage in the *Treatise* which recognized that anticipated profits are relevant for investment decisions, not *ex post* realized windfalls.[119] Y, the income of the community, was defined as $E + Q$, the expected sales proceeds. This resembles the *General Theory*'s discussion of aggregate demand as the sales proceeds which entrepreneurs expect to receive as the result of employing a certain amount of labour. Keynes noted in his lecture that in the normal case, marginal cost rises when output rises, so that there would be an inducement to increase output only if the price level was expected to rise. While Q was redefined as expected quasi-rents, 'profits' in the *Treatise* sense reappeared in Keynes' 6 November lecture as windfall appreciation, A, 'the excess of actual sale proceeds of goods selling in period plus the change in the value of capital'. According to the notes taken by Lorie Tarshis, but not those taken by Bryce, Fallgatter or Salant, Keynes then presented a consumption function, stated as $C = f(Y, A)$, where $Y = C + I$. This is the first appearance of the consumption function in Keynes' lectures. The function which Keynes presented in his lecture differed from the consumption function of the *General Theory*, where consumption depends on disposable income alone, by the inclusion of windfalls in the manner of the *Treatise*.

While only Tarshis records the consumption function in the 6 November lecture, all the sets of students' notes agree that on 20 November, Keynes expounded the 'psychological law' that consumption changes by less than income, and discussed the propensity to spend. Fallgatter recorded the consumption function as $C = f(Y)$ in his notes for that day, in notation similar to that of Tarshis' notes on the earlier lecture, but without inclusion of windfall appreciation. As in the opening paragraphs of Chapter 16 of the *General Theory*, Keynes denied that an act of saving substitutes definite future consumption for present consumption, and pointed out that not eating a dinner today does not signal entrepreneurs that they should devote resources to preparing a dinner for a particular day next week. An act of saving reduces total effective demand, whereas the classical view had been that an act of saving induces a matching act of investment.[120] In his lecture on 27 November Keynes derived the multiplier from the marginal propensity to consume, and showed how this was equivalent to Kahn's analysis of the ratio of the change in total employment to the change in primary employment.[121]

KEYNES' THEORY OF A MONETARY ECONOMY IN 1933

Keynes was already dissatisfied with the *Treatise* when it was published. The *Treatise* advocated public works spending as a second-best remedy for unemployment when a balance of payments constraint precluded monetary expansion by a single country and a co-ordinated international increase in money supplies could not be achieved, but argued for this only as an increase in investment leading to windfall profits. The multiplier analysis of *Can Lloyd George Do It?* was not incorporated into the *Treatise*, because Keynes did not yet have a way to show that the multiplier would be finite. Without a saving function or some other theory of leakages, Keynes' parable of the thrift campaign in a banana plantation, presented in the *Treatise* and in his private evidence to the Macmillan Committee, had no stopping point for a cumulative deflation, other than central bank intervention to lower the interest rate, starvation of the entire population, or, mentioned only in a fleeting remark, the thrift campaign petering out because of growing poverty. Although Keynes was motivated to write the book because of a concern that mistaken monetary policy associated with the return to the gold standard was responsible for Britain's high unemployment rate, the *Treatise* lacked a theory of output and employment.

A month before the publication of the *Treatise*, Keynes received Hawtrey's comments on the *Treatise* and an early draft of Kahn's article on home investment and unemployment. Each of these papers provided a derivation of a finite multiplier. Hawtrey's comments, expanded later in his Macmillan Committee working paper, pointed out that a fall in spending would cause an unintended increase in inventories, providing an incentive for firms to reduce output, and that the reduced output would reduce saving, eliminating the gap between desired investment and saving. Kahn's article contributed the supply curve for output as a whole in the short period, given the money wage rate and productive capacity, but Kahn did not use a personal saving function in his multiplier analysis until after his exchange with Jens Warming. Earlier, while proof-reading the *Treatise* for misprints and preparing the index, Kahn had drawn Keynes' attention, before publication, to the index number problem in the Fundamental Equations which Hansen subsequently attacked as a 'fundamental error'.[122]

Keynes had no time to revise the *Treatise* before publication, which had already been delayed a year beyond the date advertised in *Can Lloyd George Do It?*. The Macmillan Committee on Finance and Industry, of which Keynes was a member, met one hundred times from November 1929 to May 1931, according to Keynes' appointment book. Various committees of the Economic Advisory Council, including the Committee on Channel Tunnel Policy, took much of Keynes' time, especially the Committee of Economists, which met on 10 and 11 September 1930 in London, 26 to 28 September at Josiah Stamp's home at Shortlands in Kent, 7, 8, 15 and 16 October in London, 18 and 19 October at King's College, Cambridge, and 22, 23 and 24 October in London.[123] His first opportunity to present reconsidered views on economic theory, as distinct from immediate questions of policy, was in his Harris Foundation lectures in Chicago in June 1931, where he stressed the *Treatise*'s analysis of the difference between investment and saving, but also discussed Hawtrey's point that an equilibrium level of output would be reached because of the effect of changes in output on the level of saving. Without the decline in Keynes' activity in Whitehall and in politics following the formation of the National Government, and after Britain's departure from the gold standard ended Keynes' campaign for tariffs, he might not have had the time to write the *General Theory*.

After his initial push on the equilibrating effect of changes in output on saving and his identification of the unintended change in inventories as the difference between intended investment and saving, Hawtrey became less involved in the further development of

Keynes' thought. The barrier between them was Hawtrey's continued insistence that, despite his own analysis of the dependence of saving on income, public works spending would simply crowd out private investment because of a fixed pool of saving. The Cambridge 'Circus', whose discussions were reported to Keynes by Kahn each week in the Easter Term of 1931, analysed the implicit assumptions underlying the widow's cruse fallacy and pressed Keynes to admit that crucial portions of the *Treatise* depended on constant output and on consumption changing by as much as income. After the end of the formal sessions of the 'Circus', Kahn and the Robinsons pointed out to Keynes, in their manifesto on his second lecture in the Easter Term of 1932, that one of the conditions for his proof that output and investment would vary in the same direction, the assumption that consumption would change by less than earnings, was a stability condition for the economy.

Keynes' lectures in 1932 and 1933 show him struggling to construct an integrated theory of a monetary economy. The multiplier theory of effective demand, showing the increase in aggregate demand resulting from an increase in public works, exports or autonomous private investment, was only one of four crucial building blocks of this theory. To the multiplier, it was necessary to add an explanation of the existence of involuntarily unemployed resources and of how changes in aggregate demand could affect output and employment. Keynes' first lecture in the Michaelmas Term of 1932, which was the basis of the paper in the Spiethoff Festschrift, stressed the need for such an explanation, and criticized Pigou, among others, for supposing that a monetary economy behaved as if workers could bargain directly for real wages. The theory itself was not provided until the first two lectures in the Michaelmas Term of 1933, when Keynes explained why workers could not set a market-clearing real wage rate by bargaining for nominal wage rates. Workers would quite rationally resist reductions in money wage rates because, given overlapping contracts and decentralized collective bargaining, such reductions would disrupt relative wages. Changes in the price level would not have any such effect on relative wages. Furthermore, even if money wages were reduced, this would lead to a fall in prices, as firms' cost curves shifted. Relative wages as a source of downward rigidity of nominal wages, and the effect of rigid nominal wages on employment in the face of demand shocks, had been mentioned in two isolated passages in the *Treatise*, but Keynes presented this argument systematically for the first time in his 1933 lectures. In his 1933 lectures, Keynes also derived the multiplier from a marginal propensity to consume of less than one, whereas a year earlier he had been concerned merely to argue that investment and output would move in the same direction, without working out any quantitative relation between their changes. Given the multiplier link of aggregate demand to the sum of government spending, exports and investment, and a theory of how changes in aggregate demand affect output and employment, Keynes needed an analysis of whether changes in government spending would simply be offset by changes in investment. It was not enough to show by means of the saving function that increased spending would generate increased saving. It was also necessary to show that the demand for money would depend on the interest rate as well as on the level of income, so that, with a fixed quantity of money, increased government spending would not simply drive up the interest rate so much that the money market would be cleared by an unchanged level of income. The liquidity preference theory of the interest rate, based on the *Treatise*'s analysis of the demand for money as an asset, dealt with this problem. To complete the case against total crowding out of private investment by government spending, a theory of investment was needed.

Keynes' 1933 lectures on 'The Monetary Theory of Production' presented liquidity preference, the theory of effective demand and the analysis, in terms of the two classical postulates, of the inability of workers to bargain for a market-clearing real wage in a monetary economy, all in forms recognizably similar to those of the *General Theory*. Only the theory of investment, in terms of the marginal efficiency of capital, was not yet present. The theory of effective demand and the labour market analysis had not appeared in Keynes' lectures in the Michaelmas Term of 1932, and the formal model outlined in the second to last of those lectures is clearly not that of the *General Theory*. Between the Michaelmas 1932 lectures and the 1933 lectures, Keynes dropped profits, Q, the difference between investment and saving, from its central position in his theory, although it made a fleeting reappearance as A, windfall appreciation. Keynes' Easter 1932 lectures were in line with his intention, announced in April 1932 in the preface to the Japanese edition of the *Treatise*, 'to publish a short book of a purely theoretical character, extending and correcting the theoretical basis of my views as set forth in Books III and IV'. His Michaelmas 1932 lectures had a loftier ambition, the formulation of a theory of the determination of output and employment in a monetary economy, but the theory itself first appeared in his Michaelmas 1933 lectures.

I would thus argue that Keynes made a decisive advance between his 1932 and 1933 lectures. Contrary to James Meade's cautious confidence that he took most of the essential ingredients of the *General Theory* back to Oxford with him in 1931, I argue that, apart from the *Treatise*'s analysis of the asset demand for money, Keynes and his associates were engaged in asking the right questions in 1931, but not yet in answering them. Despite Lord Kahn's recent reservations, expressed in his Mattioli Lectures, I think that Hawtrey and the members of the Circus were right to argue, and Keynes was right to accept, that the widow's cruse, Danaid jar and other parts of the *Treatise* assumed implicitly that output was constant and that saving did not depend on income. In dating the formulation of Keynes' theory of a monetary economy between his 1932 and 1933 lectures, rather than between his two sets of lectures in 1932, the analysis of the lecture notes in this chapter agrees with Patinkin's review of Keynes' *Collected Writings*, rather than with Kahn's Mattioli Lectures.[124] While earlier studies have concentrated on the multiplier theory of effective demand, I would place equal stress on the development of Keynes' explanation of how involuntary unemployment can exist in a monetary economy and how, as a result, changes in aggregate demand can affect real output.

NOTES

1. Keynes (1979), xxix, 10.
2. Ohlin (1974), 891.
3. Ohlin, in Patinkin and Leith (1978), 162.
4. See Patinkin and Leith (1978) and Moggridge (1973). An earlier passing reference to surviving lecture notes in Tarshis (1948), 262, was not noticed by the economics profession.
5. Robbins (1971), 152–3.
6. Muggeridge (1940), 185–6.
7. Keynes (1931), 286.
8. Muggeridge (1940), 227. Lloyd George had a final chance for high office when Churchill offered him a place in the War Cabinet in July 1940 and the ambassadorship in Washington that December, but Lloyd George, then seventy-seven years old, had to decline, as Churchill perhaps expected.

9. E. Johnson, in E. Johnson and H. Johnson (1978), 22; Nicolson (1966), 71–2; Keynes (1981), xx, 312–15, 473–6, 482–3.
10. Nicolson (1966), 73–4.
11. Keynes (1973), xiii, 342.
12. Kahn (1984), 113.
13. Klein (1947), 38–40.
14. Hicks (1967), 197. Cf. Mehta (1983), 156.
15. Patinkin (1982), 81 and 81n.
16. Kahn (1931), 188; Patinkin (1982), 198; Cain (1979), 110–11.
17. Samuelson, in Patinkin and Leith (1978), 83; Patinkin (1982), 30–1; Hawtrey, in Keynes (1973), xiii, 150–2.
18. Copland, in Gayer (1937), 407–9.
19. A. Robinson, in Patinkin and Leith (1978), 25.
20. *Ibid.*, 28.
21. *Ibid.*, 30; cf. H. Johnson, in E. Johnson and H. Johnson (1978), 173, and A. F. W. Plumptre in M. Keynes (1975), 250. Similarly, Gerald Shove, a University Lecturer, contributed to economic discussion primarily through published criticisms.
22. Keynes (1979), xxix, 5; Tarshis, in Patinkin and Leith (1978), 50.
23. Keynes (1973), xiii, 118.
24. Keynes (1979), xxix, 4–6; the assumption of constant output is noted at p. 5; Milgate (1983), 190n.
25. Presley (1979), 82–90; Anyadike-Danes (1985).
26. Keynes (1973), xiii, 271–321; Keynes (1979), xxix, ch. 2.
27. Keynes (1979), xxix, 36, notes for Keynes' lecture on 25 April, 1932.
28. Hicks (1946), 158–62; Hines (1971), 47–50. Keynes was not persuaded when Hicks first made this point in his review of Keynes (1936).
29. H. Johnson, in E. Johnson and H. Johnson (1978), 139.
30. A. Robinson, in M. Keynes (1975), 14.
31. Keynes (1973), xiii, 338.
32. A. Robinson, in Lekachman (1964), 55. Robertson attended one meeting of the 'Circus': J. Robinson (1978), xiv.
33. Harrod (1951), 433; Winch (1969), 378.
34. Plumptre, in M. Keynes (1975); Harcourt (1981).
35. Keynes (1973), xiii, 338n.
36. See the issue of *New Left Review* (1978) in honour of Sraffa's eightieth birthday.
37. See the *Economic Journal* (1972) issue in honour of Sir Austin Robinson. Austin Robinson was a University Lecturer by 1931, but Kahn then held only a College position, at King's. Kahn, in Patinkin and Leith (1978), 147.
38. Hall (1982), 78–9.
39. Robertson (1931), 408–9.
40. Keynes (1973), xiii, 339. See I Kings 17 on the widow's cruse.
41. A. Robinson, in Patinkin and Leith (1978), 34; J. Robinson (1978), xii–xiii; Kahn (1984), 106–7.
42. Kahn (1984), 109.
43. Hawtrey, in Keynes (1973), xiii, 151–2.

44. Tarshis (1976), 1285. Tarshis also identified 'the kernel of the multiplier' in Hawtrey, in Keynes (1973), XIII, 157. See Keynes (1973), XIII, 139–49, for Keynes' initial response to Hawtrey.
45. Keynes (1979), XXIX, 10–11. See E. Davis (1980).
46. Keynes (1979), XXIX, 11.
47. *Ibid.*, 12.
48. Keynes (1973), XIII, 374.
49. *Ibid.*, 375.
50. Klein (1947), 38–40.
51. Keynes (1973), XIII, 268; J. Robinson (1980), I, ix.
52. J. Robinson (1933a), 82.
53. Keynes (1973), XIII, 270.
54. Keynes (1930), I, 305.
55. Kahn to Patinkin, 19 March, 1974, in Patinkin and Leith (1978), 147.
56. Kahn (1933), reprinted in Kahn (1972).
57. Rotheim (1981), 572.
58. Kahn (1984), 108; cf. Kahn (1985), 47–8.
59. Mehta (1983), 156. Cf. Mehta (1979), ch. 5, and Minoguchi (1981).
60. Keynes (1930), I, 160–1. Cf. Mehta (1983), 155.
61. Minoguchi (1983), 159.
62. Cain (1979).
63. Pribram, in Q. Wright (1931), 129–33, 150.
64. Kahn (1984), 109.
65. Keynes, in Q. Wright (1931), 12; Keynes (1973), XIII, 349.
66. Keynes, in Q. Wright (1931), 20; Keynes (1973), XIII, 354.
67. Keynes, in Q. Wright (1931), 22; Keynes (1973), XIII, 355.
68. Keynes, in Q. Wright (1931), 13; Keynes (1973), XIII, 350.
69. Keynes, in Q. Wright (1931), 23–4; Keynes (1973), XIII, 356.
70. Kahn, in Harcourt (1985), 59–60.
71. Harrod (1951), 146.
72. *Ibid.*, 149–50.
73. *Ibid.*, 286–7, 387. Keynes became Second Bursar of King's College, with a stipend of £100 a year, in November 1920, and rose to be First Bursar in 1925.
74. Plumptre, in M. Keynes (1975), 248–9. On one Tuesday evening each month in the 1920s, Keynes dined at the Café Royal in London with the Tuesday Club, a group formed in 1917 by Keynes, Basil Blackett and C. T. Falk, all then serving in A Division of the Treasury, to discuss questions of currency and finance. Harrod (1951), 220, 323.
75. Harrod (1951), 325; Keynes (1979), XXIX, 4; Plumptre, in M. Keynes (1975), 252.
76. Galbraith (1981), 349.
77. Bryce's paper appears in Patinkin and Leith (1978), Appendix I, and in Keynes (1979), XXIX.
78. Galbraith (1981), 90.
79. Keynes (1939); Tarshis (1939). See also Harcourt (1981).
80. E. A. G. Robinson, in Harcourt (1985), 62, where Bryce's notes are incorrectly stated to be for 1931–3.

81. Milgate (1983), 187.
82. Smith (1978).
83. Keynes (1979), xxix, 35–8.
84. The 'manifesto' is in Keynes (1979), xxix, 42–5. The covering letter for it is in Keynes (1973), xiii, 376.
85. Keynes (1979), xxix, 40–1.
86. *Ibid.*, 39.
87. *Ibid.*, 42–3.
88. *Ibid.*, 43. On p. 47, Joan Robinson refers to elasticity of supply, but does not make any formal use of the supply curve.
89. J. Robinson (1978), 2–3.
90. *Ibid.*, xv.
91. Harcourt (1985), 60.
92. Tarshis notes, 10 October, 1932. Bryce notes: 'Much new matter – change of title indicates change of attitude / important things not directly money – / important emphasis should be on production.' This opening statement is not in Keynes' notes, which are labelled as sections II and III. Keynes (1979), xxix, 50.
93. Bryce notes, 10 October, 1932. See Keynes (1979), xxix, 49–50, for two draft tables of contents from 1932.
94. Tarshis notes, 10 October, 1932.
95. Bryce notes, 10 October, 1932.
96. Tarshis notes, 10 October, 1932.
97. Bryce notes, 21 November, 1932. Tarshis' notes show that I is equal to I' the volume of output of investment goods, multiplied by P_2, the price of capital assets.
98. Tarshis notes, 12 November, 1932.
99. *Ibid.*, Bryce's notes omit ΔO from this passage, and add parenthetically 'this is a truism'.
100. *Ibid.*
101. Keynes (1979), xxix, 57–61; Patinkin (1980), 6.
102. J. Robinson (1962), 66, 88–9. See Keynes (1981), xx, 513–14, for Keynes' comments to Beveridge: 'apart from Chapter 6 ... this scarcely seems to me a grown-up discussion of the matters at issue'.
103. Robbins (1971), 155–6.
104. Tarshis notes, 28 November, 1932.
105. J. Robinson (1933b), as reprinted in J. Robinson (1978), 14, 16; Keynes (1930), i, 139.
106. *Ibid.*, 17; Keynes (1930), i, 178.
107. Cain (1979), 116.
108. Promotional letter from Harcourt, Brace and Company enclosed with review copy of Keynes (1933).
109. Keynes (1933), 10. Also in Keynes (1972), ix.
110. Keynes (1933), 19–24; Keynes (1981), xx, 544–53.
111. Keynes (1973), xiii, 408–11. Also reprinted in the *Nebraska Journal of Economics and Business* (1963), 7–9.
112. Tarshis notes, 16 October, 1933. 'Momentary position' is from Bryce notes, in place of 'monetary position' assumed in Keynes (1930) accord-

ing to Tarshis notes. Fallgatter did not attend the first lecture. Bryce, Salant and Tarshis present the two classical postulates with only trivial differences in wording.

113. This definition appears in exactly the same form in the Bryce, Salant and Tarshis notes.
114. Salant notes, 16 October, 1933 (Salant's emphasis).
115. Tarshis notes, 16 October, 1933 (Bryce's notes give 1927 instead of 1932). Bodkin (1966), 124–5.
116. Tarshis notes, 23 October, 1933; Pigou (1933), 112.
117. Bryce notes, 23 October, 1933. Salant notes: 'Struggle over money wages is one over *distribution* of real wage, not its size.' Keynes (1930), I, 271.
118. Fallgatter notes, 23 October, 1933.
119. Keynes (1930), I, 159.
120. Bryce, Fallgatter, Salant and Tarshis notes, 20 November, 1933; Keynes (1936), 210. Tarshis attributes this classical view to Robertson.
121. Bryce, Fallgatter, Salant and Tarshis notes, 27 November, 1933. Fallgatter records Kahn's name as 'Mr Carns'.
122. Kahn (1984), 69.
123. Keynes (1981), xx, 38, 326, 403. Keynes was also chairman of the Economic Advisory Council's Committee on the Economic Outlook, March to May 1930.
124. Keynes (1973), xIII, 342; Kahn (1984), 113; Patinkin (1976), ch. 8. While Patinkin argues that Keynes' 1933 lectures show Keynes' belated recognition that Kahn's multiplier analysis was logically equivalent to the saving function and the theory of effective demand, Warming (1932) and Cain (1979) point to the absence of a saving function from Kahn (1931).

6 The general theory of employment

Keynes changed the title of his lectures for the Michaelmas Term of 1934 to 'The General Theory of Employment', after lecturing on 'The Monetary Theory of Production' for two years. He made a similar change in the working title of drafts for his book-in-progress. Despite the change in title, Keynes retained the key elements of his 1933 lectures. In the first two lectures, Keynes again explained why he accepted the first classical postulate, that the real wage is equal to the marginal product of labour, but not the second postulate, that the utility of the wage just equals the marginal disutility of labour (that is, that the economy is on the labour supply curve), and again criticized Pigou for assuming that the economy behaved as though workers could bargain directly for real wages. The propensity to save and the multiplier was presented in a very similar manner to that of 1933, as was liquidity preference, the portfolio approach to the demand for money, which was covered in the final lecture on 3 December. The one novelty promised in Keynes' opening lecture was his 26 November lecture on the marginal efficiency of capital and the rate of investment. In February 1935, Keynes travelled to Oxford to address the economists there on the marginal efficiency of capital and the rate of interest.[1] By that time, the *General Theory* was largely in its final form. Interest in what Keynes was doing went much further than just Roy Harrod and his colleagues at Oxford. James Earley, who had been Marvin Fallgatter's room-mate as an undergraduate at Antioch Collsee, used Fallgatter's notes on Keynes' 1933 lectures as the basis for seminars at the University of Wisconsin in June and December 1935, rather as Adam Smith's lectures had been used by one of his students as the basis of university lectures in Moscow before the publication of *The Wealth of Nations*.[2] Joseph

Schumpeter of Harvard visited Cambridge each summer in the early and middle 1930s, on his way between Harvard and Austria, to keep informed on developments in Cambridge monetary economics.[3]

REAL WAGES IN A MONETARY ECONOMY

In his 1933 and 1934 lectures, and in the *General Theory*, Keynes opened his attack on what he called classical economics by denying that labour could adjust its real wage rate to eliminate involuntary unemployment and clear the labour market by bargaining for money wages. In two surviving draft chapters written in late 1933, but only discovered in 1976, on 'The Distinction Between a Co-operative Economy and an Entrepreneur Economy' and 'The Characteristics of an Entrepreneur Economy', Keynes characterized classical economics as the theory of a co-operative economy, in which factors of production contracted for fixed shares of output. In an entrepreneur economy, entrepreneurs hired factors for fixed nominal rates, making their offers on the basis of their expected money proceeds from sale of output.[4] Keynes argued that real wages would not adjust to clear the labour market in the wake of a large downward nominal shock. While in the *Tract*, Keynes had held that nominal interest rates adapted only slowly to changes in the rate of inflation because of the lingering effects of a century of price stability, his case against real wage adjustment in a monetary economy presented in the 1930s did not rest on money illusion.

Since Keynes accepted the first classical postulate, that profit-maximizing competitive firms wish to hire labour until the real wage is equal to the marginal net product of labour and that the economy is on the demand curve for labour, he believed that an increase in employment must be accompanied by a decrease in the real wage rate. This was because, for a given technology and capital stock, the marginal product of labour would be a decreasing function of the level of employment. Thus a drop in the price level, due to an aggregate demand shock such as a decrease in the rate of investment, would cause unemployment unless the money wage rate dropped by the same proportion. In Chapter 2 of the *General Theory*, as in his lectures and in a passage of the *Treatise*, Keynes argued that resistance by workers to reductions in nominal wage rates was rational, and did not follow from any confusion of real and nominal wages.

Wage contracts expired at different times, and were of varying length, so that changes in money wage rates would alter workers' relative wages, over which they could quite rationally have preferences. A change in the price level, resulting from a shift in aggregate demand, would affect the real value of all nominal incomes at the same time and by the same proportion. Another reason for resisting nominal wage reduction could be a recognition by workers of the futility of that measure. In Chapter 19 of the *General Theory*, on 'Changes in Money-Wages', as in his lectures, Keynes explained that reductions in nominal wages could affect prices so that real wages and employment would not be altered.

In the *Treatise*, reductions in firms' wage-bills and other costs, the earnings of the factors of production, E, would reduce firms' receipts by exactly the same amount, leaving profits or losses, the difference between investment and saving, unchanged. Profits, as a determinant of investment, were the driving force of the *Treatise*'s model, so altering E would matter only if the reduced transactions demand for money lowered the rate of interest. Keynes assumed in the *Treatise*, however, that the central bank controlled the market rate of interest. The analysis in Chapter 19 of the *General Theory* and in the lectures was a different one. There was a supply curve for output as a whole corresponding to each money wage rate. This was because, for a given money wage rate, each price level represented a different real wage rate and hence a different volume of employment which firms wished to provide. A reduction in the money wage rate shifts this upward-sloping aggregated supply curve downward, because, for a lower money wage, the same real wage and hence the same level of employment would correspond to a lower price level. Such a shift of the aggregate supply curve would increase equilibrium output only to the extent that it was a movement along a downward-sloping aggregate demand curve. If the aggregate demand curve was vertical, that is, if the real volume of spending was independent of the price level, then the price level would fall by as much as the money wage rate, and neither output nor employment would be stimulated.

For a closed economy, without international trade, the aggregate demand curve slopes downward because the price level affects the demand for nominal money balances (liquidity preference). A lower price level means that a given nominal money supply is a larger real quantity of money, which Keynes measured in wage-units (deflating nominal quantities by the money wage rate, rather than by the price level). For the public to continue to desire to hold the existing nominal quantity of money when the price level is lower, the nominal interest rate (the opportunity cost of holding money) must also be lower. A lower rate of interest is equivalent to a higher price of securities, since the market price of securities is determined by discounting the expected flow of earnings from those securities. The higher price of capital goods (lower rate of interest) causes a higher rate of investment, which, with the induced increase in consumption resulting from the increased investment, is why a larger volume of output is demanded at a lower price level. 'It is, therefore, on the effect of a falling wage- and price-level on the demand for money that those who believe in the self-adjusting quality of the economic system must rest the weight of their argument; though I am not aware that they have done so.'[5] Edwin Cannan, for example, had discussed money wage reduction as a cure for unemployment in his Presidential address on 'The Demand for Labour' (1932) without bringing in money demand, the interest rate or investment.

If the aggregate demand curve was vertical, a reduction in the money wage rate would not reduce the real wage rate or unemployment, but an expansionary shift of the aggregate demand curve would do so. The aggregate demand curve would be vertical if either investment was not sensitive to the rate of interest, or the interest rate had been driven down to a minimum level set by an interest-elastic demand for money. The case for the interest-inelasticity of investment was made by Jan Tinbergen on the basis of his pioneering econometric model of the United States economy, *Statistical Testing of Business Cycle Theories* (1939), and on the basis of questionnaires and interviews of entrepreneurs by J. F. Ebersole in the *Harvard Business Review* (1938) and members of the Oxford Economic Research Group in the first issue of the *Oxford Economic Papers* (1938). This view conflicts with Keynes' view that investment is determined by equating the interest rate to the marginal efficiency of capital, and it appears that the empirical results were an artefact of the very low, stable nominal interest rates of the 1930s. Keynes was sceptical of Tinbergen's approach, and the lead article presenting the Oxford results was by Sir Hubert Henderson, who was by then very much out of sympathy with Keynes. One of the discussants of Lord Kahn's Mattioli Lectures identified 'regarding investment as exogenous when determining the level of income' as one of two distinctive features of later 'Cambridge Keynesian thinking',[6] but there is no justification for attributing this view to Keynes himself.

Keynes' argument rested instead on the existence of a minimum nominal rate of interest. Dennis Robertson derided liquidity preference and the liquidity trap in his lectures as 'a College Bursar's theory of the interest rate', where the current market rate of interest was determined by expectations of what the rate of interest would be in the future, with interest rates, in Robertson's phrase, being held up by their own bootstraps. If the interest rate was above its expected level, and so was expected to fall and the price of bonds to rise, wealth-owners would buy bonds for the expected capital gain, driving the interest rate down to its expected level. Any interest rate expectation would thus be self-fulfilling. However, Keynes' liquidity trap, in which the demand for money is infinitely interest-elastic, so that any increase in the real quantity of money would be held without need for any change in the interest rate, did not depend simply on unexplained expectations about interest rates. As Keynes explained in his lecture on 31 October, 1932, the own-rate of interest on money is zero. Since money can be used as a medium of exchange, while securities cannot, wealth-holders would be willing to hold all of their portfolios as money if the nominal return on bonds dropped as low as that on money. Consequently, since money is not costly to store, the nominal interest rate will not drop below zero. The minimum interest rate would be slightly above zero, because of transactions costs of buying and selling bonds, and because of a risk premium against possible capital losses, since there would be some probability of an increase in the nominal interest rate, which would lower securities prices.

The classical case, as worked out by Keynes, was based on a comparison of two economies with the same nominal quantity of money and different price levels. Comparing alternative price levels is not the same, however, as examining the effect of a falling price level. If the money wage rate, and thus the aggregate supply curve, were shifting in response to a sufficiently large deflationary shock, the rate of money wage and price deflation could be large enough to bring the economy to the minimum nominal rate of interest, beyond which further price deflation would simply raise the real rate of interest and discourage investment. As noted in Chapter 1, Keynes' *Tract on Monetary Reform* explained the British recession of 1921 as due to the high real interest rate resulting from a rate of deflation which he put at over 30 per cent a year, when the nominal interest rate could not be negative.[7] The Depression presented similar problems: from 1929 to 1932 wholesale price indices fell by 32 per cent in Britain and the United States, and by 29 per cent in France,[8] rates of deflation at which even very low nominal interest rates implied high real rates.

When Britain floated the pound sterling in September 1931, Keynes promptly withdrew his tariff proposal, urging in a letter to *The Times*, followed by an article in the *Sunday Express* and a memorandum for the Treasury, that monetary expansion to lower interest rates was what the country needed. A year later, after the Bank Rate had been cut from 6 per cent to 2 per cent and the interest rate on savings deposits had fallen to $\frac{1}{2}$ per cent per annum, Keynes no longer had confidence in unaided monetary policy, because there was no further scope for reduction of the nominal interest rate. In his lecture on 28 November, 1932 Keynes expressed the view that Britain had reached a liquidity trap at the minimum nominal interest rate, since the opportunity cost of holding currency or chequing account balances instead of savings deposits was down to $\frac{1}{2}$ per cent a year. In such a liquidity trap, the aggregate demand curve would be vertical, and neither expansion of the nominal quantity of money nor a reduction of money wage rates could stimulate employment.

Keynes also used the liquidity trap to question the consistency of the classical model. If the market-clearing real wage rate was achieved regardless of the price level, as when the two classical postulates both held, the aggregate supply curve would be vertical. If the aggregate demand curve was also vertical because of a liquidity trap, either the supply and demand curves would not intersect at any price level, or else they would coincide at every price level, with the price level being indeterminate in either case. Pigou offered a refutation of this criticism in his paper on 'The Classical Stationary State' in the *Economic Journal* (1943). He argued that a lower price level, by increasing the real quantity of money, would increase private wealth and so stimulate consumption. The aggregate demand curve would thus slope downwards even if there was a liquidity trap. There would be a unique, stable intersection between aggregate supply and aggregate demand, and money wage reductions, by shifting the aggregate supply curve along a downward-sloping aggregate demand curve, could increase real output. In a two-page note the following year, Michal Kalecki pointed out that the bulk of bank money is matched by bank loans, and should not be considered part of net private wealth. An increase in the value of inside nominal debt would make lenders wealthier by the same amount that borrowers became poorer. Pigou's real balance effect applied only to gold and the liabilities of the central bank, a tiny fraction of the obligations denominated in terms of money. In a letter to Keynes about this note, Kalecki said that the existence of a national debt was irrelevant to the real balance effect if the interest on the debt was paid out of taxes. Keynes, writing to Kalecki on 8 March 1944, agreed that government bonds are not net private wealth: 'Assuming that interest is paid on this out of taxation, it cannot affect the wealth of the community one way or another. Thus, it seems to me that Pigou is in reality depending entirely on the increase in the value of gold. The whole thing, however, is really too fantastic for words and scarcely worth discussing.'[9]

In the Harris Foundation round-table discussions in Chicago in June 1931, Keynes remarked that an unanticipated deflation would redistribute wealth from borrowers to rentiers, who would save more and spend less than the borrowers would with an equal volume of resources.[10] In Chapter 19 of the *General Theory*, he returned to this point to argue that deflation of prices and money wages would redistribute real income from wage-earners and entrepreneurs with high propensities to consume to rentiers and others with lower propensities to consume.[11] Since the volume of inside debt and contracts in nominal terms would far exceed the quantity of gold and central bank liabilities, this distributional effect on consumption could swamp Pigou's real balance effect.

While the real balance analysis of Pigou did not undermine Keynes' treatment of real and nominal wages, and of how the real wage could fail to clear the labour market in a monetary economy, two problems with this part of Keynes' theory did arise soon after publication of the *General Theory*. The first was that money wage rates could start to rise before full employment was reached, particularly since, due to bottlenecks, some sectors or regions would reach full employment before the economy as a whole did. This concern can be seen in Keynes' articles in *The Times* early in 1937,[12] after the British unemployment rate had declined from a peak of 22 per cent to a still substantial 12 per cent. Even with that much remaining unemployment, Keynes worried that further expansion of government spending, for example for defence purposes, might be inflationary. Already in 1935, Austin Robinson had recommended dealing with unemployment in depressed areas by means of selective public works and subsidies, justified on the basis of a regional income multiplier, rather than by nation-wide expansion of aggregate demand.[13]

Secondly, evidence was published which appeared to contradict the first classical postulate, accepted by Keynes, that employment and the real wage rate would be inversely related. John Dunlop, writing a doctoral dissertation for the University of California at Berkeley while spending a year at Trinity College, Cambridge, tested Keynes' hypothesis that money wages and real wages are negatively correlated over the trade cycle, using British data from 1860 to 1937, and rejected it, summarizing his results in the *Economic Journal* in 1938. Lorie Tarshis, writing a Cambridge doctoral dissertation while teaching at Tufts in Massachusetts, tested and rejected Keynes' hypothesis for United States monthly wage data from 1932 to 1938. Tarshis' article appeared in the *Economic Journal* in March 1939, along with an article by Keynes discussing and accepting the Dunlop and Tarshis results. As Dunlop pointed out, Keynes' hypothesis rested not only on a negative slope for the labour demand curve, but also on an implicit assumption that money wage changes reflect trade union strength, which in turn depends on the level of employment. This second assumption was rejected, while the only direct testing of the relationship between real wages and employment in this exchange was in a postscript to Tarshis' paper, where he found a significant negative relation, with a correlation coefficient of -0.64.[14]

Mark Casson, reviewing the literature, including his own econometric work and that of Hatton on interwar Britain, concluded that 'All of the studies discussed here thus support the view that there is an inverse relation between employment and the real wage.... It is one of the unfortunate results of the Keynesian revolution that such an obvious relationship should have been questioned, when the evidence in its favour is so very strong.'[15] However, Hatton and Seaton, in a later paper, found little support for a statistically significant inverse relation between real wages and employment in twenty-one British industries for 1921–38. They also point out that, while Casson's cross-section study across British industries between the wars yielded the expected signs on variables, the real wage was only barely significant for 1924–35 but not significant for 1924–30 or 1930–5. While the real wage had negative coefficients in Casson's time-series equations for employment in five major industries, it was significant in only two of the five cases,[16] so that Casson's weak empirical results do not support his strong conclusions. While the statistical significance of the negative relation between employment and real wages is still in doubt, there are no grounds for flat statements that 'Over the trade cycle real wages are normally *positively* correlated with output and employment'.[17]

KEYNES AND THE PRE-KEYNESIANS ON REAL WAGES IN A MONETARY ECONOMY

Keynes sharply criticized Pigou and other classical economists for reasoning in real terms in a monetary economy, and assuming that unemployment was due, at least in theory, to a refusal by workers to accept a market-clearing real wage. In addition to his comments in his lectures and in Chapter 2 of the *General Theory* on 'The Postulates of the Classical Economics', Keynes appended a critique of Pigou's *Theory of Unemployment* to Chapter 19. Mark Casson denies that such criticism can validly be applied to the group he calls the Pre-Keynesian theorists of unemployment, a group consisting of the incumbents of three chairs of economics, A. C. Pigou at Cambridge, Henry Clay in Manchester, and Edwin Cannan in London:

> To someone who has not read Pre-Keynesian theory, Keynes' description of his departure from the 'classical' theory of the labour market (Keynes, 1936, ch. 2) can appear original and perceptive. To someone who has read Pre-Keynesian theory this description is simply a mixture of bad scholarship and technically incompetent theorizing.[18]

Casson explicitly excludes Pigou's major work on the subject from his defence:

> There is no standard work epitomizing Pre-Keynesian theory. Pigou was the person best equipped to write such a book, but instead he wrote *The Theory of Unemployment* (1933) – a taxonomy of the subject which makes the reader wonder how anyone could write anything so tedious and abstract in the midst of an economic crisis.[19]

Casson does not mention Cannan's Presidential address to the Royal Economic Society on 'The Demand for Labour' (1932), in which Cannan blamed unemployment on excessive wage demands and insisted that it would vanish as unemployment itself eventually forced down money wage rates. Instead, Casson reconstructs Cannan's theory of unemployment from a single book review.[20] It does not seem obviously unscholarly for Keynes to have read the principal theoretical works of Cannan and Pigou on unemployment when considering their views on the subject. Nor is it apparent that Keynes' account of classical theory constitutes incompetent theorizing, since it was the same as the following account given by Casson:

> What the Pre-Keynesians denied was that money illusion could be exploited in the long-run to reduce the real wage. They believed that if there were persistent inflation, trade unions would seek to link money wage settlements to the price level, and so would effectively stipulate for a real wage.
>
> Given this view, the logic of the Pre-Keynesian position is impeccable. Because the real wage is fixed, the supply of real output is fixed also, and because the supply of output is fixed, public expenditure will crowd out private expenditure in the product market. It is a modern fallacy that unemployment is incompatible with pure crowding out. Keynesians are correct to assert that pure crowding out will not occur with unemployment caused by a too high money wage, but likewise the Pre-Keynesians were correct to assert that pure crowding out would occur with unemployment caused by a too high real wage.[21]

In the Pre-Keynesian view, all unemployment is voluntary in Keynes' sense, because it is due to workers demanding a high real wage. Trade unions are able to stipulate for a particular real wage, so that unemployment does not result from problems of bargaining in nominal terms in the face of demand shocks. Unemployment benefits increase unemployment by strengthening the bargaining position of trade unions, as well as by lengthening the average duration of job-search. Just as Keynes claimed they did, the Pre-Keynesians, according to Casson, held that workers could negotiate for the market-clearing real wage, and that the labour market would clear, with all unemployment voluntary (in Keynes' sense).

THE THEORY OF EFFECTIVE DEMAND

In his lecture on 4 December, 1933, Keynes summarized his monetary theory of production in these equations:

$$M = f(W, p) \qquad \text{money supply} = \text{liquidity preference}$$
$$C = \phi_1(W, Y) \qquad \text{consumption function}$$
$$I = \phi_2(W, p) \qquad \text{investment function}$$
$$Y = C + I \qquad \text{national income.}$$

Keynes defined W, in that lecture, as 'state of news'.[22] Liquidity preference and the marginal efficiency of capital remained sensitive to the state of news in Keynes' later writings, so that they responded to shifts in long-period expectations, but the consumption function became dependent on the level of income alone. Thus, while volatile expectations could cause fluctuations in the level of effective demand by changing investment, the multiplier for fiscal policy to offset these fluctuations, derived from the marginal propensity to consume, would remain stable.

Keynes' consumption function, depending on the level of current income, differed from the analysis of consumption and saving given by Irving Fisher in *The Rate of Interest* (1907), later revised as *The Theory of Interest* (1930). Fisher assumed the existence of perfect credit markets, in which individuals could borrow against their anticipated future earnings at the same interest rate which they would receive on their savings. The individual would maximize utility from present and future consumption subject to a budget constraint that the present discounted value of lifetime consumption did not exceed the present discounted value of lifetime expected income. The individual would do this by allocating consumption across time until his or her marginal rate of substitution between current and future consumption was the one appropriate to the market rate of interest. The conclusion drawn from this analysis by Fisher's classical contemporaries was that saving and consumption depend on the interest rate. The conclusion that should have been drawn, and which after the Second World War was embodied in Milton Friedman's permanent income theory of consumption and Franco Modigliani's life cycle model of consumption, was that, given perfect credit markets, the relevant budget constraint for any year's consumption is not that year's income, but rather the individual's wealth (including human capital): the present value of expected income. In that case, the marginal propensity to consume out of any change in income which was perceived to be only temporary would be small, and the multiplier would be close to one.

Robert Clower has argued that consumption would be linked to current income when there is involuntary unemployment, so that workers are quantity-constrained in the amount of labour which they can sell at the prevailing wage rate. Workers first decide how much labour to offer on the basis of the prevailing wage rate and the prices of goods and services, but their actual consumption expenditure will depend on their realized proceeds from the sale of their labour services. That is, how much a worker spends on consumption will depend on whether or not he or she was able to find a job at the going wage.[23] Imperfection of credit markets could also link consumption to current income. If the interest rate for borrowing against expected future earnings exceeded the interest rate received on savings, for instance because of a risk premium, there could be individuals who would borrow against future earnings for current consumption if they could do so at an interest rate as low as that they would get on savings. Such individuals would consume a significant fraction of any increase in their current income. This would provide a justification for Keynes' consumption function and multiplier analysis. If the interest rates on borrowing and lending by consumers differ sufficiently, a substantial number of individuals could have their current consumption constrained by their current income. If there were many such income-constrained consumers, the aggregate consumption function would depend on current income (as well as on wealth and interest rates).

J. Ronnie Davis, after showing that Keynes was not the only economist to advocate public works, argues convincingly that two American economists, John Maurice Clark of Columbia and Paul Douglas of Chicago, used the multiplier theory of effective demand before the publication of the *General Theory*. Clark presented the multiplier theory in a paper on 'Cumulative Effects of Changes in Aggregate Spending as Illustrated by Public Works' to a joint session of the American Economic Association and American Statistical Association in Chicago in December 1934. The paper appeared in the *American Economic Review* the following March, and then as a chapter in Clark's *Economics of Planning Public Works* (1935) for the National Planning Boards of the Federal Emergency Administration of Public Works. There is only one problem with accepting Clark as an independent source of the theory of effective demand and as proof that Keynes only wrote what was generally known to the economics profession: Clark calls the multiplier 'The Kahn-Keynes Approach', which is the heading of a section of his paper, and cites Keynes' *Means to Prosperity* and Kahn's papers on 'The Relation of Home Investment to Unemployment' and 'Public Works and Inflation'.[24] Clark's *Strategic Factors in Business Cycles* (1934), written before he read Kahn's articles, concentrated on the accelerator theory of net investment, of which Clark had been, in 1917, one of several independent discoverers. This book does mention that if a reduction in income is followed by a smaller reduction in expenditure, the infinite series of changes in expenditure would add to a finite number, but Clark makes no mention of what leakages could account for spending changing by less than income, and the multiplier calculations are in a footnote added at the last moment after reading Kahn's 'Public Works and Inflation'.[25] Paul Douglas, a visitor to Keynes' Political Economy Club, derived the multiplier discussion in his *Controlling Depressions* (1935) explicitly from Keynes' pamphlet and the two Kahn articles, and cited the *Treatise* on an excess of saving over investment as a cause of depression.[26] The writings of Keynes and Kahn had influence even before the publication of the *General Theory*.

THE MARGINAL EFFICIENCY OF CAPITAL AND THE RATE OF INVESTMENT

Keynes' theory of investment was the last part of the *General Theory* to reach its final form, appearing in his 1934 lectures. This theory has had a bad press over the years. Dale Jorgenson dismissed Keynes as naive for relating the marginal efficiency of capital to the flow rate of investment, instead of to the capital stock. Elizabeth and Harry Johnson held that Keynes disguised a conventional treatment of the marginal productivity of capital by calling it the marginal efficiency of capital, but added parenthetically that 'As subsequent theorists have frequently rediscovered, however, he did have a scientifically useful theory of the rate of investment, carried over from the *Treatise*, in which that rate is determined by the supply response of new capital goods set by a broad variant of liquidity preference'.[27]

A recent and thorough rediscovery of the *Treatise*'s theory of investment is by Stephen LeRoy, who shows the substantial overlap between the theories of investment of the *Treatise* and the *General Theory*. According to LeRoy, 'Keynes's model does not involve theoretical error, and Keynes's statement of the model is precise and complete. The general failure of the profession to understand what Keynes had done is due primarily to the difficulty of the material; Keynes was presenting the first analysis of temporary general equilibrium under a two-sector technology with nonshiftable capital.' LeRoy, and Christopher Bliss, pointed to Chapters 19 and 20 of the

General Theory, where, as in Hicks' 'Mr Keynes and the Classics', output of capital goods and of consumer goods are each functions only of employment in that sector, which is true only if capital cannot be shifted between sectors after being created and installed. LeRoy also noted Keynes' statement in a letter to Hawtrey that the marginal efficiency of capital for the economy as a whole was the highest of the sectoral marginal efficiencies, not an average.[28] Keynes spoke in his lectures of the stream of expected quasi-rents in a sector, using Marshall's term for the profits resulting from a temporary shortage of capital assets in a sector.

Keynes defined the marginal efficiencies of capital as the internal rates of return equating the present value of the stream of expected quasi-rents to the supply price of new capital:

> I define the marginal efficiency of capital as being equal to the rate of discount which would make the present value of the series of annuities given by the returns expected from the capital asset during its life just equal to its supply price. This gives us the marginal efficiencies of particular types of capital assets.[29]

In his lecture on 26 November, 1934, Keynes criticized Irving Fisher for having the rate of return over costs, Fisher's equivalent to the marginal efficiency of capital, equate the present value of the stream of expected earnings to the demand price of capital, rather than the supply price. Keynes condemned this as a confusion of the rate of interest with the marginal efficiency of capital, and his cry of protest appears in Bryce's notes for that day underlined and separated by blank lines from the preceding and following sentences: '*Fisher's solution is just nonsense.*'[30]

According to LeRoy, the marginal efficiency of capital schedule reflects portfolio preferences and the conditions of supply of new capital goods, so that its slope is determined by the elasticity of substitution between capital and labour in capital-producing firms, not capital-using firms. In the *General Theory*, bonds and capital are treated as close substitutes, so that the price of such securities will be such as to induce the public to hold the existing volumes of securities and money. Firms in the capital goods sector then maximize profits by producing capital goods until their marginal cost equals the price of capital assets (assuming perfect competition), so that it is the flow rate of investment which is determined, not the stock of capital. In Keynes' words:

> Upon what does the demand price of capital goods depend? It depends on *two* things – on the estimated net prospective yield from fixed capital, . . . measured in money, and the rate of interest at which this future yield is capitalized.[31]

> At a scale of new investment at which the marginal cost of producing [a new investment good] is equal to its demand price . . . we have a position of equilibrium.[32]

The two points on which the *General Theory*'s theory of investment differed in substance, rather than exposition, from the *Treatise*, were the recognition that the price of newly produced capital goods must coincide with the greater of the two sectoral prices of existing capital, and the derivation of an upward-sloping supply curve for capital goods in the short period, given a specified money wage rate and, since the sector's capital stock was held constant in the short period, a decreasing marginal product of labour.[33]

Keynes felt that the marginal physical product of capital 'involves difficulties as to the definition of the physical unit of capital, which I believe to be both insoluble and unnecessary'.[34] His wariness of the problems of defining a unit of capital might well be due to the issues raised in Gerald Shove's biting 1933 *Economic Journal* review of John Hicks' *Theory of Wages* (1932), an attack on the use of the marginal productivity of capital in distribution theory so devastating that Hicks refused to reprint the book for thirty years, and then reprinted Shove's review as an appendix. Keynes avoided this by using the marginal efficiency of capital, which depended on costs of producing new capital goods, rather than on the marginal product of capital. He did not, however, manage to avoid the pitfalls of double-switching which Fisher had shown in 1907 to vitiate Böhm-Bawerk's average period of production, since calculations of Keynes' marginal efficiency of capital and Fisher's rate of return over costs could have multiple roots.[35]

Keynes thus had a model, based on an earlier treatment in the *Treatise*, which derived the flow rate of investment from portfolio balance and supply conditions in the capital goods-producing sector. His marginal efficiency of capital was not the neoclassical marginal product of capital masquerading under a new name, and his theory of investment did not rest on a confusion of stocks and flows. Since the marginal efficiency of capital depended on expected yields on capital assets, while liquidity preference and hence the rate of interest depended on expectations about securities prices, shifts in expectations could produce large effects on the flow rate of investment. Such swings in investment were Keynes' explanation of fluctuations in effective demand.

CONCLUSION

As Keynes stated in the preface to his *General Theory*, the development of his theory of a monetary economy was a natural process of evolution from his earlier work, although partly obscured by changes in terminology. To understand the development of Keynes' thought and to get a clearer understanding of the *General Theory*, that book must be read in the light of Keynes' earlier writings and lectures. For example, Keynes assumed that readers of the *General Theory* would be familiar with the monetary analysis of his *Treatise on Money*, and so presented a sketchier account of asset markets in the later book.

A Tract on Monetary Reform (1923) was the starting-point for the evolution of Keynes' monetary theory. In that book, Keynes wrote as an orthodox disciple of Alfred Marshall but went beyond exposition of accepted Cambridge monetary theory to make important original contributions. Particularly noteworthy were his treatment of inflation as a tax on money balances, of the effect of hyperinflation on the real quantity of money, and of the nominal interest differential as the forward premium or discount in the foreign exchange market. In the *Tract*, Keynes displayed an understanding of the causes, mechanics and costs of inflation which recurs in such later works as *How to Pay for the War* (1940).The fact that Keynes did not regard inflation as a danger in 1932 in the depths of the Great Depression in no way justifies the charge by Buchanan and Wagner that he neglected the costs of inflation. He was, however, also very much aware that deflation can be costly as well, and in the *Tract* ascribed the 1921–2 British recession to the effect of a high rate of deflation on the real interest rate, given that the nominal interest could not fall below zero. The *Tract*, like Keynes' pamphlet on the return to gold in 1925 and his plans for postwar monetary reform, emphasized the importance of domestic stabilization, rather than maintenance of a fixed exchange rate at the expense of domestic goals.

Keynes' *Treatise on Money* (1930) was a more ambitious attempt to explain booms and contractions as the result of the separation of investment and saving decisions, and was received by reviewers and the economics profession as a pioneering and innovative work. The *Treatise*'s analysis of bearishness and of asset markets was the basis of the portfolio approach to the demand for money and to the pricing of capital assets in the *General Theory*. The *Treatise* was flawed, however, by the lack of a theory of the level of output and of unemployment. Although Keynes was motivated to write it by his conviction that a mistaken, contractionary monetary policy connected with the return to the gold standard was responsible for the high rate of unemployment in Britain, the *Treatise*'s formal model dealt only with changes in price levels. The *Treatise* also lacked a mechanism for bringing cumulative inflation or deflation to a halt at an equilibrium price level, unless the monetary authority happened to set the market rate of interest equal to the natural rate. Keynes made no use in the *Treatise* of the multiplier effects of public works spending which he and Hubert Henderson had presented in *Can Lloyd George Do It?* (1929), because he had no demonstration that the multiplier would have a finite value.

The derivation of a finite multiplier was provided to Keynes from two sources at about the same time: Ralph Hawtrey's comments on the *Treatise* and Richard Kahn's paper on the relation of home investment to unemployment. These two papers differed in other respects. Hawtrey derived the multiplier from a marginal propensity to save, showed that an excess of saving over desired investment would lead to unintended accumulation of inventories, and the resulting reduction in output would restore equilibrium by reducing saving. Kahn contributed the supply curve for output as a whole, given a particular money wage rate, but did not include personal saving as a leakage in the multiplier process until after a journal exchange with Jens Warming. L. F. Giblin's derivation of a finite multiplier, with leakages into imports only, did not come to the attention of anyone at Cambridge, except E. Ronald Walker, an Australian economist who went there in 1931.

The 'widow's cruse fallacy', discovered both by Hawtrey and by the members of the Cambridge 'Circus', and named by Austin Robinson, showed that important sections of the *Treatise*, notably the parable of a thrift campaign in a banana plantation (which also appeared in Keynes' private evidence to the Macmillan Committee), depended on an implicit assumption of constant output. Keynes' lectures at Cambridge from 1932 to 1935 reveal him groping towards a theory of the level of output, and particularly a theory of how nominal shocks can cause real output to change in a monetary economy. In his 1932 lectures, he pointed to the need for a monetary theory of output, and criticized such predecessors as Pigou for assuming that the economy would behave as though workers could bargain directly for real wages, but he did not yet have such a theory to offer. Although the liquidity preference theory of the demand for money as an asset was well developed in the 1932 lectures, Keynes was still trying to prove that output and investment would vary in the same direction, without using the multiplier to obtain a quantitative relationship between changes in investment and changes in effective demand, or having an explanation of how changes in effective demand could alter employment.

In his 1933 lectures, Keynes explained, following an isolated passage in the *Treatise*, that money wage rates could be rigid downward without money illusion, because workers cared about relative wages, and not all nominal contracts would expire at the same time. Furthermore, even if money wage rates fell, this could stimulate employment only to the extent that it affected liquidity preference. That is, a downward shift of the aggregate supply curve would increase employment and output only to the extent that it was a shift along a downward-sloping aggregate demand curve. However, if money wage rates and prices were responding to a large deflationary shock, such as the stock market crash of 1929 or the return to the gold standard, the rate of deflation could be sufficient to drive the nominal rate of interest down to the minimum set by the zero own-rate of interest on money. In that case, the aggregate demand curve would be vertical, since an increase in the real quantity of money due to a lower price level could not reduce the interest rate. In the 1933 lectures, Keynes derived the multiplier from the consumption function, and used it to determine the equilibrium level of income. His presentation of how the flow rate of investment is determined by the equality of the marginal efficiency of capital to the rate of interest was deferred until his 1934 lectures, but drew heavily, despite difference in terminology, on the *Treatise*'s portfolio approach to the pricing of capital goods, which, given a supply curve for the capital goods sector, would give the flow rate of output of new capital goods.

Keynes' theory had four crucial elements: the multiplier theory of effective demand, the liquidity preference theory of the demand for money as an asset, the marginal efficiency of capital theory of investment, and the analysis of the inability of workers to negotiate a market-clearing real wage by bargaining for nominal wages. In a paper in Polish in 1935 on 'The Mechanism of the Business Upswing', Michal Kalecki independently developed the multiplier theory of how changes in investment affect the equilibrium level of income. However, Kalecki did not present any equivalent of Keynes' money demand and investment theory, and his explanation of the failure of money wage reductions to alter real wages was that prices were set as a fixed markup over costs, including wages, with the size of the markup depending on the degree of monopoly, unlike Keynes' explanation.[36]

Keynes' early disciples sometimes wrote as if Keynes had been the only prominent economist to advocate fiscal and monetary expansion in response to the Depression. Debunking of this myth has led to the opposite myth that anyone who supported public works was an independent discoverer of the *General Theory*. In fact, as shown above, a large number of economists were supporters of the orthodox 'Treasury view', while many academic supporters of public works, such as Pigou and Cole, were justly described as supporting theoretical views from which their policy advice could not be derived. Support for fiscal and monetary expansion was often combined with inconsistent policy advice to balance the budget or maintain a fixed exchange rate. Even when the policy advice was consistent, it lacked the theoretical basis provided by Keynes. The lack of a theory to explain mass unemployment was such that Robertson was driven to explain the Depression by satiation of human wants. Keynes was presenting a new theory, not just previously accepted theory in a new guise.

This theory did not depend on money illusion or on systematically mistaken short-period expectations. In his 1937 lectures, 'Footnotes to the *General Theory*', Keynes insisted that 'the theory of effective demand is substantially the same if we assume that short-period expectations are always fulfilled', and distinguished his short period unemployment equilibrium from the disequilibrium theories of Robertson, Hawtrey and the Swedish economists in which 'the whole explanation lies in the *differences* between effective demand and income; ... they do not notice that in my treatment this is not so'.[37] In his 1937 reply to reviews in the *Quarterly Journal of Economics*, Keynes discussed fundamental uncertainty about the future, but drew only two implications from it for his theory: the existence of a speculative motive for holding money, and the possibility of sharp shifts in investment when long-period expectations changed.[38] Keynes' achievement was to develop a theory of short-period equilibrium in a monetary economy. While reductions in money wage rates and prices could bring the economy back to full employment after small deflationary shocks, the existence of money with a zero own-rate of interest and the relative wage motive for nominal wage rigidity meant that for a sufficiently large deflationary demand shock, the economy would come to rest at less than full employment. Keynes provided a more general theory in which situations like the Great Depression were possible, and explained how policy should deal with such cases.

NOTES

1. Keynes (1973), viii, 531n. The account of Keynes' 1934 lectures is based on the Bryce and Tarshis notes.
2. Smith (1978), 27.
3. E. A. G. Robinson, in Patinkin and Leith (1978).
4. Keynes (1979), xxix; Rotheim (1981).
5. Keynes (1936), 266. As stressed by Meltzer (1981), Keynes also mentioned that money wage cuts, by affecting expectations of future wages, can reduce consumption. However, it appears preferable to follow Keynes in stressing the effect of money wage cuts on liquidity preference, rather than to rest the case against money wage cuts clearing the labour market on a particular specification of how expectations are formed.
5. Giangiacomo Nardozzi, in Kahn (1984), 211: the other characteristic cited is 'dealing with inflation *before* introducing money'.
7. Keynes (1923), 23.
8. Lewis (1949).
9. Pigou (1943); Kalecki (1944). The relevant correspondence between Kalecki and Keynes is in Patinkin (1982), 102–3.
10. Keynes (1973), xiii, 369.
11. Keynes (1936), 262.
12. Reprinted as an appendix in Hutchison (1977).
13. Casson (1983), 142–4.
14. Dunlop (1938); Tarshis (1939); Keynes (1939).
15. Casson (1983), 177–9.
16. Hatton and Seaton (1984), 5; Casson (1983), 174, 176.
17. McCombie (1985–6), 245, emphasis in the original.
18. Casson (1983), 158.
19. *Ibid.*, 157.

20. Cannan (1930), quoted by Casson (1983), 42–3, 57, 128.
21. Casson (1983), 48–9.
22. Bryce, Fallgatter and Salant notes, 4 December 1933. Tarshis missed this lecture, and copied Bryce's notes.
23. Clower (1965).
24. J. M. Clark (1935), 16–17; J. R. Davis (1971), 65–83.
25. J. M. Clark (1934), 85–6.
26. Douglas (1935), 123–4; J. R. Davis (1971), 47–60; Harcourt (1981), 612.
27. LeRoy (1983), 416; E. Johnson and H. Johnson (1978), 74.
28. Keynes (1973), xiii, 593; Keynes (1936), 135, 137; Bliss (1975a); LeRoy (1983), 407, 412.
29. Keynes (1936), 135; LeRoy (1983), 413.
30. Bryce notes, 26 November 1934.
31. Keynes (1930), i, 202.
32. Keynes (1973), xiv, 102; LeRoy (1983), 411.
33. LeRoy (1983), 413.
34. Keynes (1936), 138.
35. Velupillai (1975); Bliss (1975b), 328.
36. Kalecki (1971), ch. 3.On Kalecki, see Feiwel (1975), Sawyer (1985), and the February 1977 issue of the *Oxford Bulletin of Economics and Statistics*. Patinkin (1982) presents the case that the theory of effective demand and equilibrium income can be found in Kalecki's 1935 paper, but not in his 1933 and 1934 papers in Polish, translated as Kalecki (1971), chs 1 and 2.
37. Keynes (1973), xiv, 181–2.
38. Keynes (1937).

References

Adarkar, B. P. (1933), 'The "Fundamental Error" in Keynes' *Treatise*'. *American Economic Review*, **23**.

Akerman, Johan (1931), *Some Lessons of the World Depression*, London: Macmillan.

Akerman, Johan (1932), *Economic Progress and Economic Crises*, London: Macmillan.

Akerman, Johan (1933), *Economic Forecast and Reality, 1928–1932*, London: Macmillan.

Andersen, Peder (1983), '"On the Rent of Fishing Grounds": a Translation of Jens Warming's 1911 Article, with an Introduction', *History of Political Economy*, **15**.

Anyadike-Danes, M. K. (1985), 'Dennis Robertson and Keynes' *General Theory*', with discussion by T. Wilson, in Harcourt (1985).

Barro, Robert J. (1977), 'Long-Term Contracting, Sticky Prices, and Monetary Policy', *Journal of Monetary Economics*, **3**.

Bell, Clive (1956), *Old Friends*, London: Chatto and Windus.

Benassy, Jean-Pascal (1975), 'Neo-Keynesian Disequilibrium Theory in a Monetary Economy', *Review of Economic Studies*, **42**.

Benham, F. C. (1932), *British Monetary Policy*, London.

Benjamin, Daniel and Levis P. Kochin (1978), 'Unemployment and the Dole: evidence from Interwar Britain', with discussion by Martin Feldstein, in Grubel and Walker (1978).

Benjamin, Daniel and Levis P. Kochin (1979), 'Searching for an Explanation of Unemployment in Interwar Britain', *Journal of Political Economy*, **87**; reply to their critics (1982), *Journal of Political Economy*, **90**.

Bevin, Ernest (1933), *My Plan for 2,000,000 Workless*, London.

Blaug, Mark (1968, 1978), *Economic Theory in Retrospect*, 2nd edn, Homewood, IL: Irwin; 3rd edn, Cambridge, UK: Cambridge University Press.

Bliss, Christopher J. (1975a), 'The Reappraisal of Keynesian Economics: an Appraisal', in Michael Parkin and A. R. Nobay, eds, *Current Economic Problems*, proceedings of the Association of University Teachers of Economics, Cambridge, UK: Cambridge University Press.

Bliss, Christopher J. (1975b), *Capital Theory and Income Distribution*, New York and Amsterdam: North-Holland.

Bloomfield, Arthur I. (1947), 'Foreign Exchange Rate Theory and Policy', in Harris (1947).

Bodkin, Ronald G. (1966), *The Wage-Price-Productivity Nexus*, Philadelphia: University of Pennyslvania Press.

Bowers, R. L. (1934), review of Pigou (1933), *American Economic Review*, **24**.

Brown, Douglas, *et al.* (1934), *The Economics of the Recovery Program*, New York: Da Capo Reprint, 1974.

Bryce, Robert B. (1932–4), see note at end of References.

Buchanan, J. M. and R. E. Wagner (1977), *Democracy in Deficit, The Political Legacy of Lord Keynes*, New York and London: Academic Press.

Burns, James MacGregor (1956), *Roosevelt: The Lion and the Fox*, New York: Harcourt Brace.

Cabiati, A. (1931), 'Il neo-protezianismo del Prof. Keynes', *La Riforma Sociale* (Turin), English summary in *Economic Journal*, **41**, 511.

Cain, Neville (1979), 'Cambridge and its Revolution: a Perspective on the Multiplier and Effective Demand', *Economic Record*, **55**.

Cain, Neville (1982), 'Hawtrey and the Multiplier', *Australian Economic History Review*, **22**.

Calabre, Serge (1980), 'L'explication du sous-emploi durable par R. G. Hawtrey: Échanges extérieurs, taux d'intérêt à court terme et credit', *Revue d'économie politique*, 90ᵉ année.

Cannan, Edwin (1930), 'The Problem of Employment: A Review', *Economic Journal*, **40**.

Cannan, Edwin (1932), 'The Demand for Labour', *Economic Journal*, **42**.

Cannan, Edwin (1933), *Economic Scares*, London: P. S. King.

Carothers, Neil (1934), *Experimenting with Our Money*, New York: Farrar & Rinehart Pamphlets, no. 3.

Casson, Mark (1983), *Economics of Unemployment: an Historical Perspective*, London: Martin Robertson.

Claasen, Emil-Maria and Georges Lane (1978), 'The Effects of Unemployment Benefits on the Unemployment Rate in France', in Grubel and Walker (1978).

Clark, Colin (1977), 'The Golden Age of Great Economists', *Encounter*, **48**, 6.

Clark, John Maurice (1934), *Strategic Factors in Business Cycles*, New York: National Bureau of Economic Research.

Clark, John Maurice (1935), 'Cumulative Effects of Changes in Aggregate Spending as Illustrated by Public Works', *American Economic Review*, **25**.

Clay, Sir Henry (1928), 'Unemployment and Wage Rates', *Economic Journal*, **38**.

Clower, Robert (1965), 'The Keynesian Counter-Revolution', in Frank H. Hahn and F. R. Brechling, eds, *The Theory of Interest Rates*, London: Macmillan.

Cobbett, William (1817), *Paper Against Gold*, London: Cobbett.

Cole, G. D. H. (1930), *Gold, Credit, and Employment*, London: Allen and Unwin.

Cole, G. D. H. (1932), *British Trade and Industry, Past and Present*, London: Macmillan.

Cole, G. D. H. (1932), *Economic Tracts for the Times*, London: Macmillan.

Cole, G. D. H., ed. (1933), *What Everybody Wants to Know About Money*, New York: Knopf, and London: Gollancz.

Copland, Douglas B. (1934), *Australia and the World Crisis, 1929–33*, Alfred Marshall Lectures (Michaelmas Term, 1933), Cambridge, UK: Cambridge University Press.

Copland, Douglas B. (1951), 'L. F. Giblin: a Brief Tribute', *Economic Record*, **27**.

Copland, Douglas B. (1958), 'L. F. Giblin and the Frontier of Research on the Australian Economy: the First Giblin Memorial Lecture', *Australian Journal of Science*, **XXI**, reprinted in Copland (1960).

Copland, Douglas B., ed. (1960), *Giblin: the Scholar and the Man*, Melbourne: F. W. Cheshire.

Copland, Douglas B., L. F. Giblin and G. L. Wood (1930), 'The Restoration of Economic Equilibrium', *Economic Record*, **6**.

Copland, Douglas B., *et al.* (1952), 'L. F. Giblin: an Appreciation', *Economic Record*, **28**.

Cross, Rodney (1982), 'How Much Voluntary Unemployment in Interwar Britain?', *Journal of Political Economy*, **90**.

Darby, Michael (1976), 'Three and a Half Million Employees Have Been Mislaid', *Journal of Political Economy*, **84**.

Davis, Eric G. (1980), 'The Correspondence Between R. G. Hawtrey and J. M. Keynes on the *Treatise*: The Genesis of Output Adjustment Models', *Canadian Journal of Economics*, **13**.

Davis, Eric G. (1981), 'R. G. Hawtrey, 1879–1975', in D. P. O'Brien and J. R. Presley, eds, *Pioneers of Modern Economics in Britain*, London: Macmillan.

Davis, Eric G. (1983), 'The Macro-Models of R. G. Hawtrey', Ottawa: Carleton Economics Papers, 83–4.

Davis, J. Ronnie (1966), 'Chicago Economists, Budget Deficits and the Early 1930s', *American Economic Review*, **58**.

Davis, J. Ronnie (1971), *The New Economics and the Old Economists*, Ames, Iowa: Iowa State University Press.

Deutscher, Patrick (1984), 'R. G. Hawtrey and the Development of Macroeconomics in the Interwar Period', Ph.D. dissertation, University of Toronto.

Douglas, Paul (1935), *Controlling Depressions*, New York: Macmillan.

Drucker, Paul (1979), *Adventures of a Bystander*, New York: Basic Books.

Dunlop, John G. (1938), 'The Movement of Real and Money Wage Rates', *Economic Journal*, **48**.

Durbin, Evan F. M. (1932), *Purchasing Power and Trade Depression: a Critique of Underconsumption Theories*, London: Cape.

Dyason, J. (1939), 'A Note on the Multiplier in Australia', *Economic Record*, **15**, and note in the same volume by F. B. Horner.

Ebersole, J. F. (1938), 'The Influence of Interest Rates Upon Entrepreneurial Decisions in Business', *Harvard Business Review*, **17**.

Economic Essays in Honour of Gustav Cassel (1933), London: George Allen and Unwin.

Edel, Leon (1979), *Bloomsbury: a House of Ideas*, London: Hogarth Press.
Ellis, Howard S. and Lloyd A. Metzeler, eds (1949), *Readings in the Theory of International Trade*, Philadelphia: Blakiston.
Ensor, R. C. K. (1936), *England 1870–1914*, Oxford History of England, Oxford: Oxford University Press.
Fallgatter, Marvin (1933), see note at end of References.
Fairchild, F. R., E. S. Furniss, N. S. Buck and C. H. Whelden, Jr (1935), *A Description of the 'New Deal'*, rev. edn, New York: Macmillan.
Feiwel, George (1975), *The Intellectual Capital of Michal Kalecki*, Knoxville, Tennessee: University of Tennessee Press.
Field, Alexander J. (1981), 'The *Treatise on Money* After Fifty Years', working paper, Stanford University.
Fisher, Irving (1911), *The Purchasing Power of Money*, New York: Macmillan.
Fisher, Irving (1926), 'A Statistical Relation Between Unemployment and Price Changes', *International Labour Review*, reprinted (1973) as 'I Discovered the Phillips Curve', *Journal of Political Economy*, **81**.
Fisher, Irving (1928), *The Money Illusion*, New York: Adelphi.
Fisher, Irving (1930), *The Theory of Interest*, New York: Macmillan, reprinted (1978) Philadelphia, Porcupine Press.
Fisher, Irving (1933), 'The Debt-Deflation Theory of Great Depressions', *Econometrica*, **I**.
Galbraith, John Kenneth (1981), *A Life in Our Times*, New York: Houghton Mifflin.
Garcia-Mata, C. and F. I. Shaffner (1934), 'Solar and Economic Relationships: a Preliminary Report', *Quarterly Journal of Economics*, **49**.
Garraty, John A. (1978), *Unemployment in History*, New York: Harper.
Garvey, George (1975), 'Keynes and the Economic Activists of Pre-Hitler Germany', *Journal of Political Economy*, **83**.
Gayer, Arthur, ed. (1937), *The Lessons of Monetary Experience, Essays in honour of Irving Fisher*, New York: Farrar and Rinehart.
Giblin, L. F. (1930), *Australia, 1930*, Melbourne: Melbourne University Press.
Giblin, L. F. (1946), 'John Maynard Keynes (Some Personal Notes)', *Economic Record*, **22**.
Gifford, C. H. P. (1933), 'The Concept of the Length of the Period of Production', *Economic Journal*, **43**.
Gifford, C. H. P. (1934), 'Protection and the Price Level in Australia', *Economic Record*, **10**.
Gifford, C. H. P. (1935), 'The Period of Production Under Continuous Input and Point Output in an Unprogressive Community', *Econometrica*, **3**.
Goodwin, Craufurd D. W. (1962), 'Alfred de Lissa and the Birth of the Multiplier', *Economic Record*, **38**.
Gordon, Robert J. (1973), *Milton Friedman's Monetary Framework: a Debate with his Critics*, Chicago: University of Chicago Press. Originally published (1970–2) in *Journal of Political Economy*, **78–80**.
Gordon, Robert J. (1981), 'Output Fluctuations and Gradual Price Adjust-

ment', *Journal of Economic Literature*, **19**.

Graham, Frank (1932), *Creating Employment*, Princeton, N.J.: Princeton University Press.

Graham, Frank D. (1932), *The Abolition of Unemployment*, Princeton, N.J.: Princeton University Press.

Gregory, T. E. (1926), *The First Year of the Gold Standard*, London: Methuen.

Gregory, T. E. (1933), *Gold, Unemployment and Capitalism*, London: P. S. King.

Grubel, Herbert G. and Michael A. Walker, eds (1978), *Unemployment Insurance*, Vancouver, B.C.: Fraser Institute.

Guillebaud, Claude W. (1924), 'The Economics of the Dawes Plan', *Economic Journal*, **34**.

Guillebaud, Claude W. (1939), *The Economic Recovery of Germany, 1933–38*, London: Macmillan.

Guillebaud, Claude W. (1940), 'Hitler's New Economic Order for Europe', *Economic Journal*, **50**.

Guillebaud, Claude W. (1941), *Social Policy of Nazi Germany*, Cambridge: Cambridge University Press.

Gunther, John (1938), *Inside Europe*, rev. edn, New York: Harper.

Haberler, Gottfried (1937), *Prosperity and Depression*, Geneva: League of Nations.

Haberler, Gottfried (1946), *Prosperity and Depression*, Lake Success, New York: United Nations.

Hahn, L. Albert (1949), *The Economics of Illusion*, New York: Squier.

Hall, Michael (1982), *Cambridge*, Cambridge: Pevensey Press.

Hancock, K. J. (1962), 'The Reduction of Unemployment as a Problem of Public Policy', *Economic History Review*, 2nd series, **15**.

Hansen, Alvin (1932), 'A Fundamental Error in Keynes' *Treatise on Money*', *American Economic Review*, **22**, and reply by Keynes, both reprinted in Keynes (1973), **XIII**.

Hansen, Alvin and Herbert Tout (1933), 'Annual Survey of Economic Theory: Investment and Saving in the Business Cycle', *Econometrica*, **I**, section on Keynes reprinted (1938), as appendix to Alvin Hansen, *Full Recovery or Stagnation?* New York: Norton.

Hansen, Bent (1981), 'Unemployment, Keynes and the Stockholm School', *History of Political Economy*, **13**.

Harcourt, Geoffrey C. (1981), 'An Early Post-Keynesian: Lorie Tarshis (or: Tarshis on Tarshis by Harcourt)', *Journal of Post Keynesian Economics*, **3**.

Harcourt, Geoffrey C. (1985), *Keynes and His Contemporaries* (proceedings of the Sixth and Centennial Keynes Seminar at Keynes College, University of Kent at Canterbury), London: Macmillan.

Hardy, Charles O. (1931a), review of Keynes (1930), *American Economic Review*, **21**.

Hardy, Charles O. (1931b), 'Saving, Investment, and the Control of Business Cycles', *Journal of Political Economy*, **39**.

Hardy, Charles O. (1942), 'Fiscal Policy and the National Income: a Review',

American Economic Review, **32**.

Harnetty, Peter (1972), *Imperialism and Free Trade: Lancashire and India*, Vancouver, BC: University of British Columbia Press.

Harris, Seymour (1934), review of Pigou (1933), *Quarterly Journal of Economics*, **49**.

Harris, Seymour, ed. (1947), *The New Economics*, New York: Knopf.

Harrod, Roy (1934), review of Pigou (1933), *Economic Journal*, **44**.

Harrod, Roy (1951), *The Life of John Maynard Keynes*, London: Macmillan.

Harrod, Roy (1970), 'Keynes' Views on Money', *Journal of Political Economy*, **78**.

Hart, A. G. (1933), 'An Examination of Mr. Keynes' Price Level Concepts', *Journal of Political Economy*, **41**.

Hatton, T. J. and J. S. Seaton (1984), 'Real Wages and Employment Between the Wars: a Cautionary Note', Exeter Discussion Paper, unpublished.

Hawtrey, Ralph G. (1913), *Good and Bad Trade*, London: Augustus Kelley Reprint; New York: no date.

Hawtrey, Ralph G. (1925), 'Public Expenditure and the Demand for Labour', *Economica*, **5** (old series).

Hawtrey, Ralph G. (1931), review of Keynes (1930), *Journal of the Royal Statistical Society*, **94**.

Hawtrey, Ralph G. (1932), *The Art of Central Banking*, London: Longmans.

Hawtrey, Ralph G. (1933), 'Public Expenditure and Trade Depression', *Journal of the Royal Statistical Society*, **96**.

Hawtrey, Ralph G. (1934), review of Pigou (1933), *Economica*, **1** (new series).

Hayek, Friedrich A. (1931–32), 'Some Reflections on Mr. Keynes' Pure Theory of Money', *Economica*, **11** and **12** (old series), August 1931 and February 1932, with reply by Keynes and rejoinder by Hayek, November 1931.

Hegeland, Hugo (1954), *The Multiplier Theory*, Lund, Sweden; reprinted New York: Kelley, 1966.

Heimann, Edward (1945), *History of Economic Doctrines*, New York: Oxford University Press.

Hicks, John R. (1932), *The Theory of Wages*, London: Macmillan.

Hicks, J. R. (1937), 'Mr. Keynes and the Classics: a Suggested Interpretation', *Econometrica*, **5**, as reprinted (1967) in J. R. Hicks, *Critical Essays in Monetary Theory*, Oxford: Blackwell.

Hicks, J. R. (1946), *Value and Capital*, 2nd edn, Oxford: Oxford University Press.

Hicks, J. R. (1967), 'A Note on the *Treatise*', *Critical Essays in Monetary Theory*, Oxford: Blackwell.

Hines, A. G. (1971), *On the Reappraisal of Keynesian Economics*, London: Martin Robertson.

Howson, Susan (1973), '"A Dear Money Man"? Keynes on Monetary Policy, 1920', *Economic Journal*, **83**.

Howson, Susan and Donald Winch (1977), *The Economic Advisory Council*, Cambridge, UK: Cambridge University Press.

Humphrey, Thomas M. (1974), 'The Concept of Indexation in the History of Economic Thought', *Economic Review*, as reprinted (1983) in Thomas M. Humphrey, *Essays on Inflation*, 4th edn, Richmond, Virginia: Federal Reserve Bank of Richmond.

Humphrey, Thomas M. (1981), 'Keynes on Inflation', *Economic Review*, as reprinted (1983) in Thomas M. Humphrey, *Essays on Inflation*, Richmond, Virginia: Federal Reserve Bank of Richmond.

Hutchison, T. W. (1953), *A Review of Economic Doctrines, 1870–1929*, Oxford: Oxford University Press.

Hutchison, T. W. (1977), *Keynes versus the 'Keynesians' ...?* London, Institute of Economic Affairs.

Hutchison, T. W. (1978), 'Demythologizing the Keynesian Revolution: Pigou, Wage-Cuts and the *General Theory*', in his *On Revolution and Progress in Economic Knowledge*, Cambridge, UK: Cambridge University Press.

Hutt, W. H. (1930), *The Theory of Collective Bargaining*, London: P. S. King.

Iwai, Katsuhito (1981). *Disequilibrium Dynamics*. Cowles Foundation Monograph. New Haven, Ct: Yale University Press.

James, Robert Rhodes (1970), *Churchill: A Study in Failure, 1900–1939*, London: Pelican.

Jevons, Horatio Stanley (1933), 'The Causes of Fluctuations of Industrial Activity and the Price Level'. *Journal of the Royal Statistical Society*, **96**.

Johnson, Elizabeth and Harry G. Johnson (1978). *The Shadow of Keynes*, Chicago: University of Chicago Press.

Jones, J. H. (1964), *Josiah Stamp, Public Servant*, London.

Jonung, Lars (1981), 'Ricardo on Machinery and the Present Unemployment: An Unpublished Manuscript by Knut Wicksell'. *Economic Journal*, **91**.

Kahn, Richard F. (1931). 'The Relation of Home Investment to Unemployment'. *Economic Journal*, **41**.

Kahn, Richard F. (1932), 'The Financing of Public Works: a Note', *Economic Journal*, **42**.

Kahn, Richard F. (1933), 'Public Works and Inflation', *Journal of the American Statistical Association*, Supplement: Papers and Proceedings, **28**, 168–73.

Kahn, Richard F. (Lord) (1972), *Selected Essays on Employment and Growth*, Cambridge, UK: Cambridge University Press.

Kahn, Richard F. (Lord) (1984), *The Making of the General Theory* (The 1978 Raffaele Mattioli Lectures at Luigi Bocconi University, Milan), Cambridge, UK: Cambridge University Press.

Kahn, Richard F. (Lord) (1985), 'The Cambridge "Circus" (1)', in Harcourt (1985).

Kaldor, Nicholas (1937), 'Annual Survey of Economic Theory: the Recent Controversy in the Theory of Capital', *Econometrica*, **5**.

Kalecki, Michal (1944), 'Professor Pigou on "The Classic Stationary State"', *Economic Journal*, **54**.

Kalecki, Michal (1971), *Selected Essays on the Dynamics of the Capitalist Economy*, Cambridge, UK: Cambridge University Press.

Karmel, P. H. (1960), 'Giblin and Multiplier', in Copland (1960).

Keynes, John Maynard (1911), review of Fisher (1911), *Economic Journal*, 21, reprinted (1983) in Keynes, XI.

Keynes, John Maynard (1913), *Indian Currency and Finance*, London: Keynes (1971), I.

Keynes, John Maynard (1923), *A Tract on Monetary Reform*, London: Keynes (1971), V.

Keynes, John Maynard (1924a), 'Does Unemployment Need a Drastic Remedy?', *Nation and Athenaeum*, May 24.

Keynes, John Maynard (1924b). 'A Drastic Remedy for Unemployment: Reply to Critics', *Nation and Athenaeum*, August 9.

Keynes, John Maynard (1924c), 'Foreign Investment and the National Advantage', *Nation and Athenaeum*, 9 August.

Keynes, John Maynard (1925), *The Economic Consequences of Mr. Churchill*, London: Hogarth Press, reprinted in Keynes, *Collected Writings*. IX.

Keynes, John Maynard (1929), 'The German Transfer Problem', *Economic Journal*, 39.

Keynes, John Maynard (1930), *A Treatise on Money*, two volumes, London: Macmillan.

Keynes, John Maynard (1931), *Essays in Persuasion*, London; an expanded version is Keynes, *Collected Writings*, IX.

Keynes, John Maynard (1933). *The Means to Prosperity*, New York: Harcourt, Brace. Includes an additional chapter not in the original London version.

Keynes, John Maynard (1935), 'The Future of the Foreign Exchanges', *Lloyds Bank Monthly Review*, October.

Keynes, John Maynard (1936), *The General Theory of Employment, Interest and Money*, London: Macmillan, Keynes (1971), VII.

Keynes, John Maynard (1937), 'The General Theory of Employment', *Quarterly Journal of Economics*, 52: in Keynes (1973), XIV, and in Harris (1947).

Keynes, John Maynard (1939), 'Relative Movements of Real Wages and Output', *Economic Journal*, 49, reprinted as appendix to Keynes (1971) VII.

Keynes, John Maynard (1940), *How to Pay for the War*, London: Macmillan.

Keynes, John Maynard (1946), 'The Balance of Payments of the United States', *Economic Journal*, 56.

Keynes, John Maynard (1951), *Essays in Biography*, expanded edn edited by Geoffrey Keynes, London: Macmillan.

Keynes, John Maynard (Lord) (1971-83), *Collected Writings*, London: Royal Economic Society. Includes:

(1973) *The General Theory and After*, Vols XIII and XIV.

(1979) *The General Theory and After: Supplement*, Vol. XXIX.

(1981) *Activities, 1929-31*, Vol. XX.

(1983) *Economic Articles and Correspondence*, Vols XI and XII.

Keynes, John Maynard and Hubert Henderson (1929), *Can Lloyd George Do It?*, London: The Nation and Athenaeum.

Keynes, Milo, ed. (1975), *Essays on John Maynard Keynes*, London and Cambridge, UK: Cambridge University Press.

Klein, Lawrence (1947), *The Keynesian Revolution*, New York: Macmillan.

Lavington, Frederick (1912), 'Uncertainty and Its Relation to the Net Rate of Interest', *Economic Journal*, **22**.

Leijonhufvud. Axel (1968), *On Keynesian Economics and the Economics of Keynes*, New York: Oxford University Press.

Lekachman, Robert, ed. (1964), *Keynes' General Theory: Reports of Three Decades*, Boston: Heath.

Lekachman, Robert (1966), *The Age of Keynes*, New York: Random House.

Leland, Simeon, ed. (1933), *Balancing the Budget: Federal Fiscal Policy in Depression*, Public Policy Pamphlet, Chicago: University of Chicago Press.

LeRoy, Stephen (1983), 'Keynes' Theory of Investment', *History of Political Economy*, **15**.

Lewis, W. Arthur (1949), *Economic Survey, 1919-1939*, London: Allen and Unwin.

Lipsey, Richard G. (1972), 'The Foundations of the Theory of National Income: an Analysis of Some Fundamental Errors', in Maurice Preston and Bernard Corry, ed., *Essays in Honour of Lord Robbins*, London: Weidenfeld and Nicolson.

Lloyd George, David (1924), 'The Statesman's Task', *Nation and Athenaeum*, April 12.

Loria, Achille (1931), 'Keynes sulla moneta', *La Riforma Sociale* (Turin), English summary in *Economic Journal*, **41**, 511.

McCombie, John S. (1985-86), 'Why Cutting Real Wages Will Not Necessarily Reduce Unemployment', *Journal of Post Keynesian Economics*, **8**.

MacFie, Alec L. (1934), *Theories of the Trade Cycle*, London: Macmillan.

Marshall, Alfred (1920), *Principles of Economics*, 8th edn. London: Macmillan.

Marshall, Alfred (1923), *Money, Credit and Commerce*, London: Macmillan.

Marshall, Alfred (1926), *Official Papers*, John Maynard Keynes, ed., London: Macmillan.

Mathias, Peter (1979), *The Transformation of England*, London: Methuen.

Meade, James E. (1933), *Public Works in Their International Aspect*, London: Fabian Society pamphlet. Reprinted (1986), in Meade, *Collected Papers*, Vol. I, S, Howson ed., London: Macmillan.

Mehta, Ghashyam (1979), *The Structure of the Keynesian Revolution*, London: Martin Robertson.

Mehta, Ghashyam (1983), 'Comments on Professor Minoguchi's Interpretation of the *Treatise* and the *General Theory*', *Hitotsubashi Journal of Economics*, **24**.

Meltzer, Allan (1981), 'On Keynes' *General Theory*', *Journal of Economic Literature*, **19**; with comments by James Crotty, Paul Davidson, Don

Patinkin and Sidney Weintraub, and reply by Meltzer, *Journal of Economic Literature*, **21**, (1983).

Middleton, Roger (1982), 'The Treasury in the 1930s: Political and Administrative Constraints to the Acceptance of the "New" Economics'. *Oxford Economic Papers*, **34**.

Milgate, Murray (1983), 'The "New" Keynes Papers', in John Eatwell and Murray Milgate, eds, *Keynes's Economics and the Theory of Value and Distribution*, New York and Oxford: Oxford University Press.

Minoguchi, Takeo (1981), 'The Process of Writing the *General Theory* as a "Monetary Theory of Production"'. *Hitotsubashi Journal of Economics*, **21**.

Minoguchi, Takeo (1982), 'Some Questions About IS-LM Interpretation of the *General Theory*', *Hitotsubashi Journal of Economics*, **22**.

Minoguchi, Takeo (1983), 'Reply to Professor Mehta', *Hitotsubashi Journal of Economics*, **24**.

Mitchell, Wesley C. (1927), *Business Cycles*, New York: National Bureau of Economic Research.

Moggridge, Donald (1969), *The Return to Gold, 1925*, Cambridge, UK: Cambridge University Press.

Moggridge, Donald (1973), 'From the *Treatise* to the *General Theory*: An Exercise in Chronology'. *History of Political Economy*, **5**.

Moggridge, Donald (1976), *John Maynard Keynes*, London: Fontana.

Moggridge, Donald and Susan Howson (1974), 'Keynes on Monetary Policy', *Oxford Economic Papers*, **24**.

Muggeridge, Malcolm (1940), *The Thirties*, London: Hamish Hamilton, as reprinted (1971), London: Fontana.

Nanto, Dick N. and Shini Takagi (1985). 'Korekiyo Takahashi and Japan's Recovery from the Great Depression', *American Economic Review*, **75**.

Nicolson, Harold (1966), *Diaries and Letters, 1930–39*, London: Collins.

Ohlin, Bertil (1929), 'Reparations Difficulties, Real and Imagined', *Economic Journal*, **39**.

Ohlin, Bertil (1974), 'On the Slow Development of the "Total Demand" Idea in Economic Theory', *Journal of Economic Literature*, **12**.

Patinkin, Don (1969), 'The Chicago Tradition, the Quantity Theory and Friedman', *Journal of Money, Credit and Banking*, **1**, as reprinted (1972), in Don Patinkin, *Studies in Monetary Economics*, New York: Harper and Row.

Patinkin, Don (1976), *Keynes' Monetary Thought: a Study of Its Development*, Durham, NC: Duke University Press, Also as the Summer 1976 issue of *History of Political Economy*, **8**.

Patinkin, Don (1980), 'New Material on the Development of Keynes' Monetary Thought', *History of Political Economy*, **12**.

Patinkin, Don (1982), *Anticipations of the General Theory? and Other Essays*, Chicago: University of Chicago Press.

Patinkin, Don and J. Clark Leith, eds. (1978), *Keynes, Cambridge and the General Theory*, Toronto: University of Toronto Press.

Peden, G. C. (1980), 'Keynes, the Treasury and Unemployment in the Later Nineteen-Thirties', *Oxford Economic Papers*, **32**.

Pigou, A. C. (1912). *Wealth and Welfare*, London: Macmillan.

Pigou, A. C. (1917), 'The Value of Money', *Quarterly Journal of Economics*, 32, as reprinted in F. A. Lutz and L. W. Mints, eds, (1951), *Readings in Monetary Theory*. Philadelphia: Blakiston.

Pigou, A. C. (1920), 'Some Problems of Foreign Exchange', *Economic Journal*, 30.

Pigou, A. C. (1922), 'The Foreign Exchanges', *Quarterly Journal of Economics*, 37.

Pigou, A. C. (1927a), 'Wage Policy and Unemployment', *Economic Journal*, 37.

Pigou, A. C. (1927b), *Industrial Fluctuations*, London: Macmillan.

Pigou, A. C. (1929), 'The Monetary Theory of the Trade Cycle', *Economic Journal*, 39.

Pigou, A. C. (1931), 'Mr. Keynes on Money', *Nation and Athenaeum*, January 24.

Pigou, A. C. (1933), *The Theory of Unemployment*, London: Macmillan.

Pigou, A. C. (1937), *Socialism Versus Capitalism*, London: Macmillan.

Pigou, A. C. (1943), 'The Classical Stationary State', *Economic Journal*, 53.

Plimsoll, James (1939), 'An Australian Anticipator of Mr. Keynes', *Economic Record*, 15.

Pollard, Sidney (1969), 'Trade Union Reactions to the Economic Crisis', *Journal of Contemporary History*, 4.

Pollard, Sidney (1970), *The Gold Standard and Employment Policies Between the Wars*, London: Methuen.

Presley, John R. (1979), *Robertsonian Economics*, London: Macmillan.

Robbins, Lionel (1932), 'Consumption and the Trade Cycle', *Economica*, 12

Robbins, Lionel (1934), *The Great Depression*, London: Macmillan.

Robbins, Lionel (1935), *An Essay on the Nature and Significance of Economic Theory*, 2nd edn, London: Macmillan.

Robbins, Lionel (Lord) (1971), *The Autobiography of an Economist*, London: Macmillan.

Robertson, Dennis H. (1915). *A Study of Industrial Fluctuations*, London: P. S. King; New York: Augustus Kelley Reprint: no date.

Robertson, Dennis H. (1926), *Banking Policy and the Price Level*, London: P. S. King.

Robertson, Dennis H. (1931), 'Mr. Keynes on Money', *Economic Journal*, 41, with rejoinder by Keynes.

Robertson, Dennis H. (1933), 'Saving and Hoarding', *Economic Journal*, 43, with comments by Hawtrey and Keynes, and reply by Robertson.

Robertson, Dennis H. (1940), *Essays on Monetary Theory*, London: Staples.

Robinson, E. A. G. (1931), *The Structure of Competitive Industry*, London: Nisbet and Cambridge, UK: Cambridge University Press.

Robinson, E. A. G. (1946), 'John Maynard Keynes, 1883–1946', *Economic Journal*, 56, reprinted (1964), with postscript in Lekachman.

Robinson, E. A. G. (Sir Austin) (1985), 'The Cambridge "Circus" (2)', in Harcourt (1985).

Robinson, Joan V. (1933a), 'A Parable on Saving and Investment', *Economica*, **13**.

Robinson, Joan V. (1933b), 'The Theory of Money and the Analysis of Output', *Review of Economic Studies*, **1**, as reprinted (1978), in J. V. Robinson.

Robinson, Joan V. (1933c), *Economics of Imperfect Competition*, London: Macmillan.

Robinson, Joan V. (1937), *Essays in the Theory of Employment*, London: Macmillan.

Robinson, Joan V. (1962), *Economic Philosophy*, London: C. A. Watts.

Robinson, Joan V. (1978), *Contributions to Modern Economics*, Oxford: Blackwell.

Robinson, Joan V. (1980), *Collected Economic Papers*, 2nd edn. Cambridge Mass.: MIT Press, and Oxford: Blackwell.

Roos, Charles F. ed. (1933), *Stabilization of Employment*, Bloomington, Indiana: Principia Press.

Rotheim, Roy J. (1981), 'Keynes' Monetary Theory of Value (1933)', *Journal of Post Keynesian Economics*, **3**.

Ruebner-Pederson, R. (1934), 'The "Fundamental Error" in Keynes' *Treatise*', *American Economic Review*, **24**.

Rueff, Jacques (1931), 'L'assurance-chômage, cause du chômage permanent', *Revue d'économie politique*, 41ᵉ année; see also Jacques Rueff, 'Chomage permanent: nouvelle discussion', *Revue d'économie politique*, 61ᵉ année.

Rueff, Jacques (1964), *The Age of Inflation*, Chicago: Regnery.

Salant, Walter (1933), see note at end of References.

Samuelson, Paul A. (1947), *Foundations of Economic Analysis*, Cambridge, Mass.: Harvard University Press.

Saulnier, Raymond J. (1938), *Contemporary Monetary Theory*, New York: Columbia University Press.

Saunders, Charles B., Jr., (1966), *The Brookings Institution: a fifty-year History*, Washington, DC: Brookings.

Sawyer, Malcolm C. (1985), *The Economics of Michal Kalecki*, Armonk, NY: M. E. Sharpe, also published as a double issue of *East European Economics*, (1985), XIII, nos 3–4.

Saxon, Olin Glenn (1962), *Keynes at Harvard: Economic Deception as a Political Credo*, 2nd edn, New York. Published anonymously by the Veritas Foundation, which attributed the pamphlet to Saxon in the posthumous dedication to him of the next Veritas Foundation study, *The Great Deceit: Social Pseudo-Science*, New York, 1962.

Seligman, Ben B. (1962), *The Revolt Against Formalism*, Chicago: Quadrangle Books.

Shackle, G. L. S. (1967), *The Years of High Theory, 1926–39*, Cambridge, UK: Cambridge University Press.

Silk, Leonard (1985), 'The Balanced Budget Risks', *New York Times*, October 16.

Smith, Adam (1978), *Lectures on Jurisprudence*, R. L. Meek, D. D. Raphael and P. G. Stein eds Oxford: Oxford University Press.

Spahr, Walter E. (1934), *The Monetary Theories of Warren and Pearson*, New York: Farrar and Rinehart Pamphlets, no. 1.

Spreng, F. (1976), 'R. G. Hawtrey and British Macroeconomics', Ph.D. dissertation, University of Pittsburgh.

Sraffa, Piero (1926), 'The Laws of Return Under Competitive conditions', *Economic Journal*, **36**.

Stamp, Sir Josiah (1931), review of Keynes (1930), *Economic Journal*, **41**.

Stein, Herbert (1969), *The Fiscal Revolution in America*, Chicago: University of Chicago Press.

Stewart, Michael (1967), *Keynes and After*, Harmondsworth, Middlesex: Penguin.

Sweezy, Paul (1934), review of Pigou (1933), *Journal of Political Economy*, **42**.

Tarshis, Lorie (1932–5), see note at end of References.

Tarshis, Lorie (1939), 'Changes in Real and Money Wages,' *Economic Journal*, **49**.

Tarshis, Lorie (1948), 'An Exposition of Keynesian Economics,' *American Economic Review*, **38**.

Tarshis, Lorie (1976), review of Keynes (1973), xiii. *Journal of Economic Literature*, **14**.

Tarshis, Lorie (1978), 'Keynes as Seen by his Students', in Patinkin and Leith (1978).

Tinbergen, Jan (1939), *Statistical Testing of Business Cycle Theories*, 2 vols, Geneva: League of Nations, reprinted New York: Agathon Press, 1968.

Topp, Niels-Henrik (1981), 'Julius Wulff and the Multiplier Theory in Denmark 1896–1932', *History of Political Economy*, **13**.

Trevithick, James (1975), 'Keynes, Money Illusion and Inflation', *Economic Journal*, **85**.

Velupillai, K. (1975), 'Irving Fisher on "Switches of Techniques"'. *Quarterly Journal of Economics*, **89**.

Walker, E. Ronald (1933), *Australia in the World Depression*, London: P. S. King.

Walker, E. Ronald (1935), 'Public Works and Recovery', *Economic Record*, **11**.

Walker, E. Ronald (1936), *Unemployment Policy*, Sydney: Angus and Robertson.

Warming, Jens (1932), 'International Difficulties Arising Out of the Financing of Public Works During Depressions', *Economic Journal*, **42**.

Wicksell, Knut (1907), 'The Influence of the Rate of Interest on Prices', *Economic Journals*, **17**, as reprinted (1965), in James A. Gherity, ed., *Economic Thought: a Historical Anthology*, New York: Random House.

Wicksell, Knut (1934–35), *Lectures on Political Economy*, with an introduction by Lionel Robbins, London: Routledge.

Wicksell, Knut (1936), *Interest and Prices*, R. F. Kahn, trans., introduction by Bertil Ohlin, London: Macmillan, reprinted (1965), New York: Kelley.

Williams, John H. (1931), review of Keynes (1930), *Quarterly Journal of Economics*, **46**.

Winch, Donald (1966), 'The Keynesian Revolution in Sweden', *Journal of Political Economy*, **74**.

Winch, Donald (1969), *Economics and Policy: An Historical Survey*, London: Fontana.

Wood, J. Cunningham, ed. (1983), *John Maynard Keynes: Critical Assessments*. 4 vols, London: Croom-Helm.

Wootton, Barbara (1931), review of Cole (1930), *Economic Journal*, **41**.

Wright, A. Ll., (1956), 'The Genesis of the Multiplier Theory', *Oxford Economic Papers*, **8**.

Wright, Quincy, ed. (1931), *Unemployment as a World-Problem*, Chicago: University of Chicago Press.

Wright, Quincy, ed. (1932), *Gold and Monetary Stabilization*, Chicago: University of Chicago Press.

Unpublished student notes on Keynes' lectures taken by: Robert B. Bryce, 1932–34; Marvin Fallgatter, 1933; Walter Salant, 1933; Lorie Tarshis, 1932–35.

Typewritten transcriptions of these notes are deposited with the Royal Economic Society, Marshall Library of Economics, Cambridge. Bryce's notes are deposited at the MacOdrum Library, Carleton University, Ottawa, Canada.

Index

Gesell, Silvio, 78
Giblin, Lyndhurst Falkiner, 3, 105–
  8, 113, 114, 118, 129–30
Gifford, C.H.P., 134–5
Gold standard, 4, 5, 9, 14–17, 23,
  29–30, 40–1, 47, 48, 59, 61, 62,
  63, 64, 65, 66, 67, 69, 70, 75–6,
  78, 80, 90–2, 93, 96–7, 118,
  156, 163, 164, 187–9
Goschen, Viscount, 6
Graham, Frank, 79, 80
Gregory, T.E., 65, 100, 125, 156
Growth, 26, 28–9, 131
Guillebaud, Claude, 17, 131
Gunther, John, 49–50

Haberler, Gottfried, 72, 130
Hansen, Alvin, 44, 54–5, 56, 58,
  124, 164
Hardy, Charles, 48, 52–3, 58
Harrington, John Lyle, 73
Harris, Seymour, 72, 77
Harrod, Roy, 77, 78, 79, 89, 134,
  145, 146, 172
Hatton, T.J., 179
Hawtrey, Ralph G., 2, 3, 17, 34–5,
  53, 60, 77, 87, 98, 100, 105,
  107–11, 114, 118, 119, 120,
  124, 127, 129–30, 132, 134,
  136–7, 139–42, 145, 163–5,
  167, 185, 188, 190
Hayek, Friedrich A., 52, 56–8, 65,
  70, 82, 100, 124, 137, 147, 151
Heckscher, Eli, 156
Hegeland, Hugo, 117
Henderson, Hubert, 3, 37, 66, 92–
  103, 112, 175, 188
Hicks, Sir John R., 77, 128, 133,
  156, 185, 186
Hobson, John, 50
Hoover, Herbert, 47, 63–5, 70, 71
Horner, F.B., 130
Hotelling, Harold, 72
Hutchinson, T.W., 76, 100
Hutt, W.H., 67

Imports, 37, 90–1, 99, 102, 105–9,

114, 116, 117, 129, 140, 143,
  153, 156, 158
Income, 11, 53, 55, 64, 71, 72, 79,
  82, 98, 102, 105–8, 110, 111,
  115, 116, 129, 136–8, 140, 144–
  5, 149, 151, 153, 155, 158–9,
  161–2, 166–7, 174, 175, 178,
  181–4, 189–90
Index construction, 12, 18, 23, 56,
  113, 120, 164
Inflation, 4–5, 7–13, 14, 17, 18, 33,
  40, 41, 53, 61, 66, 71, 74, 89,
  99, 112, 116, 126, 140–1, 158,
  173, 178, 187–8
Interest rate, 50, 51–3, 55, 58, 65,
  69, 75, 81, 82, 87, 90, 91, 94,
  95, 98, 105, 109, 111, 116, 124–
  5, 128, 133, 134, 140, 144, 152–
  3, 155–6, 163, 166, 172, 173,
  174–7, 182–3, 185–9
International finance, 4, 39, 48, 69,
  90–91, 95, 98–9, 106, 108, 114,
  116, 140, 148–58
International trade, 4, 11–12, 30,
  39, 90–1, 93, 97, 105–6, 108–9,
  115, 116, 143, 156, 174
Inventories, 34, 36, 109, 111, 128,
  129, 136, 164
Investment, 22, 24–9, 31, 34, 35–42,
  50–1, 53, 54, 55, 58, 74, 75,
  81–2, 90, 91, 95–6, 98–100,
  110–12, 114, 116, 120, 127–9,
  136–7, 140–5, 149–51, 154–7,
  159, 162–3, 165–6, 172–5, 181,
  183–90
Iwai, Katsuhito, 21

Jevons, Herbert Stanley, 81
Jevons, William Stanley, 80–1
Johannsen, Frederick, 117
Johannsen, N.A.J.L., 118
Johnson, Elizabeth, 184
Johnson, Harry, 9, 10–11, 53, 96,
  133–4, 184
Jorgenson, Dale, 184

Kahn, Richard, F., 3, 38, 54, 76, 87,
  103, 105, 107, 109–20, 124,